Grandparents' Guide To Gifted Children

James T. Webb, Ph.D.
Janet L. Gore, M.A., M.Ed.
Frances A. Karnes, Ph.D.
A. Stephen McDaniel, J.D., A.E.P., E.P.L.S.

Great Potential Press, Inc.
Scottsdale, Arizona
www.giftedbooks.com

Great Potential Press, Inc.
www.giftedbooks.com

Grandparents' Guide to Gifted Children

Cover design: ATG Productions, Inc.
Interior design/layout: Lisa Liddy, The Printed Page

Published by Great Potential Press, Inc.
P.O. Box 5057, Scottsdale, AZ 85261
www.giftedbooks.com

Printed and bound in the United States of America

08 07 06 05 04   5 4 3 2 1

Library of Congress Cataloging-in-Publication Data

Webb, James T.
  Grandparents' guide to gifted children / James T. Webb, Janet L. Gore,
Frances A. Karnes.
       p. cm.
  Includes bibliographical references and index.
    ISBN 0-910707-65-0 (pbk.) — ISBN 0-910707-68-5 (large print) 1.
Grandparent and child. 2. Gifted children. 3. Grandparenting. I. Gore,
Janet L., 1941- II. Karnes, Frances A. III. Title.
  HQ759.9.W375 2004
  306.874'5—dc22
                                        2004008854
ISBN: 0-910707-65-0 (paperback)
ISBN 0-910707-68-5 (large print)

Dedication

To all the authors' grandchildren—
the ones we have thus far:
Alex
Anna
Annika
Aryanna
Caleb
Dominique
Emma Leighanne
John Morris
Katelyn
Lauren
Mary Ryan
Matthew
Olive
Paris
Pip
Sadie
—and to the others who are yet to come.

Acknowledgments

The authors wish to thank their grandchildren, for without them this book would never have been written. The joy they have added to our lives is boundless. We look forward to many more years and also to more grandchildren.

We also appreciate the stories that other grandparents have shared with us about how they nurtured, supported, and guided their gifted grandchildren. They have helped us to appreciate the complexities that can arise, as well as giving us creative and practical suggestions to enhance the time we spend with our grandchildren.

Our thanks go to Sandra Warren for her ideas on ways that grandparents can be advocates for their gifted grandchildren. We are grateful to Lisa Rivero for her many suggestions throughout the manuscript, as well as for her editing and indexing skills. And to Jen Ault Rosso, whom we have come to rely on for her dependably astute and detailed copyediting.

Table of Contents

List of Tables

No cowboy was ever faster on the draw than a
grandparent pulling a baby picture out of a wallet.
~ Author Unknown

Perfect love sometimes does not come
until the first grandchild.
~ Welsh Proverb

Few things are more delightful than
grandchildren fighting over your lap.
~ Doug Larson

When the grandchildren went home,
it was like the sun stopped shining.
~Raymond Fowler

Introduction

From the moment you first learn you are about to be a grandparent, you know your world is changing. Your adult child is about to become a parent, and you, too, will have a chance to be important in this new child's life. There are many joys of grandparenting, but one of the greatest is two-way unconditional love—

the best gift either a child *or* a grandparent can ever receive. Having already experienced the heavy responsibilities of parenting and providing for a family, grandparents can be more relaxed with grandchildren, with the luxury of knowing that they will be sending the child back to his or her parents when their special time together is over—a luxury to be treasured indeed, and one unique to grandparents.

Nana, Poppy, Pawpaw, Grampa, Grandma—whatever your grandchild calls you—you are special to a grandchild. Every culture recognizes and values this unique relationship between grandparent and grandchild. Most grandparents will say they never expected to feel this strongly about a grandchild, but now that they have one, they absolutely delight in the experience. They will say unabashedly, "Being a grandparent is just the best!"

How do we explain this special bond? Is it the love that the elder feels from the child? The total acceptance and unconditional love the two, young and old, find in each other? Is it the sense of family and the promise of future generations of family that are being carried on? The answer is probably all of the above.

In this book, we will look at many aspects of grandparenting and propose to you, our readers, that grandparents are increasingly important to grandchildren in today's world, whether they live near or far, in this country or in some other part of the world. We especially want to emphasize the importance of grandparents to those children who seem unusually bright, who are developmentally ahead of their age peers, and who show other characteristics of children who are talented or gifted. Like any other exceptional children, these unusually bright, talented grandchildren have distinctive needs, and their grandparents can play a special role in both understanding and meeting those needs. But first, we want to talk about the importance of grandparenting in general.

There seems to be an innate urge to be a grandparent. Couples in their fifties and sixties unashamedly say to their unmarried children, "Hey, I'm ready to be a grandparent. When are you going to settle down and have a family?" If their children are already married, they drop hints that they would be happy to have grandchildren. These older couples, upon seeing small children in restaurants, will say to each other or to no one in particular, "Oh, look at that little boy over there. Isn't he adorable? And look at how bright his eyes are!" "I wonder when Lisa and Carlos are going to start a family? I hope they don't wait much longer." Or, " I'm all for the kids having time to travel and get going in their careers, but it's sure easier to have children before 40, while you still have the energy."

We even know of some parents of adult children who have a "grandchild hope chest" of homemade baby quilts or soft stuffed toys, saved for the day when there is a new baby. These "wannabe grandparents" may even forthrightly say to their children, "You know, your father and I aren't going to be around forever. We'd at least like to see one or two grandchildren before we pass on."

With adult children these days waiting longer to marry and have their families, there are quite a few 60- and 70-year-olds wanting their children to "hurry it up." After all, *they* were married in their twenties and were parents of teenagers by their forties. If these children had started a family at the same age, there would be teenage grandkids by now!

It is hard to wait patiently while the younger generation tries to figure out what they want out of life, a career, and marriage. The parents in their sixties are ready to be grandparents and pass on their wisdom and family values to the next generation. If their kids wait too long to have children, they'll be too old to go camping or play ball with their grandkids!

On the other hand, there are probably a few grandparents who actually have to *become* grandparents before they realize just how special the grandparent relationship is. They may be absolutely amazed to discover that holding a newborn grandchild leaves one breathless in awe. This is indeed a miracle—the child of your child! Look how she looks so much like her father! Or her grandmother! At times like these, grandparents realize the continuity of the human race and of the family. They also know, better than the new parents at this point in time— because they have lived it—the hard work and responsibilities these new parents face.

A grandparent's emotions are a mixture of pride, joy, worry, concern, and excitement, but above all of these, love and caring. With each passing month there are special events, as the new grandchild grows, develops, and learns to smile and coo, roll over, grab a toy, crawl, talk, and walk, and then later how to ride a tricycle, read and solve problems, and make friends with other children. From the beginning, it is special just to share and enjoy the excitement of the new world with them. You coo and talk to the baby. You explore the world with the toddler. You read picture books to the three- and four-year-old. You discover just how much your six-year-old granddaughter or 10-year-old grandson looks up to you and turns to you for answers, advice, or sometimes for comfort.

You may notice that your grandchildren admire you, want to spend time with you, and listen carefully to what you say—perhaps more than they listen to their parents, or more than your own children listened to you when you were a parent. Grandparents are indeed unique in their relationship with grandchildren, perhaps because parents are always there to do the everyday chores, set the house rules, and handle the discipline. Because grandparents are usually around less often, this in itself makes them special. The child may also particularly value his parent's parent, attributing special respect or wisdom to this older person.

The grandparent relationship is entirely different from the parent relationship. Most grandparents are far more relaxed with their grandchildren than they were with their own children. You probably have more time to spend with them than you did with your own children. When you were a parent, you had all kinds of pressures—stresses of career, of earning and managing money, of a young marriage, financing a home, and having to juggle career and home responsibilities. Now, as a grandparent, you may have completed your career, or you may be in a new "retirement career." Your lifestyle, housing, and finances are probably stable. You have learned and experienced many things in your life thus far—about people, business, lifestyle and personal values choices, travel and cultures, politics and religion. You have had your share of struggles and successes with all of those things. By now, you are probably fairly comfortable with yourself and the choices you have made. All of this accumulated knowledge, experience, and perspective in itself takes away a certain amount of stress. The result is that you almost certainly have more relaxed time—more *quality* time—to spend with your grandchildren than you did with your own children. You may be able to afford time on a weekend to build a birdhouse, play a board game, or make something in the kitchen. You may even have a whole day or a whole weekend now and then. Don't feel guilty. Enjoy it. You have earned it. This is the way of families for generations.

Your own children are grown and, with any luck, are busy making their way in the world. As a grandparent, you have a new and very enjoyable responsibility—your grandchildren. Whether you live near or far from them, they need you. They need your ideas, your experience, your thoughts, and your wisdom. The subtle (and sometimes not so subtle) acts of passing information, beliefs, and attitudes along which occur in grandparenting are vital; that is how family values and history get passed on from one generation to the next.

The connection between grandparent and grandchild is so valuable that children without grandparents often seek out that kind of relationship from an aunt or uncle, neighbor, or friend of their parents. Some children with real grandparents living several states away may also have "surrogate grandparents" in neighbors who live next door. Mr. and Mrs. Wilson in the

"Dennis the Menace" cartoon strip are surrogate grandparent figures for Dennis and his friends. Some children "adopt" grandparents from their school, Scout troop, religious institution or a nearby retirement home. These substitute grandparents are just as important and valuable as grandparents who are actually related to the child. In today's blended families and stepfamilies, some lucky children find themselves with as many as four or more sets of grandparents, if their parents have married more than once.

Some particularly fortunate children will actively know their great-grandparents. TV personality Hugh Downs, in his delightful book, *Letter to a Great Grandson*, reminds us that great-grandparents are often involved these days.

According to an AARP survey,[1] 11% of grandparents these days are actually raising their grandchildren or providing day-to-day care on a regular basis. There are times when a parent is unable to be a parent, and grandchildren come to live with a grandparent full time. Perhaps the child's parent died in an accident or became seriously ill, or perhaps there is some other reason. In these cases, the grandparent becomes both parent and grandparent. We'll have a special chapter devoted to them later on.

Whether you see the children seldom or often, whether you live near or far, your relationship with your grandchildren is extremely important. Interestingly, physical proximity doesn't seem to be a huge or overwhelming factor in the quality of the grandparent/grandchild relationship. Grandparents can live near or far and still have a positive influence on their grandchildren. In some situations, the grandchildren live close enough that you are able to see them frequently. In other circumstances, the children live in another state, and you must relate to them by talking on the phone or by e-mail. Whatever your current relationship with your grandchildren, this book is written for you. With the world becoming increasingly complex, and diversity within families more common, the grandparent relationship may be more important than ever before.

This book emphasizes the special relationship between grandparent and grandchild and focuses on strategies to use with grandchildren who are bright, gifted, or talented. However, many of the ideas and tips we offer will apply to any grandchild, gifted or not. And some of the ideas and suggestions will be important specifically for a grandchild who is truly gifted and talented. Our reasoning is that gifted children are part of a small group and, like any person in a small, minority group, are usually aware that they are different from others. This difference can make them feel like the "odd child out" and can seriously affect their life-long self-esteem. Parents, grandparents, and others who understand that the child sometimes feels different and left out will be able to help when they understand what the child needs and why.

The fact that you have begun to read this book suggests that you think one or more of your grandchildren may be gifted or talented, or that you at least want to know more about what the term "gifted" means. If you are not sure whether your grandchild is gifted, we talk specifically in this book about common characteristics of gifted and talented children, different types of gifted children, and various levels of giftedness. But whether or not you have a gifted grandchild, you will want to make sure that your grandchild will receive the support and attention needed to develop his or her special talents. We applaud you for that, and we hope that by reading this book, you will find a variety of ways to encourage your grandchild's development.

If you are a grandparent who wants to be important in the lives of your grandchildren, this book is for you. Grandparents need to know about smart, gifted, and talented children for the same reasons that parents and teachers do. These children want adults who understand them and their learning characteristics, as well as their social and emotional needs. Grandparents can provide some of the additional social and intellectual challenge and support needed. So whether your grandchild is developmentally advanced—gifted and talented—or not, you will find valuable grandparenting tips here.

We know, too, that sometimes neighbors or friends act as grandparents to children—surrogate grandparents, if you will. Sometimes children do not have grandparents, or the grandparents are too ill or frail to be involved. Sometimes an aunt or uncle or friend of the family takes on a grandparent role. Because of this, we use the word "grandparent" to mean any adult who is significant to the child who may sometimes take on a grandparent-like role.

From our work with thousands of parents and grandparents over the last two decades, we've come to recognize that grandparents have an increasingly important role in families and that they are uniquely qualified to share in the joy of supporting and encouraging bright young minds, particularly those of their own grandchildren. Grandparents know first hand how challenging and exhausting parenting can be. By sharing some of the responsibility for encouraging and nurturing the child, grandparents can support what parents are already doing, and thus ease the burden on parents.

Thanks to major advances in medicine and health care, grandparents expect to stay active and live far longer these days than their own parents or grandparents.[2] They will have more time to know their grandchildren. In addition, today's grandparents also tend to have more resources and perhaps more leisure time than did their counterparts in previous generations. When these factors are added together, one realizes that grandparents today have the possibility of being a major influence in their grandchildren's lives.

All grandparents want the best for their grandchildren. They want them to have plenty of opportunities to develop special talents and abilities, to develop emotionally with good self-esteem and interpersonal skills, and to realize their full intellectual, social, and other potentials.

If the grandchildren are unusually bright, gifted, and talented, then grandparents need to have some familiarity with the common characteristics and behaviors of gifted and talented children. Many or most of these traits, such as curiosity, intensity, and idealism, have both positive and negative aspects to them. Yet such traits are not necessarily problems if others understand that they come from the child's high ability and expectations.

Recognizing potential while a child is still young will help to ensure, through planning, that your grandchild will have access to important opportunities along the way. Numerous books have been written for parents and educators of gifted and talented children. With more and more grandparents in the 21st Century actively involved in their grandchildren's lives, we think it is time that grandparents of developmentally advanced, gifted, talented, and creative children have a book of their own.

As a grandparent, you may notice the special abilities and potentials of your grandchildren sooner than others—perhaps even before parents or teachers. This is partly due to the special relationship between a grandparent and a grandchild, and it is partly due to your greater life experience with people of all ages.

It is interesting to know that research indicates that there are many more gifted and talented children than we have previously thought, and that as many as half are not recognized by parents or teachers as having high potential in one or more areas. Some of these bright, talented children will never be recognized or identified as gifted and so will lose out on important opportunities. It is sad to think that high innate ability is not always recognized, developed, or properly nurtured—giftedness essentially stymied. It happens because so many people in our society simply do not know about the common characteristics, behaviors, and special needs of children who learn at a faster pace or are more creative. These children are not "better" than other children; they simply learn differently and deserve to have material that matches their learning style and speed.

One would expect a society to be actively searching for intellectual promise in its youth, but that does not appear to be the case. Why? Probably because so many people hold the belief that mental ability or talent will just develop on its own, without any particular notice, support, or intervention. Our experience tells us, however, that, just as with ability in basketball or music or any other area, academic and creative ability first need to be recognized, then coached and nurtured with help from others in order to be developed. In schools where high potential is both noticed and nurtured, where all children are allowed to progress at the appropriate pace for their own needs, gifted children will thrive. When high-ability children are not encouraged and challenged to do their best, their high potential may be wasted.

The term "gifted" does not mean the same thing in all children. As you will see below, the concept is actually quite broad and encompasses a large array of abilities and talents. We will briefly describe some of the "many faces of gifted," as well as some common myths about giftedness. If educators, parents, pediatricians, and psychologists think that a gifted child is always a child who reads lots of books or uses big words, or if they fail to understand that gifted-ness has many different faces and many different dimensions, these adults will not be able to pro-vide appropriate guidance or recommendations. Many times, if there are no professionals sup-porting the child, the child's parents and grand-parents are left to provide the needed support.

There are many different kinds of gifted chil-dren with gifts and talents in many different areas; and within the set or group of children called "gifted," there exists a huge range of abil-ity and intelligence. The range starts with those who might be called mildly or moderately gifted, then moves on to highly gifted, to exceptionally gifted, and finally to "off the top" gifted, who are called profoundly gifted.

Fortunately, contemporary psychologists are learning more every day about the broad range of abilities and behaviors found within the broader field of "gifted." For example, some gifted chil-dren are significantly above average in *all* academic subjects, while others seem to excel or be gifted in only a single area. Some gifted chil-dren show strong talent and advanced ability in an area such as music or art or in other areas not traditionally emphasized by schools, such as visual-spatial ability, creative thinking, leadership, or problem solving ability. These children may like to invent things or create plays or games or come up with new ideas. Teachers may view these types of children as difficult because of their free, "outside the box" thinking or their willingness to ask probing questions or even to challenge adults. Sometimes these children are seen as behavior problems, when in fact they are simply very bright and doing what is normal and natural to them. They may not always realize social conventions or tact. They may be reprimanded for their bright comments and may feel that they are not okay. Having adults—including grandparents—who understand them will be important to such children.

When does giftedness appear? Most gifted children show their unusual ability in reading, vocabulary, memory, or some other area quite early in life. They will seem advanced in one or more areas when compared to age peers—that is, other children their same age. Being developmentally advanced is a strong indicator of potential for unusual aptitude throughout childhood as well as throughout the person's life. Of course, there are exceptions. Some highly gifted adults, such as Thomas Edison or Albert Einstein, did not have a history of being unusually precocious in childhood, at least not in their regular schoolwork.[3]

To further complicate matters regarding an understanding of the term "gifted," there are children who are "twice exceptional" who may, for example, be gifted as well as handicapped, or gifted as well as learning disabled. Many teachers are incredulous upon first hearing this, because their understanding of the term "gifted" is "a child who is bright in all academic areas." But not all gifted children are bright in all areas. And in fact, some of the children who are visually impaired, deaf, or physically or emotionally challenged are also intellectually gifted and learn quickly and at higher levels. Some children with serious learning disabilities are also gifted. This "twice exceptional" situation can of course cause problems with the child's self-esteem, because although the child is very smart, he or she has difficulty, for example, expressing him- or herself in writing. And sometimes an intellectually gifted child will also show behaviors that resemble Attention Deficit Hyperactivity Disorder (ADHD).

With "twice exceptional" children, it is usually their disabilities that are noticed and emphasized in school and at home rather than their talents. The advanced abilities and talents may be disregarded or not even recognized, when by rights, these "twice exceptional" children need and should receive special assistance in two areas—in the area of the disability as well as in the area of strength or talent.

As if that weren't enough, there is one more complication regarding the term "gifted." Some young children are incorrectly diagnosed as suffering from a behavioral problem such as ADHD, when they are actually gifted and not ADHD at all! They have been misdiagnosed (usually by well-meaning people) because they act out in the classroom by not paying attention, disrupting others, or getting up out of their seats and wandering around. It is often their lack of challenge—and resulting boredom—in the classroom that causes them to act out and behave in ways similar to children who truly do have an attention disorder—ADD or ADHD. A professional with training in the characteristics of gifted children as well as in attention disorders is needed to tell which label is correct—that is, whether the child is "twice exceptional" with both ADHD *and* gifted characteristics, or just one—either ADHD or gifted.

We have said that many gifted children are never recognized. But how many gifted are there? The population of gifted individuals is estimated to be 3% to 5% of the general population, a relatively small percentage. This is certainly part—but only a part—of why gifted and talented children often receive less attention and support than one would expect.

Teachers, administrators, and school psychologists are likely to be better trained these days in recognizing and showing concern for children with learning disabilities than in recognizing and showing concern for children who demonstrate advanced learning abilities. The result is that the rapid learners are often left to fend for themselves. Some of them learn to dislike school, simply because so much of the curriculum consists of material they already know and understand.

Pediatricians and child psychologists are another group of professionals that seldom get specific training about the characteristics and needs of gifted and talented children. Some may learn about it on the job as they interact with parents who come in with these developmentally advanced children. Unfortunately, it may take a decade or more before all of the relevant professionals get the training and information they need.

Fortunately, the two professional fields of psychology and education are beginning to catch up with what is known by experts in the field of gifted education who have studied and worked with gifted children. Certainly, not every psychologist or educator has received training. However, it is promising that the American Psychological Association now has an office in Washington, D.C. staffed by a specialist in gifted education, and state and national gifted associations are increasingly offering workshops and seminars in continuing education for psychologists. There is hope that in another few years more educational psychologists will have this much-needed training.

Because most children spend a great amount of their childhood in school, one would hope that teachers are generally knowledgeable about how to identify and educate our brightest children. Regrettably, most teachers lack the necessary information and have little training. They learn very little about gifted learners in their pre-service teacher training. Though they may read a chapter in a textbook or hear a lecture about exceptional children, more attention is usually given to problems of slow learners than to children who learn rapidly. For years, the prevailing belief in schools has been that gifted children will "get it on their own" and don't need any special accommodations. As a result, many teachers incorrectly believe giftedness is something that will "take care of itself," and that no teaching modifications are needed for children who are unusually bright. These teachers fail to realize that all children, including gifted children, need adults who understand their different learning strengths and styles, and then need guidance to maximize their learning potential.

Some schools and teachers worry that special programs for gifted children are elitist. They will say, as a way of refusing to have special services for gifted students, that more equity and fairness is needed because "*WE believe that ALL children are gifted.*" In saying this, however, they are using the term "gifted" incorrectly. All children are unique and special, and all have some ability to learn, and certainly all children deserve the best education we can provide for them so that they reach their potential. But not all children are gifted in the sense of advanced learning ability. All children do not read two to four grade levels above their age peers. All children cannot grasp algebra in first, second or third grade, or enjoy chess, or have unusual musical ability. Children do not all learn the same way or at the same rate. They have varying rates of learning and retention.

Equity does not mean all children should get the same exact curriculum. Equity and fairness means providing all children with curriculum that matches their skill and ability levels. There seems to be some misunderstanding in schools about providing an "equal opportunity" education versus an "equitable" education. To us, equal opportunity means that all children are encouraged to progress according to their readiness. In fact, many schools hold gifted children back by requiring them to wait while others catch up. For more on the subject of gifted children and equity in public schools in America, we recommend the book *Genius Denied: How to Stop Wasting Our Brightest Minds.*[4]

There are still other misconceptions and misunderstandings about gifted children. In society at large, for example, there is still a naïve notion that gifted children are always "a joy and a pleasure to have in the family" and that they "seldom have problems in school." The idea apparently is that parents who have a gifted child should simply feel fortunate to have such a child. Few people understand that the intense nature of gifted children can be quite problematic for a family, and that these children are not always a pleasure to be around and do not always succeed in school.

The truth is, many gifted children DO need special understanding and often DO need educational accommodations. They are not always easy to parent or to educate. This is why informed parents and grandparents are especially important.

As you read this book, some of you may come to a new realization that, as children, you were gifted in a time when no special provisions were made for gifted children. Or you may realize that your own children were gifted and received little or no special help. You may think, "If only someone had known," or "If only I had known, I might have understood myself or my own children better." You may not only better understand and appreciate your grandchildren, but you may also gain new insight into some of your own gifted child experiences.

*It's funny what happens when you become a
grandparent. You start to act all goofy and do things
you never thought you'd do. It's terrific.*
~ Mike Krzyzewski

*They say genes skip generations. Maybe that's why
grandparents find their grandchildren so likeable.*
~ Joan McIntosh

*I am neither especially clever nor especially gifted.
I am only very, very curious.*
~ Albert Einstein

Chapter 1
You and Your Grandchild

There are many myths about parents of gifted children, as well as about the children themselves. One prevalent myth is reflected in the statement, "Well, *all* parents believe they have a gifted child." The sarcasm behind this statement would seem to indicate that any parent who thinks that her child is gifted is obviously wrong and is merely practicing wishful thinking. The child is not gifted; the parent simply has an inflated and distorted view of him. Or the person making the sarcastic comment thinks, "Gifted-schmifted! What's gifted, anyway? It doesn't even exist." However, in our experience and in that of many others in this field, parents more often tend to *underestimate* their child's abilities than to overestimate them. Parents will say things like, "Well he's bright, but he's not gifted!" or they may say, "Gifted? I don't think so! She daydreams all the time and forgets her homework. Her mind is usually someplace other than where it should be." Sometimes, parents who have not had much contact with other families with same-age children may be truly unaware that their child is developmentally advanced. In our experience, when a parent says her child is gifted, the parent is usually correct. Most parents don't go around bragging about it to others; in fact, they hesitate to discuss it, except maybe with the child's teacher.

Grandparents, who often have a broader life perspective, may be the first to notice some of the characteristics of unusually bright children— things like an advanced mechanical ability, a high reading level, or an extraordinary in-depth interest in a topic. They may also notice the child's remarkable curiosity, perceptive abilities, or unusual sensitivity or creativity. Grandparents know from experience that while many children are smart or bright, some children are truly distinctive in their advanced development, and these children are truly gifted, with a few of them having potential at the highly gifted level. Grandparents may have noticed the same unusual traits in their own children (who are now the grandchildren's parents) or in themselves as young children. They can say, "That reminds me of how Amy was when she was that age."

Another reason grandparents are often more able to recognize a child's potential is because they tend to focus more on what the child is able to *do*, while parents and teachers are more likely to notice what the child *cannot do*—the mistakes or lags in development that lead them to think that the child is not gifted. They might say, for example, "He may be advanced in one or two areas, but he's certainly not gifted."

Parents often have mixed feelings about having a child who is very bright. They would sometimes prefer that their child not be gifted; they would like their child to just be "normal." They may be worried about raising a child who is exceptionally bright or talented. It is generally easier to raise an average child than an exceptional one. They may downplay any special achievement by the child with the comment, "Don't let it go to your head," which in effect tells the child that it would be best not to show talent too much of the time so as to not outdo or be different from others. These sorts of conflicting messages can be confusing to a child. On the one hand, she scored well above others on a test and is proud; on the other hand, her parents are dismissive of her achievement. How shall the child think of herself? Is it good to be smart? Or not? A grandparent can offer needed support to such a confused gifted child.

As for teachers, we hear over and over again of well-meaning kindergarten teachers who tell parents, "I don't think your son is gifted. Although he does well academically, he is socially very immature. I think he needs to repeat kindergarten so he can learn to socialize with other children." The teacher then cites the child's crying or emotional outbursts as proof of the immaturity, all the while failing to acknowledge that this five-year-old already knows everything that is being taught in kindergarten and is reading at a second- or third-grade level. The child's emotional outbursts most likely come from extreme frustration over having to "learn" things he already knows. At five, since he does not yet know how to advocate for himself with adults, he has a childish tantrum in frustration. Parents who find themselves in this situation can become quite distraught and may not know what to say or do. Grandparents can be listeners and can offer a different perspective, particularly after they are more familiar with the ideas in this book.

Bright Children Have Special Needs

Very bright children see and experience the world differently from other children. They are good observers and may notice things that others do not, such as physical features and emotional or intuitive nuances in others' body language. They question "why" more often. They also tend to do things differently from other children and often are non-traditional. For example, gifted children in school will often ask "too many" questions, they may challenge the teacher or even the principal, they may find that they have little in common with other children, and they may invent games or daydream when work is not interesting to them.

All of the above behaviors can get these bright children into trouble with teachers and administrators in school. Yet we say we want our gifted children to be creative; we want them to experiment and discover. The problem is that teachers are sometimes not good at viewing these behaviors as expressions of the child's innate curiosity. They see the behaviors as simply rude.

Gifted children have a need to know. They have many questions, and they want answers to their questions. Grandparents who are "tuned in" to these grandchildren will enjoy answering their questions and supporting their interests. This is why grandparents (or surrogate grandparents) have the opportunity to be so special in the lives of their grandchildren. As we have already suggested above, children who are particularly bright and creative—those we call gifted and talented—are often quite literally neglected in their own learning at school. This happens, first because teachers don't *know* that the child is gifted; second, because they have no training in what to do with a high-ability child; and third, because it is widely believed among many educators that gifted children don't need different learning experiences than other children. Even teachers who have received special training in educating gifted children often do not provide appropriate opportunities for them.

Training in how to adapt curriculum to different levels—often called differentiation—has been available at education conferences and in teacher training workshops since the mid 1980s. However, current research shows that although these teachers understand and support the intent of differentiation, they seldom practice it in classrooms.[5] Changing one's teaching methods is hard. It is much easier to give all children the same assignment than to create different levels of each assignment. Schools that match the curriculum or the program to the child's ability level are rare.[6]

Children who are intellectually gifted or who are especially talented in an area such as music do need special time and attention both in school and at home. Most of all, they need someone who will provide them with support and who will help them gain access to the books, materials, activities, and other opportunities they may need to develop their abilities. They may want music, art, or acting lessons; they may need books from the public library to pursue a special interest; or they may need a tutor to help them advance in mathematics or learn a foreign language. These children have an inner drive to learn, sometimes far beyond what the school can offer.

In the preface, we mentioned one particularly widespread myth about gifted children—that "they will make it on their own." The assumption behind this myth is that since they are bright, gifted children will be able to figure things out for themselves and teach themselves what they need to know. While it is possible that some gifted children may do so, most will not. Although they are bright and sometimes seem older than their years, they are still children, and they still need adults to help them access information. Young children's experience in the world is simply not extensive enough yet for them to know the options open to them. They need caring and interested adults to facilitate their learning.

Gifted children not only need encouragement for their intellect and advanced abilities, they also need support for and help in dealing with their strong emotions. One thing we know about the social and psychological makeup of gifted children, which we'll talk about in more detail in the next chapter, is that they are both more *intense* and more *sensitive* than other children. We also know that gifted children have trouble making friends with age mates who don't necessarily share interests as advanced or diverse as theirs. Not many five-year-olds, for example, like to play chess, study ant farms, ask questions about constellations in the sky, are emotionally and morally concerned about tragedies they see on the evening news, or play difficult mathematical games. But gifted five-year-olds may, and often do, have such interests. Few 10-year-old children delight in creating puns, want to talk about world events, skip a grade in school, or attend an advanced music camp. Children who are gifted often do.

Gifted and talented children usually become keenly aware when they are still young that they are somehow different from others—though they aren't sure quite how or why—and sometimes they learn to hide their talents and special interests in order to fit in with other children. If they do too much "hiding their quickness" or "blending in with others," the result may be that they end up holding back their own intellectual development and academic progress.

Most gifted children could easily do work three grade levels beyond where their age peers are working. With their ability to work at higher levels, gifted children need curriculum that fits their abilities and interests, and they need the opportunity to progress at a rate that fits their learning ability. Schools that are willing to offer some flexibility in academic options are helpful. In a school with flexibility, a child who is gifted in math might be allowed to work on harder or higher-level math, for example, but might stay with age mates for the other subjects.

Gifted children frequently find more inter-personal success and happiness when they do blend in with others. After all, like everyone, they want to have friends, and they soon learn that if they know too much or can do too much as compared to other children, the other children won't like them. But camouflaging their brightness and differentness causes gifted children to be untrue to themselves; they are often aware that they are sacrificing their innate intellectual curiosity in order to be accepted. Conflicts such as this may result in gifted children having low self-esteem or simply not feeling right about themselves. If gifted children do find themselves standing out as different from their peers in school, then it is particularly important that people in their family life accept them fully—with all of their gifted traits—and encourage them to develop and use their abilities.

Many people are surprised to learn that gifted children are sometimes even punished for the very things that make them what they are, even though they are trying to fit in with their class-mates and friends. It is certainly ironic that some parents and teachers treat many of the character-istics of gifted children as liabilities rather than assets. Teachers, parents, siblings, and peers often react to gifted children as though they need to be "taken down a peg" or "put in their place" because they "act like they are smarter than others." These bright, curious, and creative chil-dren are often criticized for being "too sensi-tive" or "too intense," for "endless daydreaming" or for having a "weird sense of humor." Criti-cisms like these can be called "killer statements"[7] because they chip away at the child's self-concept and convey a sense that the child would be more valued if only he or she could be more like other children—not gifted.

If a child hears killer statements repeatedly, the damage to a sensitive child's emotional well-being and self-concept can be considerable. However, when parents and other significant adults in the child's life understand that behaviors and traits such as intensity, sensitivity, curiosity, and questioning are normal—even typical—for gifted children, these adults can be more accepting and tolerant of the child's personality. Family members and friends of the family, then, can be understanding and can become a support system for the child.

Your Gifted Grandchild in School

Gifted children are typically excited about their first day of school. They are filled with questions and can hardly wait to get to kindergarten, where they will be able to learn and do new things. However, these children are often sorely disappointed. They are surprised to be told to be quiet and not ask so many questions or to give the other children a chance to answer. In the grades after kindergarten, the teacher tells them that they are not allowed to read ahead in their books. How frustrating this must be for a bright child.

School, of all places, ought to be a wonderful and exciting place for a bright, curious, creative child. Sadly, it often becomes instead a place where conformity and fitting in—called "socialization"—are more valued by educators than innovation, curiosity, and excellence.

Sometimes gifted children are neither valued nor even accepted at school—the very place that one would hope would be a haven for a bright, gifted, and talented child. Why are they not valued more? Regrettably, as we have mentioned earlier, most teachers and administrators have little or no knowledge of the common behavioral characteristics or learning needs of gifted children. Though they all have knowledge and some training about children in the lower 3% of the population—those generally referred to as intellectually challenged or mentally retarded—very few teachers or administrators have attended any courses or training workshops about learning needs and strategies for gifted children. Because they simply lack the information and knowledge, these educators often view the gifted child's intense, curious, creative, or sensitive behavior as rather troublesome, quirky, or odd. These behaviors, in their opinion, are problematic, but nothing that would prompt them to alter lesson plans or classroom activities.

Sometimes a gifted child is even labeled by teachers as having a behavior problem, such as Attention Deficit Hyperactivity Disorder (ADHD), when in fact the child is acting out restlessness she feels because she already knows what is being taught. She wants to learn new things and at a faster pace. Kindergarten and first-grade teachers often tell parents that the gifted child simply needs to learn to "fit in" or "get along with others" or that she "needs time to mature." These teachers reason that the child could not possibly be bored and certainly should not be allowed to work ahead. Some parents have become so frustrated with the lack of understanding from the schools that they have chosen to take their children out of school and teach them at home.[8] And indeed, some highly and profoundly gifted children are better off being schooled at home or with a combination of subject area tutors. Knowing the level or degree of giftedness in these children is important, for schools likely cannot meet the needs of a profoundly gifted child, even with acceleration or grade-skipping.

As for working ahead, research absolutely does not support the view that bright children should not be allowed to work ahead. Several studies indicate that from 50% to 75% of a gifted child's time in the regular classroom is spent waiting for others to catch up, even as early as kindergarten and first grade.[9]

It is probably obvious by now that having a teacher who knows something about gifted children (either intuitively or through coursework), who understands their needs, and who has training in how to teach them will be very important to a gifted child. Sometimes teachers and schools do understand, nurture, and support the inquiring minds of these children, and they ignite an excitement for learning that lasts for many years. Supportive parents and grandparents will be similarly important.

Losing Our Elders

How do grandparents figure in to all of this? Can grandparents really help grandchildren at home and at school? Certainly they can't be seen as meddling in areas where they shouldn't. Isn't it enough for grandparents simply to love and enjoy their grandchildren?

15

At a recent parent conference, a speaker said, "We have lost our elders, and because of that, we are now at risk for losing our children." Today's elders seem to have no special role. Psychologist Mary Pipher expressed a similar sentiment in her best-selling book, *Another Country: Navigating the Emotional Terrain of Our Elders.*[10] Pipher pointed out that whereas in earlier times, grandparents were valued members of the family involved in daily work routines, play, and social activities with the rest of the family, now they often live far away and have little or no input into the extended family, or they live in retirement homes where they interact and socialize primarily with other retired people. Pipher writes about how in previous generations, grandparents remained important and contributing members of the family, working on the farms or in the cities, cooking, sewing, gardening, canning and baking, repairing machinery, doing household maintenance, and hosting family dinners. At family gatherings, people would sit after dinner and talk about shared family experiences, family stories, and family history, including what happened to this or that individual, or how one or the other achieved success or dealt with tragedy or failure.

The children would play nearby but would over-hear many of these stories. Family values, ideas, traditions, and a sense of belonging were thus conveyed from the older generations to the younger. The children all knew about other members of the extended family, including the aunts, uncles, and cousins. They knew about family differences and disagreements. They knew how their own family fit within the larger family context.

With increased mobility and family members moving back and forth across the country for jobs or other reasons, much of that earlier family life, unfortunately, is gone. Society has changed dramatically over the past century, and family structures with it. When those of us born in the 1940s and 1950s were children, we knew the names and faces of many members of our extended family—aunts, uncles, cousins, nieces, and nephews—and we usually saw them at least once a year. Even though people died much younger back then, some of us knew our grand-parents. Often, an entire extended family lived and worked in or near one small town, went to the same church, and ate Sunday dinner together. Family members who died were buried in the family cemetery. The word *family* meant extended family, not just immediate family.

As family members moved from farms and small towns to the cities for better paying jobs and a better lifestyle, and later moved even farther across the country, people slowly lost touch with the aunts, uncles, and cousins. And as those who lived in the cities improved their lifestyle and their children went off to college, we lost touch with our own siblings and nieces and nephews because they now lived hundreds or thousands of miles away. Keeping in touch was more difficult and done through infrequent phone calls.

The grandparents of this newly spread-out family often stayed behind in the small town or the place they had moved to from the farm, but their children and grandchildren now lived in distant places. Family visits with grandparents occurred only once or twice a year rather than daily or weekly and were with family subsets, not the entire family group. Unless there was plenty of money for plane tickets and someone took the initiative to organize family reunions and get-togethers, large family gatherings just didn't occur. Today, there seems to be a small trend beginning toward families making efforts to live near each other again, usually with grandparents moving to the town where one or more of their children live.

Young adults in the 21st Century have gained a great deal of freedom in terms of where they live and work and in the kinds of work they do. At the same time, however, they have lost the benefits of having parents or other family members close by to take an interest in their children and to share family holidays and other special occasions. The effects of this greater freedom and mobility on a personal, family level are that now family members are so disconnected that they cannot act as an extended family support system for each other when there are troubles or difficulties. When someone goes to the hospital, family members can't just get in the car to rush over. When two people are having relationship problems, family members aren't there to act as a buffer. Individual family members may turn to friends and counselors where they once turned to family.

Statistics tell us the average family in the United States now moves once every six years,[11] and as a result, many grandparents probably live so far away that most grandchildren see them only occasionally. Grandparents, meanwhile, who might be able to provide a sense of stability, belongingness, and sanctuary for grandchildren, find it difficult to communicate as much as they would like to from such a distance. The result is that grandparents have far less time with their grandchildren than their counterparts in previous generations.

Add to that the increased rate of divorce and remarriage. A divorce—sometimes more than one—occurs in almost half of all U.S. marriages these days, resulting in further splintering of families. Divorce has difficult and long-lasting consequences for the divorcing parents, their children, extended family, and for the subsequent relationships of grandparents with the grandchildren of divorced parents. Joint custody creates additional difficulties when the parents live in different cities or states. We know instances in which children of divorce spend a year in one state with one parent and the next year in another state living with the other parent. Other children of divorced parents may live a week or a month with one parent, the next week or month with the other. Many children live with mom during the week and visit dad on weekends. And if the divorced parents live on the same block, children might spend every night with Mom at her house but go home every day after school to Dad's house. Although children are resilient, these back and forth adjustments are difficult. There are often different rules in the two homes, and the constant shifting can be unsettling to young children.

Divorce almost always involves emotional distress, disappointment, and disillusionment in the entire family. A child, particularly a teenager, may think, "Since my family has disappointed me in this way, I will protect myself by diminishing the importance of my family, including my extended family." As a result, children may be unsure of how much they can trust their own parents and, later, the young men or women they may date and consider as potential marriage partners. Such children, in our experience, would like to turn to grandparents for stability, love, and comfort if the grandparents were nearby.

Regrettably, many children in divorced families have not had the opportunity to get to know their grandparents. Perhaps the divorced parent has not allowed grandparents free access to the grandchildren or has not encouraged visits. Perhaps the

21

grandparents have taken sides in the divorce or in other ways have not kept in touch. In some cases, unfortunately, a grandparent must wait until the grandchild becomes an adult for the relationship to develop.

If all of this sounds somewhat discouraging, we agree that it is. But the examples above are the reality of the society we live in today. In our eyes, this reality accentuates the importance of grandparents. Grandparents, who have grown up in different times with different values, can offer the current generation some very helpful viewpoints, perspective, and wisdom.

For example, present society increasingly seems to idealize young adults who are actively—sometimes frantically—accomplishing their life's goals, which usually include having a house in the suburbs with at least one or maybe two cars (one of them an SUV), all the latest in electronic equipment, a big screen TV with a DVD player, one or two (or more) cellular phones, a recliner in the living room, a barbecue in the backyard, and maybe a swimming pool. The children in these families will have the latest computer and video games, the most stylish clothes, the latest hairstyle, and will participate in organized soccer or football or other lessons. There are many con-sumer-related pressures.

We grandparents can remember times when there were far fewer of these pressures to own material things. Our parents worked in the town we lived in, or at least nearby. We had one TV, not four or five, and it was black and white. Pro-gramming was limited, so we watched TV, at most, one or two evenings a week. As children, we spent more time running around outside playing with our friends. When we were inside, we made forts with sheets over furniture or played with dolls or Lincoln Logs®. We went to the library and brought books home to read. There were no video games. To us, it seems chil-dren in the 21st Century are being deprived of important simple pleasures of imaginative play or making one's own toys and playthings.

Grandparents can remind their own children that having lots of video games, CDs, and DVDs is far less important than interacting with a child in a board game or cooking together or having a family discussion of items in the news. A grand-parent can show a child how to make puppets from paper bags or fabric scraps, or how to make houses or forts from cardboard boxes or sheets thrown over a dining room table. Grandparents can show children how to plant seeds in a paper cup or plant a garden in the backyard. A grandparent can take a child on an overnight camping trip. A grandparent can teach a child to knit or embroider, or make a birdhouse, or build stilts out of wood. Grandparents can teach many such simple pleasures to their grandchildren, and in these ways, grandparents can counteract the culture of television, excessive materialism, or consumerism and instant gratification.

TV ads and movie characters in the 21st Century nurture a fast-paced—but very disjointed—lifestyle. Visual and broadcast media portray beautiful, handsome, vibrant young adults who rush busily hither and yon for their careers or to enhance their social lives.

Grandparents remember less frantic and less materialistic times. At the risk of sounding quite nostalgic, our parents worked hard. Our mothers hung clothes out on the line and mended socks. They grew fresh vegetables in a backyard garden; we ate homegrown canned tomatoes and beans throughout the winter. We knew all the neighbors, and our playmate's parents felt free to tell our parents if we ever misbehaved at their house.

Not every family had a telephone, but when they did, it was a party line. We did not feel obligated to answer the phone every time it rang.

Technology, too, has its plusses and minuses, and again, grandparents can offer a different perspective. We grandparents remember a time in the 1970s when futurists predicted that computers and other technology would eliminate so many jobs that we would all work a four-day work week. There would be childcare centers at all major work sites and extra vacation time each year. We would have huge amounts of leisure time.

It has not turned out that way. In fact, work schedules have become increasingly demanding in their pace, and now the workers—sometimes both parents—commute by car or mass transit for an hour or more each day to a job where they work eight or more hours a day, then bring work home. There is a sense of urgency, even on weekends. Information is everywhere—on the TV and radio, in the newspapers, on the Internet—and parents feel a constant pressure to be informed and in touch with their jobs, world events, and with other adults. People walk down the street talking on their cell phones. For some people, there is no time in which one is not "connected" to the media or technology.

These days, virtually every household has one or more phone lines with phones in every room, including a separate line for the fax machine and a computer with high-speed Internet access. New homes are built with cable TV and high-speed Internet connections built in.

From a grandparent's perspective, all of these marvels of communication—so much an accepted and exciting part of modern society—have actually become barriers to communication within the family. Parents find themselves responding to what seem to be urgent business matters at the expense of quality time spent walking, talking, or reading together, or just listening and observing the world around them. Stephen Covey pointed out in his best-selling book, *Seven Habits of Highly Effective People,*[12] that we often find ourselves responding to what feels *urgent* rather than what is *important.* A game of checkers after dinner with a child and helping a child with homework may be more *important* than that business call that comes in and seems so *urgent.*

The fast-paced world of this 21st Century has created a loss of perspective about value s—

particularly for our grandchildren—as well as a loss of family togetherness. Grandparents are able to recognize that what seems urgent at the moment is not so important in the long run. Grandparents have the luxury to move at a slower pace that allows observation, contemplation, time to sort out what is really important, and a wealth of experiences from which to draw. For those interested in reading more, Mary Pipher has written eloquently on this topic in her book, *The Shelter of Each Other: Rebuilding Our Families.*[13]

Along with the huge information explosion of the 20th and 21st Century—with satellite feeds of CNN and MSNBC—has come still another unintended consequence. When we turn on our television sets, we are connected to our world so rapidly and so extensively that our children hear and see events on the daily news that in earlier days were simply unimaginable. In one evening news broadcast, children might see video replays of terrorist attacks, war, famine, death from AIDS, and news of child kidnappings. It's too much for adults to digest, let alone a child. And bright children, with their sensitivity and intensity, compassion, and sense of moral justice, will be strongly affected by these things in the news and will need adults to talk with them about the events.

In our own childhoods, we never had to face such a daily news barrage of beatings, murders, mutilations, disease, war, and even global annihilation. What is this doing to the minds and souls of our young children? The effect of all of this world tragedy is even greater for a child who is bright, sensitive, intense, and who internalizes things heard and seen. Grandparents may be able to shield the child from some of this barrage of distressing information by suggesting that parents keep TV news and certain programs off-limits to the children; or if not, by talking to the child about the thoughts, feelings, and emotions that such terrible images bring up.

The Unique Role of Grandparents

A former Chief Executive Officer of a major midwestern company told his employees how his granddaughter had taught him a very important life lesson. She insisted that he watch her on the trampoline, but asked him not to say anything. This grandfather watched his granddaughter jump for nearly an hour. Then she dismounted, took her grandfather's hand, and as they walked back toward the house, she said, "Gramps, you're the most special person in my life. No one else would watch me." The CEO told his employees, "What I learned is that the most precious thing you can give to another person is your time and your undivided attention."

As grandparents, we should take that lesson to heart. Most of us now *do* have the time, and we *can* give our complete attention, at least some of the time. We may be able to give other things as well, but *time* and *attention* seem to be the most important, particularly in a frantic world where everyone is rushing about. Time and attention implies acceptance, too, which gifted and talented children need desperately. The time and attention you can give will help them to feel valued and will contribute to their later self-esteem.

Not all grandparents are retired, and many who have officially retired tell us that they are now busier than ever before, often with new enterprises or hobbies. Many grandparents are still busy influencing the world with their own businesses and talents. They have second careers in business, consulting, politics, lobbying, volunteer work, writing and publishing, creative pursuits like painting, and serving on community boards. Despite all of these activities, we grandparents owe some time to our grandchildren, for their own future. In nurturing grandchildren, grandparents also affirm the parents who are raising the child. There is an informal partnership consisting of parents and grandparents, and the child feels secure in a connection to both. He now knows that he is loved and cared for by both, which can only help his self-image.

In addition to time and attention, we can also give a sense of perspective, tradition, an appreciation of values, and an indication of support. Pulitzer prize-winning newspaper publisher Hodding Carter once said, "There are only two lasting bequests we can hope to give our children. One is roots, the other is wings." With regard to grandchildren, we give them roots in family, in geographic place, and in traditions and values, and we give them wings through acceptance and the belief that they will be able to make good choices once they have a strong foundation from which to draw.

Grandparents who are involved in the lives of their grandchildren are truly needed in families all over the world. They have a chance to be influential in the lives of their grandchildren.

You had a chance to influence the world through your own children. You now have a second chance to influence the world through your grandchildren. Your role will be a background role when compared to that of the parents, but your role is important nonetheless.

The thought of being an influential grandparent may seem daunting. Some of us had wonderful grandparents whom we remember vividly, and we may want to be like them. Others—indeed quite a number of us—did not know our grandparents because in the 1930s, 40s, and 50s, grandparents died young, sometimes of illnesses that can be treated today. Some of us do not have role models for being grandparents. And some of us who knew our grandparents don't want to model ourselves after them. They were memorable characters, perhaps, but not role models for how grandparents should be.

A positive grandparent (or grandparent surrogate) can be a major influence in helping grandchildren feel accepted, loved, and safe. Grandparents can provide the continuity between generations, the sense of family, and the perspective that allows solid family and community values to develop. A grandparent's experience, wisdom, time, and attention

are all critically important in the life of a growing child. Distance is not an insurmountable
deterrent. The special attention we are talking
about can occur long distance, across hundreds
of miles, thanks to those modern communication tools mentioned earlier—cell phones, computers, digital and video cameras, CDs, audio
tapes—and even the "old fashioned" way—hand-
written letters, postcards, birthday and other
special occasion cards, and packages sent by way
of "snail mail," which has not yet gone the way
of the Pony Express.

Building a Bond with Your Grandchild

Many of us are fortunate in that we are able to
see and be with our grandchildren occasionally.
Sometimes we see them weekly or monthly. Each
visit provides an opportunity to be special to a
grandchild and to build a relationship.

The single most important way you can be
special to a child is through spending time with
that child. Slightly more than a quarter of grandparents say they prefer spending time with a
grandchild *without* his or her parents.[14] Perhaps
you can take one grandchild at a time on a special outing—to a movie, the library, a children's

32

museum; or on a trip fishing, camping, hiking, and looking at stars; or even on simple errands to the store. Perhaps you register for a trip specially arranged for grandparents and grandchildren such as those organized by Elderhostel or other organizations. Or perhaps you can plan your own special trip. Maybe it is simply playing a game of cards or eating a meal together at a restaurant. The important thing is that you are giving your grandchild a segment of time when he or she has your undivided attention. It doesn't have to be a long period of time. The frequency of such events will be more important than the length of time spent on each one. Even five or 10 minutes each day of shared experiences and acceptance can rapidly develop and nurture a very valuable and satisfying relationship. You don't even have to do anything special; just being there is a strong statement. We know of one grandparent whose home serves as the place the child comes after school every day while the mother works. This place will be a constant for the child from kindergarten through high school and represents valuable time indeed for the child and the grandparents both.

Some grandparents give their special time a formal name. One grandmother we know periodically schedules a "Board of Directors" meeting with her very bright granddaughter where they discuss options and make decisions about their special vacation time together. This grandmother wants to make sure that her granddaughter has high aspirations, and these meetings are special times when she will have her grandmother's undivided attention, as well as a time when the child gets to set part of the agenda.

If you have more than one grandchild, it is important to allocate time for each one. This is more easily done when grandchildren live close by than when some live near and others live far away. If you have grandchildren you see frequently, let them keep track of whose turn it is next. They are more likely to remember than you are. If you are able to see your grandchildren only very occasionally, it is still important to try to balance your special time so that each grandchild has approximately equal time. When some are near and others far, you will probably make the effort to travel to see the distant ones and stay for a week or more.

It is best, if there are two grandparents, for each grandparent to spend exclusive time with each grandchild. If grandparents are always together during this time, then the child does not get the opportunity to know each one as an individual. By doing things separately, each grandparent can develop a relationship unique to him or her. If the grandchildren live nearby, Grandma might be the one who reads books aloud to them, while Grandpa is the one who takes them to the park. The same principle can apply to long-distance grandparenting relationships. Grandma can talk to the child about school and friends, and Grandpa can ask about sports or hobbies. Each grandparent should follow his or her own natural inclinations and interests with the child. If Grandma doesn't care much for fishing but does enjoy baking cookies with her grandchildren, then she should bake cookies with them. Grandpa may enjoy teaching his grandson how to play cribbage, or to paint, or to plant in the garden. Grandma may want to teach the children how to watch and identify birds. Engaging grandchildren in activities you enjoy will allow them to have experiences that they otherwise would not, and these experiences will help broaden their ideas about what adults might enjoy.

Most grandparents are naturals at praising and encouraging grandchildren. It is easy to notice all of the marvelous and wonderful things that our grandchildren can do, and also to overlook their faults. Whether grandparents are near or far, messages of encouragement—both verbal and nonverbal—are important ways to recognize the importance of the relationship. It has been said that the parents' job is to raise and discipline the child, whereas the grandparents' job is simply to enjoy the grandchildren.

Praise does not need to be in words. A smile or a wink, a "thumbs up" or a "high five" can be as powerful as a written note or a spoken comment. We can show how much we value our grandchildren in other ways, too—by accepting their feelings, listening to their opinions, and attending their sports activities. The combination of enjoyment and acceptance with approval is what creates the relationship that is so special between grandchildren and grandparents.

Enjoyment and acceptance do not mean you should praise everything about your grandchildren. Silence is sometimes golden. Your grandchild, for example, may simply want someone to listen without offering opinions. Or you may express a difference of opinion by not expressing anything at all—a silent expression of disagreement. Sometimes you may be able to say something that instructs or gives gentle advice. You may even be able to say or do some things that the child's parents cannot. When 10-year-old Tyler shows poor table manners despite his parents' admonishments, a quiet word from Grandpa about the importance of good table behavior will have a lasting effect.

Most of all, be aware of what you are modeling in your relationship with your grandchild. Always treat your grandchild with respect, even when you disagree with behaviors, style, or language. Grandchildren, particularly when they reach the pre-teen and teen years, may have opinions or may engage in activities that grate on your personal sense of values and traditions. If you can remember when you were a teenager, you may recall some of your own behaviors at that age that were at odds with the traditions that existed in your home. It is natural for pre-teens and teens to experiment with different attitudes and behaviors as they begin to find their own identity.

We recommend that you avoid being the disciplinarian unless it becomes an absolute necessity. Discipline is a job for parents. You may want to criticize your grandchildren's behavior or their parents' methods of raising them, and you may want to offer advice that has not been requested. Though it is very tempting, we recommend staying out of the discipline area unless the situation becomes so critical that you simply must intervene. For example, if your grandson is about to engage in a dangerous activity, such as playing touch-tag on the roof, you will intervene quickly. However, in the case of a messy room, you will avoid insisting that he clean up his room before you take him on a special outing. It will be easier to remember if you keep in mind that your primary role is that of a supportive grandparent. (Note: The above suggestions regarding discipline do not apply, of course, if you are acting as the parent.)

Half a century ago, when several generations lived in the same house—when grandparents lived in the homes of their children, or the children lived in the family home with their parents—grandparents acted as an ever-ready back-up support system for the child. When parents disciplined the child, the grandparent was there to hold the child while she cried or was sad and remorseful. Grandma's lap was there to crawl into. It wasn't that the grandparent undermined the parent's discipline; rather, the child had a safe haven to go to when she was hurting emotionally so that that she knew she was still loved.

Like the above example, your role as a grandparent gives you the opportunity to have a special relationship that is different from the parent relationship. Think back to your own childhood and consider whether there was someone in the family—a special aunt, uncle, or grandparent, or even someone outside the family—who loved and accepted you unconditionally, without criticism. If so, you can probably see now how important this person was, or perhaps still is, in your life. At the time, you may have brushed aside or pretended to ignore the praise or special attention that this adult gave you. But now, in retrospect, you appreciate the importance of that person to your later growth and development. He or she may have even been a role model for you. In the same way, you have an opportunity to be a significant adult in the life of a grandchild or in the lives of several grandchildren.

You are familiar with the saying, "It takes a village to raise a child." As children grow, they naturally look to other adults for support and to gain a broader understanding of who they are and how and where they fit in this world. They examine their own family and its values and traditions in relation to other families. It is certainly important for children to have positive and caring adults as examples—adults they can trust always to have their best interests in mind. Grandparents are an important part of the caring "village."

Every child is born a genius.
~ Richard Buckminster Fuller

*Doing easily what others find difficult is talent;
doing what is impossible for talent is genius.*
~ Henri-Frédéric Amiel

*There are two kinds of talents, man-made talent and
God-given talent. With man-made talent you have to
work very hard. With God-given talent, you just touch
it up once in a while.*
~ Pearl Bailey

Chapter 2
Is My Grandchild Gifted?

You might think that all grandparents believe that they have a gifted child, perhaps even a budding genius. Our experience, working with grandparents and with our own grandchildren, suggests otherwise. Yes, some grandparents might overestimate their grandchild's ability, but most do not.

In fact, there is a good reason to encourage grandparents to recognize their grandchildren's abilities—because as we said at the beginning of Chapter 1, parents tend to underestimate and downplay their children's talents and intelligence rather than bring it to the attention of teachers or others.

Is it really so important to know and recognize whether a child has high potential?

In our opinion the answer is a resounding "YES," and we will talk more about why a bit later in this book.

How soon can you tell whether a child is gifted?

Well, it depends upon the child—how gifted, and in what areas.

Is it important to identify a child as gifted at an early age?

Though it usually is not particularly important to do so in a child younger than age four, in our opinion, it can be quite important for children who are between the ages of four and six, and it is certainly important before the age of nine.

What do you look for in a child to determine giftedness?

With most children, you can figure it out—even at a very early age—simply by looking at their behaviors. These behaviors may not tell you the exact level of giftedness, but they will tell you generally whether or not you have a gifted grandchild.

Are there tests you can give?

Yes, but tests are seldom necessary for preschool children. Tests are primarily used to convince others (institutions such as schools) who may be doubtful or to provide specific information for educational planning.

Here are some guidelines that will help you answer questions such as these. They will also help you determine if your grandchild is gifted.

Early Signs

The development of an infant's brain is quite startling in its ability to make sense of the world's sounds, sights, odors, tastes, and textures.[15] Sometimes grandparents—and parents—can tell quite early in the child's life that the child is unusually bright and curious. Studies have found that infants who are brighter look intently for longer periods of time at their surroundings than do other infants. Scientists[16] have now found evidence to support the comment made by parents for years that "He has such bright and curious eyes!" or "She seems to really see and understand things even as an infant."

Length and intensity of gaze does not, in and of itself, allow you to conclude that your infant grandchild is a genius. However, it is one indicator. And some children who do not show this early intensity of gaze *are* in fact gifted. We remind readers, too, that all children show developmental spurts and lags. That is, they do not develop in a smooth, continual pattern of growth, either physically or mentally. Sometimes they are advanced beyond what would be expected of a child their age, but later may fall back to age-expectancy. This is one of the reasons why pediatricians, psychologists, and educators are often reluctant to talk about a child as "gifted" before the age of eight.

Still, some children are simply far too precocious for their behaviors to be nothing more than an early developmental spurt. Parents and grandparents have accurately reported to us that their two-and-one-half- or three-year-old child is reading (the child taught himself by just asking questions) or that a 12-month-old child is speaking in complete sentences using five to 10 words. These things are possible. These children are developmentally advanced to the point of being verbally gifted. Furthermore, it is extremely unlikely that these abilities will later decline or diminish so that these children will ultimately "even out" with other children their age. Instead, the child will continue to be advanced in this area of strength.

Most gifted children who are advanced in one area will also be advanced in several other areas. In general, gifted preschool children are about 30% more advanced developmentally than the norm on developmental checklists used by pediatricians.[17] Sometimes they are remarkably advanced, although wide variability exists.[18] Some gifted children learn letters, numbers, and colors earlier than other children—often on their own, not from anyone teaching them—and notice things or ask questions that are normally noticed and asked by much older children. Mothers often complain that their ears feel tired from all of the questions and chatter of their preschool gifted children.

About half of all gifted children begin reading by age five, though some start to read as early as age two.[19] You may notice that your grandchild is substantially ahead of what Dr. Spock or others say she should be doing at that age. As a grandparent, because of your greater life experience, you may be the first to notice this precocious behavior. If parents have had little experience with young children, they may think that what the child is doing is normal rather than exceptional or extraordinary.

Some grandparents (and teachers) may think, and even worry, that a child's precocious behaviors are due to parents' coaching or drilling the child (with reading flashcards, for example). In our experience, this is rarely the case. Almost always, the behaviors show themselves simply because the child is curious, ready to learn, and has asked lots of questions which parents and grandparents or others have taken the time to answer. In many cases, parents have also exposed the child to many different environments and have conversed with him or her in a respectful manner.

Characteristics

When we speak of gifted and talented children, we are not just speaking of children who are academically gifted—that is, children who do well in their school subjects. We are speaking of intellectually gifted and talented children, using today's newly expanded views of intelligence. In the early 1900s, intelligence was defined primarily by IQ as shown on a standardized test. The usual tests back then looked mostly at verbal and academic problem-solving skills. The meaning and understanding of intelligence has changed dramatically since then.

These days, the meaning of intelligence has been broadened. Similarly, the notion of giftedness has been broadened to more than just academic achievement, so that now there is more recognition of creativity and of giftedness in leadership, the arts, and areas like practical problem solving. We expect the concept of intelligence to continue to change as scientists and psychologists learn more about learning and the brain.

Even though academicians will continue to debate the many different aspects of intelligence and giftedness, there is agreement that high intelligence exists. There is also agreement that intelligence may be expressed in many different ways—not just in one way such as reading or mathematics. A theorist at Harvard University, Howard Gardner,[20] has said that there are at least seven—and perhaps more—different types of intelligence: Verbal, Mathematical, Musical, Spatial, Bodily-Kinesthetic, Interpersonal, and Intrapersonal. A person may be gifted or advanced in one or more of these areas.

Gardner's theory has been helpful to schools and to children. It has put the focus back on the individual child by reminding educators to pay attention to the different learning strengths, learning styles, and learning preferences of all children. In doing so, teachers have become more aware that children learn differently and that some children learn more rapidly and might be advanced or gifted in an area. In schools today, we find teachers increasingly using methods that take into account Gardner's "multiple intelligences."

Even though there are multiple intelligences, most educators and other professionals agree that gifted and talented children generally share a common set of characteristics, or behavioral traits, and that most gifted children show most of these traits most of the time.[21] Following is a list of the common traits or characteristics of gifted and talented children, with examples of how the traits manifest themselves.

Strong Verbal Abilities

Most gifted children start speaking earlier than other children. Most, but not all. Some actually start speaking later than other children, but then when they do speak, it is with unusually large vocabularies and often non-stop. As they grow more proficient, gifted children's sentences tend to be complex, and they demonstrate an understanding of nuances that distinguish words, such as the difference between "irritated" and "angry." Gifted children will sometimes insist upon the use of the absolute precise word. Their strong verbal abilities usually lead them to be early readers, and they read extensively, sometimes five picture books or one chapter book in one sitting. Even before they can read, they usually delight in (and even insist upon) being read to, and they are thrilled when they learn their letters and numbers.

A book titled *Some of My Best Friends Are Books: Guiding Gifted Readers from Preschool to*

High School[22] describes this love of reading. Parents and grandparents who introduce children to the library or who give books for special occasions are giving children a long-lasting gift.

Unusually Good Memory

Gifted children are sponges for learning. They enjoy soaking up information. They learn quickly and easily, and they remember things with less practice than their age mates. One grandparent remarked at how quickly her granddaughter remembered the location of items when they played the game of *Concentration®*. Another grandparent said, "I don't have to look up telephone numbers. I just ask my eight-year-old grandson." Many of you already know that when you read a bedtime story, your gifted grandchild will quickly notice if you skip a page or change or omit any part. The child can often fill in the missing phrase or sentences for you.

Intense Curiosity

Gifted children are very inquisitive and are continually asking, "Why?" Their questions often show an advanced ability to think and reason. For example, "Why do we call it toothpaste? It ought to be teethpaste." "What makes stars twinkle?"

"Why does your face have lines?" Questions such as these can be on any subject and may at times seem impolitely curious, making adults uncomfortable. Yet to the child, the questions seem perfectly reasonable. He or she has not lived long enough to understand social rules that govern things seen as inappropriate or tactless.

Gifted children often have such a wide range of interests that there do not seem to be enough hours in the day. They even fight going to sleep as long as possible so as to continue to learn! Their interests frequently go far beyond what is typical for their age, and they may even create their own experiments—sometimes to the dismay of adults. Their curiosity may prompt them to take apart the toaster or the fishing reel or the telephone just to see how it works, or they may try mixing different foods together to see how they taste, look, or feel.

Passionate Imagination and Creativity

Preschool gifted children will very often have an imaginary playmate, and sometimes more than one. The imaginary playmates may have imaginary pets and live in an imaginary town or city. If playmates are not easily available, the child will create games with her imaginary playmates.

We know of one young girl who claimed that she came from the Rabbit Family before she lived with her present family. We know another gifted child with two imaginary friends. Conveniently, these two, Lena and Deeka, were the ones who "did it" if something was broken or out of place. Still another child insisted that the imaginary friend eat at the dinner table, and the child's mother had to set another place setting.

Parents and grandparents may worry that the child's imaginary playmates indicate emotional problems or that the child is not receiving enough intellectual stimulation. Almost always, this is not at all the case. As long as a child can give and receive affection, imaginary playmates simply reflect high intelligence and creativity.

Remarkable Sense of Humor

By age five or six, the gifted child's strong imagination and creativity may be expressed in an unusually mature sense of humor, and by age eight or 10, the child may even be inventing riddles or puns. A young gifted child might say, for example, "Do you know the stomach's favorite color? It's burple." And then the child will laugh for five minutes. Or the child may find it hilariously funny to tell you the story of two Eskimos sitting a kayak who were chilly, but when they lit a fire in the craft, it sank. (This proves once again that you can't have your kayak and heat it, too.) Gifted children like these can wear parents out with the number of puns they create.

The zany sense of humor and creativity of a gifted child can produce more than groans. Sometimes good judgment is sacrificed for a joke, a prank, or an experiment. One six-year-old experimented with the acoustics of her tap-shoes by dancing on the hood of the family car in the garage. Needless to say, her parents were not amused. Another child tried mixing Jell-O on the carpet. These are true stories; we have not made them up. Parents and grandparents will need to remind themselves that the child's curiosity and creativity are what prompts these behaviors, and they must try to understand that sometimes these intense children will act before they think through the consequences. They generally *do* learn from their experiences.

Creativity can also cause gifted children to question customs and traditions, often causing adults to wonder themselves as they try to provide answers. "Why do we have to get dressed up to go to church?" "Why does the fork always have to be to the left of the plate?" "Why can't I wear a plaid shirt with striped pants?" "Why can't children correct grown-ups if we know they are wrong?" And be forewarned that gifted children are not satisfied with "That's just the way we do it." They will want to know the reasons and will question those reasons.

Gifted children see the world through a lens that is simply different from that of most people. The brighter and more creative they are, the more likely they are to come up with non-conventional solutions to problems or different ways to behave in situations. Their solutions may or may not be workable.

Throughout all of the above examples, it is important to remember that these gifted children are *truly unaware* that the way they see the world or the way they behave is any different from how others see the world or behave. Since they have always seen the world through their own eyes, their way of thinking and being is normal to them. To their way of thinking, everyone else should be able to think and see problems and solutions as easily and in the same way as they do. For example, your five-year-old granddaughter will likely be genuinely surprised to discover that other children in kindergarten do not know how to read as well as she does. Or your 10-year-old grandson, who can see the next three possible chess moves, simply cannot understand why his friend doesn't visualize the steps necessary to checkmate and win the game. Gifted children's impatience with others is sometimes due to the fact that they simply assume that everyone else sees things the way they do. It will take a few more years of experience living in the world for them to learn that this is not the case.

Longer Attention Span

It is not just gifted infants who gaze intently with longer attention spans. Gifted children of any age show longer attention spans—in things *they* are interested in, not necessarily what you or I think they should be interested in. Many gifted children will spend long periods of time reading, building models, or drawing, often "forgetting" their household duties and not even hearing you call their name. Their concentration is so intense and focused in their area of interest at the moment that it can be all-consuming for them— at least until they discover the next area of interest, which then also becomes all-consuming. A gifted child who is engrossed in a good book simply does not hear a parent's reminder to set the table or do some other chore. The parent may need to stand in front of the child, make eye contact, and then state the request.

Gifted children note and care about details that aren't important to others. After reading the second Harry Potter book four times, a 10-year-old proudly announced that she could now name all of the courses that Harry and his friends studied at Hogwart's School. Most readers don't care about such details and certainly wouldn't bother to read a book four times to be able to list them.

Complex Thinking

Gifted children seek complexity. As preschoolers, they often devise complex structures or try to organize people and things into very complex systems. They may, for example, invent a game— but the game will have complex rules and then one or two exceptions to the rules. However, when the gifted child tries to organize the other children—who have difficulty understanding the game, much less the rules—the result is chaos, frustration, rejection, and hurt feelings. Again, the gifted child doesn't know that he experiences the world differently, and he becomes frustrated with the other children.

This search for complexity leads gifted children to become bored rather easily, particularly with routine tasks such as practice drills. Many gifted children like to have several activities going on simultaneously. Particularly frustrating to the adults around them is that they often will leave many of those tasks just partially completed. For example, they may start to assemble a jigsaw puzzle, then abandon the scattered pieces to go to the piano to pick out a one-finger tune. The child may then return to a game, where she is playing an imaginary opponent and moves pieces for both herself and the opponent.

Sensitivity

Gifted children are sensitive. They may show a compassion toward others that is unusual for their age, and they may also be quite sensitive to the expectations of others. Their sensitivity may cause them to pick up on others' feelings so keenly that they seem to have an almost intuitive sense. One grandparent described her 12-year-old grandson as "the diplomat" because he could sense tension between family members and would begin negotiations to try to prevent the looming conflict.

Gifted children are particularly sensitive to ideas of fairness and a sense of justice. They may be distraught because a classmate was teased or bullied, or they may cry when they see a homeless person who appears hungry. Gifted preschoolers may become upset over things they see on the evening news, or they may cry when they see a beautiful butterfly smashed on the car windshield.

Professionals are now beginning to recognize that the brighter the child, the more sensitive he or she may be. Thus, the child who is highly gifted notices even more in the environment and reacts even more strongly.

The sensitivity of gifted children can easily lead to hurt. If other children tease or taunt them or won't eat lunch with them, it hurts them very deeply. They may suddenly break off a longstanding friendship because of a quarrel, and they may remember criticisms and slights for long periods of time. The sensitivity extends even to physical stimuli. For example, quite a number of gifted children are particularly sensitive to lights, sounds, odors, or even touch. Parents have told us that they have to remove the tags from the backs of their gifted children's shirts, or that their children complain if their socks have seams, or if certain clothing material rubs against their skin. Other children are bothered by the sound of fluorescent lights or are intensely bothered by aftershave, perfume, or other scents.

Intensity

Perhaps the most striking aspect of gifted children, and one that underlies all the others, is intensity. Gifted children simply are more intense than other girls and boys. Whatever these children do, they do it intensely. Whatever they believe, they believe intensely. When they converse, they state their opinions with great intensity. One mother explained, "My child's life motto seems to be 'Anything worth doing is worth doing to excess!'"

Gifted children do seem to be "excessive personalities." If they are involved in chess, that is all they want to do. If they are interested in insects, that becomes their passion. The intensity extends to sibling rivalry, temper tantrums, and power struggles with adults. Even their sleep patterns are characterized by intensity. When they sleep, they are more deeply asleep and more difficult to awaken. Dreams are more vivid and often are in color (not everyone dreams in color). Some professionals have noted that gifted boys are so deeply asleep that they seem more likely to sleepwalk or to be bedwetters than other children. As a side note, about 20% of gifted children need significantly less sleep than other children, and about 20% need significantly more sleep than other children.

The intensity of gifted children prompts them to have great enthusiasm and can be a very positive characteristic, but it can also lead them to be impatient with others. They may have difficulty understanding why other children do not share their interests, or don't easily grasp solutions to problems, or don't master a task as quickly as they do.

The intensity can also cause them to be impatient with themselves. Sometimes they are perfectionists, even at an early age. They can see in their mind's eye what they might be able to do, but they can see just as keenly how they are falling short of their ideal. For example, young gifted children often are impatient with their fine-motor skills. They know they would like to play the piano but are very frustrated when their fingers do not cooperate. One two-year-old gifted boy, for example, insisted that his parents read "Twas the Night Before Christmas" to him over and over again for what seemed to be hundreds of times. He corrected his parents if they left out a single word or phrase. But he refused to try to recite it himself. Then, one day, much to the family's surprise, he stood in his high chair and recited the entire thing from beginning to end without error. He had it down. Perfect. Some gifted children who are fearful of taking risks feel they must master a skill first before showing others. The need to be perfect with these children is strong.

Gifted or Just Smart?

With some children, even at an early age, it is easy to tell that the child is not only gifted but is highly gifted. With other children, it can be more difficult. Perhaps a child has unusual abilities in mechanical areas rather than verbal, or has unusual artistic talents rather than strong mathematical ability, or perhaps the child is intellectually strong in areas that can only become apparent as the child matures. It can be difficult to see a child's potential before the child has an opportunity to gain some experience in that area. For example, Greta's grandparents knew that she always enjoyed music, but they had no idea how musically talented she was until she began taking Suzuki violin lessons at age four.

Carol Strip and Gretchen Hirsch, in their excellent book *Helping Gifted Children Soar*,[23] list characteristics of gifted children, and then they provide tables that contrast the characteristics of gifted children with those of children who are called "smart." They emphasize that the primary difference between a smart child and a gifted child lies in the depth and intensity of these traits, and their advice is to look for the degree to which the child displays the traits. For example, smart children are more curious than average children, but gifted children are even more curious, and about more things and in far more depth. Smart children may like to read books, while gifted children are avid consumers of books. The difference between "smart" and "gifted" is generally a matter of degree of the intensity and complexity of the interest or other trait. The following characteristics, adapted from *Helping Gifted Children Soar*,[24] provide examples of key differences.

Questioning Style

Smart children ask questions that have answers. Gifted children ask questions that may not have easy answers, such as about abstract ideas, concepts, and theories. They may ask, for example, why light travels faster than sound, and whether this always is true, even in outer space.

Learning Speed and Application of Concepts

Smart children learn step-by-step until they grasp a concept. Gifted children may jump directly from Step 2 to Step 10 because by the time they've completed Step 2, they've already figured out the solution to the problem. Gifted children may not want to write down all of the steps that they took in solving a problem because they have figured it out in their head. To them, writing it down wastes valuable time.

Emotional Outlook

Smart children show emotion but generally are able to get past an upsetting incident fairly easily and quickly. Gifted children experience heightened, sometimes all-consuming emotions that may hamper other areas of thought or work. Their intense concerns intrude into their thoughts for days or weeks or even longer after an event.

Level of Interest

Smart children ask questions and are curious about a number of things. Gifted children show intense curiosity about nearly everything or immerse themselves in an area that interests them. For example, Sarah, at age seven, has already started a serious collection of frog larvae, and she loves to read books about amphibians or to talk to adults about natural history topics. She already is talking about becoming a zoologist when she is older.

Language Ability

Smart children learn new vocabulary easily but choose words that are typical for their ages. Gifted children use extensive, advanced vocabularies, understand verbal nuances that escape others, enjoy wordplay and puns, and often talk

over the heads of their playmates (and sometimes over adults, too). When adults try to talk in
code by using large words or by spelling words,
gifted children quickly break the code.

Concern with Morality, Justice, and Fairness

Smart children state firm opinions about what's
fair, but those opinions usually relate to personal
situations, such as, "He got more cake than I
did." Gifted children show concern about fairness and equity far more intensely and on a
more global scale. They are able to grasp the
subtleties of complex moral and ethical questions, such as those relating to war or environ-
mental issues, and they defend their viewpoints
fervently. Pedro, age nine, has been quite upset
while watching evening television because the
advertisements are not completely candid and
seem to try to persuade people by making claims
that are only partly true. He wants to complain
to the network.

How Many Gifted Children Are There?

How often do gifted children occur in the
population? How unusual or exceptional do
their abilities or potentials need to be in order

for them to be considered gifted? Do gifted children need special schools? Are they difficult to raise? Do they have mental health problems? Would they be better off just being "normal" and not "smarter" or "different"? Should we try to help them be "normal"?

The answers to these questions aren't always easy. Not all smart children are gifted, and not all gifted children are geniuses. Where one draws the line is open to debate. How unusual an ability must be in order to be called "exceptional" is somewhat arbitrary. Most experts agree, however, that children with abilities that put them in the upper 3% to 5% of the population should be considered gifted.

As for how many gifted are out there, we can estimate that two, or three, or even five children out of every 100 will be gifted to some degree, while probably about one or two children out of every 1,000 will fall in the highly or profoundly gifted category. These figures amaze most people because they show that gifted children are more common than previously thought.

For years, it was presumed that a gifted child—what some people would call a genius—was very rare—so rare that you would not want one in your family because he or she would be considered "odd" by society and would probably cause the family much grief due to their "weirdness." This belief was very strong in the 19th and early 20th Centuries. Along with this was the theory that if you were so unlucky as to have such a child, you should do everything possible to keep the child as normal as possible because there was also a theory of "early ripe, early rot." In other words, if the child were allowed to develop his genius while still young, he would surely fall apart emotionally as a young adult and perhaps develop some sort of mental illness or even need to be institutionalized.

We have come a long way in understanding giftedness since those days, but unfortunately, the stigma of being different remains. There is still a strong societal belief that it is best for everyone to be "normal" and to follow ordinary, expected behaviors for one's age group. If a child is unusually bright, it is best to keep the child as normal as possible and not allow her to skip grades in school, so the theory goes. This approach essentially holds the child back from developing her potential.

More recent research has shown these former beliefs and stereotypes to be wrong, but they still persist in the subtle messages society sends its gifted individuals. This may be because (1) many of us incorrectly equate the term "gifted" with the concept of genius, and (2) we do not realize that the proportion of children who are gifted (i.e., 3% to 5%) is the same as the proportion of children whose low abilities and potentials lead them to be classified as mentally retarded or exceptional at the other end of the intellectual spectrum. Both groups are exceptional; both groups have special needs because of their unusual intellect. Both groups need special educational attention. Both groups need help from caring adults to fulfill their potential. Both groups benefit from having teachers with special training in their unique needs. Both groups are equally different from "average." Just as with the seemingly large numbers of children identified in schools as "Special Ed" at the other end of the spectrum, giftedness may not be as rare as many have thought, particularly if schools were to look for and identify the exceptional children who are gifted.

Perhaps the lack of understanding of giftedness is also because many of us have not understood until recently that a wide range of ability exists within giftedness—i.e., mildly gifted, moderately gifted, highly gifted, exceptionally gifted, and profoundly gifted. Not all gifted individuals are the same, and not all gifted individuals are geniuses by any means. There are similar distinctions at the lower end of the intellectual spectrum, where we see variations in learning capacity between mildly retarded, moderately retarded, and severely retarded. We readily accept that children at the lower end of the intellectual spectrum need educational modifications delivered by teachers who have training and expertise in that area. Likewise, we know that children at the higher end of the intellectual spectrum thrive best when they receive modifications to their educational program, delivered by teachers with training and expertise in that area.

Fortunately there has been some progress in the area of gifted education training in the past three decades. Many universities now offer graduate degrees with specialization in gifted education, and a majority of states have legal mandates stating that public schools must identify and serve children who show abilities in the gifted ranges, though the level of service is sometimes minimal. This is a far cry from the days when there was a fear of "early ripe, early rot" (though remnants of that earlier belief still exist in the society at large). We can probably assume, and certainly we hope, that there will continue to be increased acceptance and understanding of gifted individuals and that a whole variety of new and better education options will be available to gifted children in the current decade and in those to come.

In our society, which stresses equality for all persons, it is important to remember that being gifted does not mean that one is inherently "better" or "worse" than any other individual. Gifted individuals have strengths and weaknesses and problems just like anyone else. What is different about gifted individuals is simply that they have the ability to learn and progress rapidly in their areas of strength, and in that way, they appear different from others. All individuals are valuable. Our society needs a variety of talents, abilities, and careers to support its operation. Developing the talents and abilities of gifted individuals will allow them to contribute their best work.

Types of Giftedness

In addition to the characteristics of gifted children (which also apply to gifted adults, by the way) that we described above, we will mention some broad categories of giftedness. The ones below come from a national organization that advocates for gifted children.

As we mentioned earlier, children can be talented or gifted in many different ways. Some children have unusually high abilities in only one area; others are precocious in several areas. The National Association for Gifted Children (www.nagc.org) provides a general classification of the types of giftedness, similar to the description developed some years earlier by the U. S. Office of Education, by defining a gifted person as "someone who shows, or has the potential for showing, an exceptional level of performance" in one or more of the following five areas:

➤ General intellectual ability.
➤ Specific academic aptitude.
➤ Creative thinking.
➤ Leadership ability.
➤ Visual or performing arts.

This definition clearly encompasses a wide range of giftedness that extends beyond the notion of simple academic intelligence. A child might be gifted in one or more of the above areas. Seldom is any one child gifted in all of the areas, but many are gifted in two, three, or even four of them.

How do these five major areas of giftedness differ? Following is a summary of each. As you will see, several are closely related.

Intellectual

Children who are intellectually gifted score well on intelligence or aptitude tests; they also do well academically. Some areas measured by intelligence tests, however, are not skills that are emphasized by schools. For example, mechanical or artistic aptitude is not likely to be given as much weight by school or intelligence tests as verbal aptitude.

Academic

Children who are academically gifted do very well in traditional academic areas, such as reading, writing, and arithmetic, and they usually earn high grades and do well on achievement tests given by the schools.

Creative

Children who are creatively gifted tend to be divergent thinkers and are often involved in many diverse activities. Because they think "outside the box," they may or may not do well in traditional academic settings. Standardized tests don't always reflect their true abilities because these children may try to "outthink" the test or think of new or unusual answers. Portfolios of their creative work or formal or informal performance showing their talent and skill, particularly in fine and practical arts such as art, music, computer programming, or keyboarding, are better ways that teachers and parents can recognize exceptional creative abilities. To be creative, one must first have a skill, and the creativity comes about when the person does something unusual with that skill.

Leadership

For many years, it has been recognized that some children are gifted leaders. These children have an ability to recognize and interpret interpersonal cues, personality styles, and interpersonal situations, and they know how to lead others in various situations. This skill has also been referred to as "emotional intelligence."[25] As with creativity, emotional intelligence is most likely to be recognized through observation of the child.

Visual and Performing Arts

Children who are gifted in fine and performing arts have most often been referred to in the past as "talented," but in the last 30 years or so, such talent areas have been considered as part of the gifted umbrella. Often, these children are also quite creative, have high leadership abilities, and may also be intellectually or academically gifted. Assessment of gifted abilities in the fine and performing arts is done primarily through performances and portfolios that demonstrate the child's unusually high abilities.

Twice Exceptional Gifted Children

Some gifted children are also exceptional in another sense—they are "twice exceptional" in that they have a disability as well as one or more traits of giftedness. Children who are deaf, blind, learning disabled, or who suffer from cerebral palsy can be gifted in math or reading or music or in overall intellectual ability. Their keen intellect, creativity, academic or artistic ability, or leadership may be partially hidden because of their inability to speak or write fluently. Students with dyslexia, for example, may still have very advanced knowledge, thinking skills, and problem-solving abilities. The dyslexia means they may have difficulties with traditional learning or in showing their knowledge in a formal school setting. In fact, some experts[26] have found that the more highly gifted the child, the more likely it is that the child's abilities will cover a wide span. Sometimes this spread of abilities is so great that the child is gifted in many areas and yet also is learning disabled in one or more areas. In such cases, it is important that the person doing testing and test interpretation be knowledgeable about traits of giftedness.

The needs of gifted children who are twice-exceptional are, of course, greater than those of other gifted and talented children. Twice-exceptional children are at risk because others are likely to greatly underestimate their potential, and consequently, they are less likely to receive the academic support and stimulation that is needed to develop their abilities. Twice-exceptional children are at tremendous risk for low self-esteem. They will tend to minimize their abilities because others may treat them as less able or because they are not able to express their intellect adequately to show their high ability to others. Often, they will focus their self-image on what they are unable to do—on their failures or mistakes—rather than recognizing how skilled they are in other areas.[27]

It is particularly important for twice-exceptional gifted children to be seen by a qualified psychologist for testing. Assessment will verify the child's strengths as well as areas of disability, and results will help parents and teachers to develop a plan for the child's education. Sometimes a child's disability can mask his or her giftedness and prevent abilities from being recognized and encouraged at home and at school. And sometimes the giftedness can mask a disability. We are not recommending that grandparents should intrusively assume the role of parents in getting the child evaluated by a psychologist. But sometimes it is the grandparents, rather than the parents, who will recognize that a child with disabilities is also gifted. Grandparents certainly can, and should, talk to the child's parents to help them become aware of any particular things that the grandparent has noticed.

If nothing is going well, call your grandmother.
~ Italian Proverb

*Too many people grow up. That's the real trouble with the
world; too many people grow up. They don't remember
what it's like to be 12 years old. They patronize, they treat
children as inferiors. Well I won't do that.*
~ Walt Disney

Chapter 3

Some Areas of Concern for Gifted Children

You are probably reading this book because you already know you have a gifted grandchild. The child you have in mind is mentally quick and observant, retains an unusual amount of information, has a delightful imagination, and is wonderfully creative in play and conversation. This child is eager to learn and has a zest and a passion for life. When your grandchild approaches projects and activities, it is with great enthusiasm and intensity. Her emotions, both positive and negative, are also intense. If these phrases describe your grandchild, she is demonstrating many of the common traits of a gifted child.

This child has positive energy and seems full of promise. You have no doubt that she will do very well in this world when she becomes an adult. You predict that she will enjoy a wonderful career as a physician, lawyer, artist, university professor, or valued community leader, where she will be able to use her academic, social, and leadership potential, as well as her energy and enthusiasm.

We certainly wish this kind of happiness and success for our grandchildren, but unfortunately, many bright, talented, and gifted children actually perform far below their potential later in life as gifted adults. Why is this? What happens? In simplest terms, even though these children are smart, development of their great potential is often hindered, unintentionally, by various factors at home and at school. It appears that many gifted youngsters have intellectual needs, as well as social and emotional needs, that are simply not recognized by others and therefore do not get addressed. We believe that gifted children who are surrounded by parents and educators who understand them in all of their complexities are more likely as adults to realize their potential. They can then put their intellectual, creative, artistic, and leadership abilities to use in ways that are both personally satisfying and productive for society.

Gifted children, with their extreme emotional sensitivity and idealism, often notice great gaps between how things are and how they ought to be—in their family, their school, their community, and the larger world. Because of their keen minds and their sharp thinking and reasoning abilities, they find themselves acutely aware of mediocrity, greed, poverty, corruption, violence, abuse, pollution, hypocrisy, and other flaws in society. They become discouraged and disillusioned that no one else cares or that these problems can never be fixed. They may feel an overwhelming sense of hopelessness. As a result of this "What's the point?" attitude, many intellectually gifted youngsters choose to underachieve in school, and some drop out of high school, college, or even society altogether. They may search for a life or career where they don't have to deal with social hypocrisy or other aspects of society that make them uncomfortable.

Our 30-some years of experience with gifted children indicate that meeting the social and emotional needs of these sensitive and intense children is at least as important as meeting their academic needs—perhaps even more. You personally may know some gifted adolescents or adults who seem to struggle with various aspects of their lives and with finding their place in the world. As adults, these individuals may act out their rebellion by living on the fringes of society or rejecting what they see as mainstream life— avoiding competition, the news media, or even the long-standing values and traditions of their families. Some eventually find satisfaction in unconventional ways, such as through the arts as musicians, actors, or craftsmen. Others may find fulfillment in a sustainable, rural life, raising animals and growing their own food. There is room for all of these lifestyles in a society that needs change and betterment. But what is lacking in the social and emotional lives of these individuals that sometimes causes them to reject traditional achievement and choose a totally different path from what adults and mentors in their earlier lives had predicted or envisioned?

Of course, not all gifted children are doomed to experience personal problems or to rebelliously become social misfits, hermits, or underachievers as adults. Many bright children who have received support and opportunities will develop the confidence needed to enthusiastically pursue nontraditional careers and lifestyles. Many are happy and well adjusted. But those who are unhappy typically feel misunderstood or rejected by others. Some are seen by their teachers as behavior problems because they ask too many questions, challenge, or make smart comments. Some who love verbal argument and debate get into power struggles with adults, particularly if they feel that their rights have been violated or that something is not fair. Some may dislike others who tease or bully them. And some gifted children receive poor grades or purposely fail classes simply because they become discouraged with an educational system where they don't seem to belong.[28]

Perfectionism

Some gifted children struggle with perfectionism, putting pressure on themselves and perhaps others to behave or perform perfectly. Even when very young, some of these children will work for a long time on a difficult task like printing their name or building a tower from blocks, discarding in great frustration their previous, less-than-perfect attempts. Even without pressure from others, gifted children are quick to see and understand how a task or project should be accomplished and what the final result should look like. They can just as easily see how they are falling short of that goal. They have set a standard of perfection for themselves. Even if they are too young to have the necessary skills or coordination, or if their standards are unreasonably high, some of these children see themselves as failures for falling short of the goal. In fact, some of them are so hard on themselves that they actually develop headaches or stomach problems.

Too much emphasis on achievement by others can also encourage perfectionism, so parents and others should be careful not to push children, but instead encourage them to follow their own initiative.

Occasionally, perfectionism is expressed in procrastination, sometimes called fear of failure. The child's reasoning is that if he doesn't try, then he cannot fail. Or if he postpones a task or decision, or if he thinks about it longer, then he can do it better or more perfectly later. Families of gifted children can often find themselves waiting in frustration for a child to finish a task that, in their minds, could easily be left in its current, imperfect but yet acceptable state. At other times, families may be distressed that their child is procrastinating with a task that appears to be very simple.

Many parents of gifted children have observed that their child will spend more time trying to figure out a new and better way of doing a task than it would take simply to do it. Aryanna, for example, spent so much time devising a way to videotape the position of her fingers as she practiced on the piano that she had almost no time left before her recital to actually rehearse her piece.

One mother recounted the story of her nine-month-old son learning to walk—taking about four perfectly balanced steps across the room, falling down, and then not trying again for three more months. It was as if this young child was not going to try again until he could walk without falling. This child wanted to be perfect and would avoid attempting things until he was certain that he could do them well. Similarly, older children learning to ski often don't want parents or siblings to watch their lessons, but prefer to wait until they can ski well before they show others.

Do parents teach children to be perfectionists, or are perfectionists just born that way? Most perfectionistic gifted children, in our experience, seem to have innate predispositions in that direction and thus put pressure on themselves. However, our experience also shows that "apples don't fall very far from the tree" and that usually, one of the child's parents—or someone else in the family—is also perfectionistic, thereby providing a model for perfectionism.

Is perfectionism always a serious problem for the child? Not always. It depends on how much stress these high goals cause for the child or the family, or how much they hinder the child from making progress. In the book *Perfectionism: What's Bad about Being Too Good,*[29] the author describes the major pitfalls of too much perfectionism. But for some children, she notes, the ability to set high standards is also an asset. Certainly, we want our future astronauts, architects, physicians, teachers, scientists, and business executives to have high standards in their work.

The danger occurs when perfectionism is so strong that it becomes almost a handicapping condition for the child. Silverman[30] talks about the difference between healthy perfectionism and a paralyzing perfectionism that can hinder one's ability to work productively. As grandparents, you will want to encourage the healthy kind of perfectionism, the kind that serves as motivation to achieve one's best, but not the kind that results in headaches or stomach upset. One way to do this is to share stories from your own life to illustrate that a certain number of mistakes and practice attempts are necessary when learning any new skill or project. You can say, "I remember when I first learned to ride a two wheeler. I thought I would never learn. I tried and tried. I fell at least 50 times, but I was so excited when I finally learned how to do it." Stories and examples like this can help children understand that doing something perfectly the first time is almost an impossible expectation, so they can ease up on themselves a bit.

For the child who is overly sensitive to even small mistakes, you can point out your own insignificant oversights or slip-ups, like forgetting someone's birthday or an item on a grocery list. Mention these to the child, and through your modeling, show the child that the mistake is not a huge embarrassment or a devastating humiliation. Showing the child that you—and virtually everyone else—make mistakes helps put things in better perspective. You might say, "I made these cookies yesterday and forgot to put in the baking powder. I got interrupted with a phone call. We'll just eat them anyway and laugh at Grandma's mistake. I'll be sure to double check all the ingredients next time. Do they still taste all right to you?"

To help an older child who suffers from perfectionism, talk about mistakes that you have made in your life, noting that mistakes are almost always helpful because we learn from them. Some of the most important discoveries in science, medicine, and other fields have come from unintended mistakes. Silly Putty®, Coca Cola™, Frisbees®, Slinkys®, penicillin, microwave ovens, potato chips, and many other modern inventions and discoveries all came from mistakes and misunderstandings.[31]

You can also mention to the child that no one successfully plays a musical instrument or becomes a fabulous athlete until they have lots and lots of practice, usually years and years. Tiger Woods started learning to play golf at about the same time he entered school; Michael Jordan initially was not very good at basketball and was cut from his high school basketball team.[32] It was only through years of practice that he became a championship player. Professional athletes and musicians, as well as people who are successful in business, computers, and other fields all need a great deal of practice to be successful at their jobs, and they never stop trying to improve. They can't just do it once and expect to perform well the first time.

Sometimes gifted children, with their quickness and ability to succeed at most tasks with little effort, give up too readily when they first come up against something that doesn't come easily or naturally to them. Talking about mistakes as practice in this way helps gifted children accept that there may be some things in life that they will encounter that are difficult for them.

Are all gifted children perfectionists? No. Many are not. We have seen children—particularly those who are the more divergent thinking, creative, and imaginative youngsters—who seem to give little care or attention to detail or neatness and who even show a pattern of unconcerned sloppiness. These children look unorganized. They are quite comfortable with moving quickly from one thing to the next, leaving behind many unfinished tasks. It is as though once their interest in an area is satisfied, they feel that their efforts there were good enough. These children may at times need encouragement to stick with a task longer, as opposed to a perfectionistic child who will often stay, and stay, and stay with a task too long.

It is clear that perfectionism can be a problem for some gifted children, but parents and other adults can help them learn to deal with it more effectively.

Relating to Peers

Peer relationships and friends are another common problem area for gifted children. As grandparents, we want our grandchild to be able to get along with others and to have friends. We may be concerned that she does not like to play with children her own age, but chooses instead to stay home and read a book. Or she may prefer interacting with older children or spending time talking with adults—both of whom are closer as intellectual peers—rather than her age peers. Other children view her as being too bossy and someone they don't want to be with. As grandparents observing this, we worry. We think, "She needs to learn to get along with other children. She needs to be well-liked by others if she is to be successful in this world."

These are all, of course, valid concerns, but they need to be tempered a bit. The first question to consider is this: Who is a peer for a gifted child? Does it need to be a child the same age? How many other first graders are interested in chess? Or astronomy? Or bird watching? We need to look for peers in an area of interest. Are there other children interested in chess? Are there teens? Or even adults? Who and where are they? In our experience, gifted children will need different peers for different activities.

As adults, we have a variety of friends for our different interests. The people we go to the symphony with are not necessarily the same people we go hiking with, and these are different still from the friends we have at work. We adults usually have several different peer groups. It is the same for gifted children. They may have one group of friends their own age with whom they play in the neighborhood, but they may prefer to be with older children to play sophisticated computer games, or with adults to play chess.

Parents and grandparents often tell us that they worry that their child does not have enough friends. They say, "He would rather stay home with his Legos® than play with children his age." We remind these adults that they themselves have probably been to more than one social event where they wished they were home reading the book on their bedside table. So perhaps we shouldn't worry so much if a child sometimes likes to read or play alone. Research by Barbara Kerr shows that gifted women who later became eminent as adults had one thing in common; it was that as children, these women all seemed to experience large amounts of "alone time," reading or thinking or following other pursuits. This research is described in Kerr's book, *Smart Girls: A New Psychology of Girls, Women, and Giftedness.*[33] We, too, have noted that many gifted children, even though they are quite capable of interactive play, often choose to spend substantial amounts of time alone in solitary play, manipulating objects or creating things, or just reading quietly.

Most of us can relate to the immense satisfaction we can get from burying ourselves in a good book and identifying with the characters or themes. The title of Judith Halsted's book, *Some of My Best Friends Are Books*,[34] captures this idea well. Both a librarian and a gifted specialist, Halsted understands the importance of reading to gifted children for intellectual and social and emotional growth. Her book describes the gifted reader and contains short summaries of about 300 books indexed by K-12 reading levels, as well as by themes or topics.

Another common social/emotional characteristic of gifted children is that many of them are more introverted than children in general.[35] When a tendency toward introversion is combined with the frequent lack of fit between gifted children and their age peers (in terms of interests, skills, knowledge, sensitivity, and intensity), it is not surprising that gifted children, particularly those who are highly gifted, may find that they have little in common with their age peers. So although gifted children should certainly learn the social skills of getting along and being socially friendly with everyone, we shouldn't expect them to become best friends with all, or even most, of their age peers.

Yet another problem for gifted children is that their vocabularies and other abilities are sometimes so advanced that they quickly leave age peers behind in these areas—a gap that can create social communication problems. It only makes sense that these children gravitate toward adults and older children whose vocabulary and interests more clearly match their own. Yet mixed-age relationships are problematic in other ways. They may separate the gifted child from classmates his own age, reducing the number of friendships with his age group, and may make him seem as though he is trying to appear too grown up. They may put him with pre-teens or teens, who are ready for talk about topics too mature for a young child. Parents and grandparents will need to monitor contact with older children.

Spending time in adult company can condition a child to assume a parental tone or a bossy role with other children and can cause other children to withdraw. Children don't usually like to be bossed around by another child Still, it is important that the child be with others—regardless of their ages—who share her interests and passions.

Sometimes a parent or grandparent can help the child by talking about friends, noticing which ones she enjoys for which activities, and affirming that that is acceptable. Some gifted children remain friends with children they knew in kindergarten and the elementary grades, even though the gifted child subsequently skips a grade or goes to a higher-level classroom for one or two subjects each day. A gifted child will often attend birthday parties or play after school with age-level friends, but will enjoy more academic pursuits with another group, maybe children they met at a special weekend program. Merely having an awareness that a gifted child may want different kinds of friends for different activities will be helpful.

Who, then, are the best peers for a gifted child? Are other gifted children the best peers? Sometimes, yes. This is particularly so if the other gifted children are about the same intellectual level and share many of the same interests. Situations which group several gifted children together are exciting for them, though the level of excitement is often exhausting for any adults who happen to be around. The intensity of two or three gifted children grouped together is, of course, magnified; they seem to eat, sleep, drink, breathe, and live each other's lives. The energy level is palpable, and the noise level is usually quite high. From the gifted child's point of view, it is very exciting to find someone else who can jump from topic to topic as rapidly as he and who has new information, interests, or skills to share. What parents and grandparents can do to help is to offer some structure, as well as some constraints. "You can build Legos® until lunchtime, and then all of you together can help make your sandwiches." Or, "Here are some supplies for your fort, but if it gets too noisy, you'll need to go outside to play."

Grandparents often do not realize it, but they, too, can be peers for their gifted grandchildren. Many grandparents delight in playing board or card games with their grandchild or being childishly silly with their grandchildren, enjoying the play and laughter of childhood, then switching back to seriousness when the situation requires it. Grandparents understand peer relations—they have had numerous and diverse peers during their life—and they understand as well as anyone that there are many ways to live successfully that don't hinge on being liked by peers.

Underachievement

We know that some gifted children are underachievers in areas where they could easily excel.

Why do children with such high potential under-achieve? Probably the single most important factor in underachievement is peer pressure, or wanting to fit in. The culture in most schools today, unfortunately, is one of conformity; pressures to wear the right clothes or to act the right way are enormous. One of the biggest reasons for underachievement, both for boys and girls, is the desire to fit in.[36]

The problem for bright girls was first noted years ago by the columnist Ann Landers, who wrote, "It's not too smart to be too smart—not if you're a girl and you want to fit in." And it is regrettable but true that the self-worth of girls is often established by the quality of the boy or man she can attract.[37] The problem for gifted boys, it seems, is that they must learn to respect, accept, and then adopt most aspects of "The Boy Code" if they are to be popular.[38] This means that boys must be learn to be independent, engage in daring behaviors, strive to attain dominance, and take care not to show "sissy" behaviors such as warmth, empathy, or dependence upon others. It also helps if boys are at least somewhat athletic. The big team sports are the most accepted—

football and basketball. But individual sports like tennis and golf are also acceptable.

Notice that none of the peer values listed above for girls or boys emphasize academic achievement. No wonder so many gifted boys and girls underachieve. Peer values are especially important to children and adolescents. In the Hispanic or African-American cultures, these pressures have an additional consequence—if you are a high achieving black or Hispanic male, you may be seen by your peers as "acting too white" and thus betraying your own culture. As a result, you may be rejected by your own ethnic group.

As long as schools continue to sort children by age alone for academics—i.e., all seven-year-olds belong in second grade—rather than by a child's achievement and ability, and as long as we continue to support social expectations that the most athletic boys and the cutest, prettiest girls will be the popular ones, our schools and other social systems are de-valuing those children who are different simply because they are bright. Should bright children have to play sports, be sociable, and "dumb down" in order to be accepted by society?

It appears that despite claiming support for academic excellence, our schools and our society actually prefer everyone to be the same and, in doing so, unknowingly encourage the underachievement of bright, talented, gifted boys and girls. Society seems rather confused as to whether it values its gifted children at all. If we look closely, we can see that much of the popular culture is focused on mediocrity in ways that are actually hostile to intellectual pursuits. Noted author and comedian Steve Allen[39] pointed out that TV and radio shows pander to the lowest common denominator and sometimes consciously reject talent and quality in order to reach the largest audience. Movie and pop music stars get more media coverage than NASA astronauts or photographs of Mars. Only when there is a disaster, like the Challenger explosion, does NASA get as much front-page media coverage as winning NBA teams. Only then do young people see heroes who are not sports or music stars. Only then do they see the education preparation, the years of training that are needed to become an astronaut—a career valued by society. Michael Jordan of the NBA is better known than Dick Scobee, who commanded the ill-fated Challenger spacecraft. It must be confusing to gifted youngsters to be told on the one hand that they should develop their intellectual, creative, academic, or artistic potential, while on the other hand they are bombarded with pressures to conform to an average stereotype, fit in with the group, and go along with current popular culture.

Throughout elementary, middle, and finally, high school, gifted students are often criticized for being "who they are." They hear from others that they worry too much, care too much, think too much, are involved in too many things, have a strange sense of humor, are too idealistic or critical or judgmental, and are basically just too different from others. When a highly sensitive young person hears these kinds of phrases over and over from parents, teachers, and peers, she begins to wonder if what they say is true. The bright, sensitive child will begin to doubt herself and wonder if there is something fundamentally wrong with her. She already knows that she is different. Now she asks herself, "Am I too sensitive? Am I strange? Should I try to be different?"

Is it any surprise that some of these youngsters have social or emotional difficulties with those who judge them? More than anything, they need at least one or two adults in their lives who believe in them, who appreciate their talents and traits, who support them emotionally, and who love them unconditionally—something grandparents uniquely can do. Furthermore, as a grandparent, you can talk about times and places when your own different way of being was not what was popular at the time.

You can also remind your grandchildren of the importance of achievement and the pursuit of quality and excellence, even though it may not be popular. Some books that are helpful on this complex issue of underachievement are *Why Bright Kids Get Poor Grades,*[40] *Giftedness, Conflict and Underachievement,*[41] and *Guiding the Gifted Child.*[42]

Discipline and Power Struggles

Self-discipline is necessary for a person to be able to go against peer pressure and to achieve, both in and outside of school. However, children are not born with self-discipline. They learn this important life-skill only after years of practice and encouragement from significant adults around them. With good intentions of helping children learn self-discipline, however, many parents—and sometimes grandparents—find themselves drifting into unhappy power struggles with their gifted children.

If it sometimes feels as if your grandchild is a seven- or eight-year-old lawyer skilled in refutation, you or the child's parents may be in for a series of power struggles. With this type of child, discipline often involves extensive, protracted, and painful discussion. As the grandparent, you probably want to support the parents and help them avoid getting caught up in a lengthy and relationship-damaging power struggle. But you don't want to intrude into the parents' realm, unless you actually are acting as the parent, as we talk about later in this book. You might, however, be able to help the child's parents understand that most gifted children are strong-willed. It's part of their inborn intensity, and later in life, it will probably be an important asset for them. Now, though, your grandchild's skilled attempts at asserting himself, manipulating others, or defying authority may be a major cause of strife within the family.

Let's say that your grandchild doesn't want to eat a certain food that is being served during a family dinner. Or the child is resisting bedtime.

Or the parents want their high school junior home from the party by 11:00 P.M., but the child wants to stay out until midnight. The child argues that the food makes him sick, or that there are special circumstances that should allow her to stay up later, or he maintains that everyone else will be staying at the party until midnight, and he will be totally embarrassed to be the only one not there.

Every loophole and exception is explored. Parent and child both stick to their arguments. The discussion turns to anger and shouting. Trying to set limits in cases like these often can be very difficult. Furthermore, the irony of these situations is that the more a parent cares about the child, the more likely it is that there will be a power struggle. Parents impose their will on a child because they want what's best for the child. Usually, these are issues for the parents; occasionally, though, grandparents must set—and enforce—limits, and they must encounter these discipline issues first-hand.

As the grandparent, we hope that you have a relationship with your children that will allow easy conversation—even about a matter as delicate as discipline within the family. If so, perhaps you can raise some questions that can help you and the parents gain some perspective. How much should parents and grandparents push? How do you know when to back off? These are important questions, and ones that are difficult to answer. The answer will vary with the child, and sometimes what you can insist on one day may not be enforceable another day.

Because of this, *we suggest you use your relationship with the child as your barometer.* We believe that your relationship is the most important thing you have with a child, and the most important aspects of your relationship are your *communication* with each other and the *mutual respect* that you demonstrate for each other. (This is true with people of all ages, not just children.)

Certainly you and the parents want your grandchild to manage himself better, or to attempt certain activities, or set his goals higher or try harder. But if by nudging or pushing your grandchild too hard, you are risking serious damage to your relationship, then the all-out war is too costly. If you lose the relationship, you have nothing left. And once it is lost, a relationship is hard to rebuild. Above all else, you need to preserve your relationship with your grandchild; it is the single most important thing that you have.

We are not trying to be Pollyannish here. We do recognize that sometimes the child does need limits that must be set and enforced consistently, regardless of the child's arguments. Generally, however, this is a matter for the parents, even though the grandparents may secretly believe that too many—or too few—limits are being set by the parents. Unless you are a grandparent who is also actually raising your grandchild as a parent, you will generally be better off limiting your role as disciplinarian in the situation. If you are functioning as the parent—and an increasing number of grandparents are doing so—then you will want to read more about discipline in Chapter 6 of this book.

To remain uninvolved can sometimes be difficult if you strongly disagree with the parents' discipline approach. Are they too harsh? Are they too lenient? Are they inconsistent?

Before you think about stepping in, it is important do a reality check. Perhaps you need to change your mind about discipline. Ask other parents and grandparents, and listen with an open mind. Perhaps the parents' style is right for this particular child at this time, or perhaps times have changed. Many of us were raised with a "spare the rod; spoil the child" strict discipline approach. We may feel that the parents are too lenient and our grandchild is being spoiled. But we may be wrong.

More often, in our experience, grandparents think that the parents are too harsh with the child. Perhaps, for example, you feel that the parents publicly humiliated your grandchild at dinner last week in a restaurant. Of course, you should not go behind the parents' back to say anything like, "I'm sure your mother didn't mean what she said. I'll speak to her about it." But what should you do?

We hope that you will strive to develop a relationship with your adult children in which you can talk about discipline issues. You can let them know how much you admire them for trying to teach your grandchildren appropriate self-discipline, rather than having discipline imposed from the outside. You can ask them how effective their approach has been. And perhaps you can raise a question about whether their discipline approach might affect their relationship (or your relationship) with the child. You might want to give them child-rearing books or articles or videos. Remember, good communication with your children is very important if they are to listen to your viewpoint. Also remember that they will be parents for a long time, probably well after you are gone. If after all of this you still disagree, at least you may be able to provide a gentle sanctuary for your grandchild, but without getting drawn into the child's relationship with his parents.

As a grandparent, you may also find opportunities to encourage your grandchild to participate in developing limits for herself. You might ask your grandchild, "How far do you think you should ride on your bike?" "How will you plan it so that you can be home before dark?" "What can you do that will reassure us so that we won't worry or get upset?" Encourage her to think not only about how a limit will affect her, but also how it might affect the people around her.

Dependence upon Praise and Accomplishments

The importance of learning self-motivation is as important as learning self-discipline. Gifted children—like all young children—want to be accepted and liked by others. They try to please others through something they do well that others will recognize and value as important. The accomplishment might be intellectual achievement or academic performance or a talent such as musical prowess. Is this what we want them to do? Yes, we want them to develop their abilities, but we want them to develop the talent for themselves, because they want to, not just to please teachers, parents, or grandparents.

Sometimes adults emphasize the achievements of gifted children so often and to such an extent that the child becomes dependent upon praise and works chiefly for the purpose of pleasing others. The child mistakenly thinks that he is valued only when he pleases others or does what they expect him to do. When a child has a particular talent, parents notice the child's talent and nudge him to do more, whether it's studying violin or astronomy. Although they may not intend to, a family of a gifted child can easily drift into a pattern of rewarding performance and achievement to such an extent that the child feels valued primarily for his ability to play the violin, or to spell difficult words, or some other skill. The child quite naturally but incorrectly concludes that he exists to please others. Such a child will have a hard time breaking away from this pattern to develop a career and life for himself alone. Parents don't mean to send the message that the child exists mainly for their pleasure, but when there is a charming, talented child so unusually gifted and delightful, it is hard not to give the child the wrong message.

Grandparents, aunts, uncles, and others can also fall into this trap if they continually ask Steven to demonstrate his mathematical abilities, or Maria to define words, or Josef to display his talent at painting. This can be a precarious position for a child if her self-worth depends heavily on the praise of others, rather than on how she views herself. It is as though her entire self-concept hangs only on one hook—doing things well.

Even if parents and grandparents know better than to emphasize grades or performance to such an extreme degree, they may still give the child an impression that his giftedness and brightness is his primary asset. Some parents and grandparents even pointedly emphasize the child's achievements, as well as the label "gifted" in family conversation. In our opinion, this is not healthy for the child or for the family. In her book *The Drama of the Gifted Child*,[43] Alice

Miller describes problems that can occur when parents of gifted children overemphasize their abilities and achievements. Some of these families "remind" everyone of their child's giftedness so frequently that they seem to satisfy their own egos by doing so. And some parents live vicariously through their child's accomplishments, asking the child to do what they want him to do, rather than letting him develop a separate identity and interests.

Although it is difficult to do with bright, charming young children, parents and grandparents should be careful not to focus too much on accomplishments and to watch that they do not unintentionally enmesh themselves in their children's lives. Gifted children can be such good students in school and such a joy to have around that parents and grandparents can easily lavish them with praise for their accomplishments. Some parents and grandparents may even support a "prima donna" attitude, in which they excuse the child from having to do ordinary tasks because "She's so special!" This will not, however, prepare her well for later life.

Gifted or not, children are still children. They need to know that the adults, the parents, are in

charge and that they not only must take responsibility for their own actions, they also must
assume a fair share of tasks and chores around the
home. Ideally, children are a part of a family
system where everyone pitches in and contrib-
utes, where parents are role models for behavior,
and where individual and family goals are obvious. Parents' and grandparents' long-term goals
for children should include preparing them to
be able to manage their own lives as adults, earning a living at a career, and functioning independently of parents, teachers, or other adults
and becoming what Dr. George Betts[44] calls
autonomous, life-long learners.

In her book *Dr. Sylvia Rimm's Smart Parenting*,[45] Dr. Rimm notes that praise can be too
much of a good thing. Some children, particularly high achievers, can become addicted to
praise. She wisely advises that you praise the
values you would like the children to adopt
rather than simply praising the *behaviors*, and that
you be moderate—rather than excessive—with
your praise. For example, when your child takes
his plate to the kitchen, you say, "I appreciate
your helping the family keep the house tidy,"

instead of simply thanking him for taking his plate to the kitchen.

Frequent praise can certainly encourage a child who is learning a new skill, but once the skill is reasonably well developed, the child should learn to praise herself. Similarly, says Rimm, do not praise gold and garbage alike. Children develop self-esteem when they master tasks that are difficult for them, not when they accomplish easy ones.

In a long-term study of Presidential Scholars—a group of high school seniors with top scores on the National Merit Examination—Felice Kaufmann[46] found that many of these extremely academically talented young people became so used to receiving recognition for their performance in high school that when they no longer received awards in college or graduate school, they felt "lost." Following college graduation, these award winners discovered in the workplace that excellent performance was simply expected and that praise and recognition were rare—a discovery that led some of them to feel depressed. Kaufmann concluded that these talented, high achieving young people had learned to equate their personal self-worth with academic awards and recognition. When there were no more awards to be won, they felt lost and unfulfilled. When Kaufman asked them what advice they would give to parents and teachers of other young or adolescent gifted students, they said that they would encourage the students to develop other interests outside of academics so that they would have more to live for in a future life than grades, achievements, or awards.

You do want your grandchildren to achieve. But it is important to help them learn not to become too dependent upon praise and recognition. As you have probably learned, life is much more meaningful when you are doing things that you enjoy and believe in. Gifted children must learn to find and follow their own passions in life, not ones that others have told them that they should follow. They must learn that tangible accomplishments are only a small part of one's life achievement. Grandparents can help gifted children explore hobbies and other areas of possible interest so that they can find their passions.

Sensitivity and Intensity

Being around gifted children is like being on a roller coaster. It's exhilarating and sometimes even frightening, but it's almost never dull.[47] It's the same for the gifted children themselves. The sensitivity and emotional intensity of gifted children certainly adds exciting dimension and depth to their lives. On the other hand, that same sensitivity and intensity can result in problems for them and for those around them. We see the intensity and sensitivity not only in their play with others, but also in their attitudes toward themselves and even in their reactions to everyday events. The authors of *Guiding the Gifted Child*[48] poignantly describe gifted children's reactions to everyday events: "the wonderment at the changes of fall foliage, tears of emotion upon first hearing a Mozart piano piece, or the absorbed fascination with a prism of light." They also recall a six-year-old boy who, when his pet mouse died, said, "Mom, for a person my age, I've seen too much death!"

Parents and grandparents often are the first to notice that their gifted children seem overly sensitive. They may take a minor insult much too seriously, or worry excessively about the fairness of a situation, or react strongly to a stressful situation in the family. Criticism, whether open or implied, or even suspected, hurts them terribly, and they "read" feelings contained in the nuances of body language, glances, and tone of voice, even when too young to understand the words.

This area, that of extreme sensitivity, is one that is particularly likely to be misunderstood by important adults—parents, grandparents, peers, and teachers. Gifted girls may be told they are simply being too dramatic or emotional. Gifted boys are told that they need to grow up, "be a man," and not be so quick to shed tears.[49] Both gifted girls and boys are often told, "You're just too sensitive!" when they show emotional reactions that seem out of proportion to what might be considered normal.

In school, teachers often label extremely sensitive pre-school or primary school children as "immature" or "babyish" and fail to recognize the extreme sensitivity as an indicator of giftedness, not a sign of being "too immature for school." Teachers will sometimes advise parents to hold this very sensitive child back a year, when what the child may actually need is to be moved ahead. The child may be terribly frustrated because the work is too easy, and he may show his frustration through tantrums or tears because he does not yet have the words to express his feelings.

A gifted child's intensity can also be a problem. Whatever the child is involved in may be carried to an extreme, and the child just cannot grasp the concept of moderation. Some gifted children will be passionately interested in only one area and will neglect others. Whether it is learning about Indian tribes or reading everything that has been written about dinosaurs, a gifted child is often deeply involved in the subject. Other gifted children are more like "grasshoppers" in their interests—that is, they jump from leaf to leaf, or from interest to interest. Yet whatever their interest at the time, it is one of intense involvement. This kind of focus will cause gifted children to neglect household chores or even homework, and as a result, parents or others may criticize them harshly for being forgetful or neglectful.

How can grandparents best help these intense, sensitive children? By allowing the children to be what they are—sensitive and intense—without criticizing them for it. By not comparing them with others, and by letting them know you believe in them. By accepting their feelings. Too often, teachers, parents, and others have told these children to stop being the way they are, conveying to them that there may be something unacceptable about them when they are too intense in their reactions. This sends a confusing message to the child: "I love you, but I'd love you more if you weren't so intense or so sensitive."

Steven Covey, in his chapter in the book, *If I Knew It Was Going to Be this Much Fun, I Would Have Become a Grandparent First*,[50] recommends that we avoid what he calls five emotional cancers when dealing with our families. The five cancers are: criticizing, complaining, comparing, competing for a sense of worth, and contending or arguing.

From our experience, we know that the intensity and sensitivity of gifted children can be quite frustrating to others around them. Eventually, as time goes on, these children will learn to modulate their feelings and behaviors and to take into account how their behavior impacts others. With time and maturity, their intensity and sensitivity can be great assets. In the meantime, parents and others must try to remember that most of the world's best-known writers, artists, poets, musicians, philosophers, politicians, entrepreneurs, and inventors were individuals who showed sensitivity and intensity.

Intensity of beliefs and convictions are needed to bring about social and political change. Sensitivity is a valued asset in interpersonal and intrapersonal relationships. It is also an asset in health and helping professions. Intense single-mindedness is essential for inventors, scientists, and those who work in medicine, computers, and many creative fields like architecture. Individuals who are creative, sensitive, and intense often make great contributions to their local communities, institutions, and to the world.

So how can grandparents help? They can give the gifted grandchild two very important gifts— *acceptance* and *perspective*. Listen to a child's worries and concerns, and offer the child acceptance for her passions and emotions. Tell the child about your own life experiences, your own false starts and mistakes. Make sure first that the child wants to hear these stories by saying, "Would you like to hear about a time when Grandma had really strong feelings about something and disagreed with other people?" Then tell about the time you marched for Civil Rights, or the time you stood up for a friend. In doing so, you will help the gifted child learn to understand, accept, and value herself, including her sensitivity and intensity.

Tradition-Breaking

Every society gains its culture through various traditions and "rules" about how people act, speak, and even think. These customs and regulations are a big part of the glue that holds cultures together. You've heard the saying, "When in Rome, do as the Romans do." The message is that if you do what is expected in that particular culture or society, you will stay out of trouble and have better success.

Some traditions have become part of our city and state laws. We stop at red lights. We pull over for an emergency vehicle with lights flashing. Others traditions are business-related. We tip the waiter, hairstylist, and taxi driver; we stand up to shake the hand of a new client. Still other traditions are neighborly gestures, like taking a plate of cookies to the new family down the street. Traditions help us feel safe and connected to others, and they make the world a more predictable place. They provide structure for our lives such that we know what to expect of others and what they, in turn, expect of us. Religious traditions, ceremonies, codes of ethics, and written laws all help us know how we are supposed to behave in different situations or settings.

However, some of our traditions are rituals carried over from past ages that may seem illogical, irrational, or at least arbitrary to gifted children who may question these traditions. Why is it that only men wear neckties but never dresses? Why do I have to wear a tie to church? Why can't I wear my baseball hat? Why is it that women carry purses and wear lipstick? Why do the women do the majority of housework and childcare?

As gifted children approach adolescence, some are irritated by the inconsistencies, illogical behaviors, and even hypocrisy that they see around them. They recognize that sometimes, when adults act in traditional ways, they often put up a pretense—a social facade—that can be dishonest. For example, we ask, "How are you?" when we really do not want to know, or we will be on-the-surface friendly with someone we don't really like. It may be a boss or other person with whom it wouldn't be too smart to be unfriendly, but young gifted children don't see the sense of this sort of thing unless someone explains it to them. Grandparents may be the significant adults to indicate to the child the reasons not to talk back to your teacher or your boss, even though you may think (or even know) that he is wrong.

Challenging tradition can be beneficial, too. The world is surely better because creative, caring, and courageous persons have challenged traditions. Rosa Parks challenged the division of blacks and whites on buses in the South. Martin Luther King Jr. challenged traditional beliefs and assumptions about African Americans and brought positive change through the Civil Rights Movement. Joseph Lister in England challenged the notion that diseases were not spread in hospitals. The Wright Brothers challenged the tradition that humans could not fly in machines that were heavier than air. Amelia Earhart challenged the belief that women could not fly. Most advances in our society came about because someone challenged a belief and set about to prove it wrong. Progress in knowledge and in society simply would not happen if traditions weren't challenged.

Gifted children often begin in the early grades to question rules, customs, and traditions At a young age, they are willing to forsake the comfortable predictability of traditions in order to search for improved ways of living and being. They may want to help the homeless; they may think of a project to raise money for a special cause. We want our gifted children to be creative problem solvers, because major advances are needed. But sometimes the persistent questioning and tradition-breaking by gifted children causes discomfort for family members, teachers, and others who may find the behaviors embarrassing, uncomfortable, or threatening to their own beliefs or ways of life. Parents of gifted teenage boys, for example, may find it hard to allow their son to wear a long ponytail or an earring. Parents of gifted girls may despair that their once attractive, traditional girl now wears only tattered hip-hugging blue jeans and tight midriff-baring shirts. Or we may find their anti-establishment views to be unpleasant.

Grandparents have lived long enough to have seen and experienced changes in many traditions, including hair length and clothing styles, and we know that these changes will always occur. Grandparents remember a time, for example, when women wouldn't think of eating alone in a restaurant and when stores were not open on Sunday. As recently as when our own parents were children, women did not have the right to vote. A grandparent's knowledge of "olden days" can help the parents of their grandchildren realize that positive change usually does come, though it doesn't always come as quickly as we would like.

Perhaps the most important thing grandparents can do is to help these strong-minded children, with all their beliefs and opinions, realize that there is a cost-to-benefit ratio involved in some behaviors. Certainly there are benefits to challenging traditions, but there are also costs. One of the costs is that people tend to avoid those who are nontraditional because they feel a bit uncomfortable around them. If you are going to be nontraditional and challenge the status quo, you are no longer predictable to others, and you are therefore someone to be avoided or at least treated with caution. Some may think that you are purposefully being nontraditional as a way of showing anger or resentment. They may be fearful of you or in other ways avoid connection with you. You may have difficulty finding a job because you project an inappropriate or unconventional image.

Some gifted children challenge traditional gender roles. Gifted young people, both boys and girls, tend to be more androgynous in their interests and attitudes than other children. Gifted girls not only like traditional "girl interests," but also may enjoy tomboy things and traditional male sports such as football or rough-and-tumble outdoor activities. Gifted boys tend to have broad interests that may include things like cooking, gardening, and imaginative play in addition to the traditional "male interests" like cars, bikes, and wrestling. Because some of these interests violate the traditional patterns for girls and boys, it will be important for significant adults to help gifted children think about how they want to pursue these interests. Will they conform to the traditional expectations? Will they openly and flagrantly rebel? Will they choose to express their interests and abilities in some settings and not in others? In spite of advances in this area of gender roles, it is still sometimes hard for a woman to be a police chief or for a man to be a nurse.

Sometimes their broad and diverse interests will lead gifted boys and girls to wonder if they are gay or lesbian. Some will be; others will not. It can be quite a challenge for a gifted child and her family to sort out whether the sensitivity and non-gender-traditional interests are a function of being gifted, or whether the child is gay, or both. In either case, parents and grandparents should support the child emotionally, letting her know that she is appreciated, supported and loved, whatever her interests or gender orientation. The percentage of gay individuals is the same within the gifted population as within the general population. For those who are interested, the National Association for Gifted Children (www.nagc.org) has a Task Force that provides information on gay, lesbian, bisexual, and transgendered gifted youth.

Gifted teenagers, with their wonderful creativity, will often select diverse and unusual friends and are likely to rebel openly at home or at school, particularly if there are power struggles in either place. They may dye their hair, wear funky clothes, renounce their family or society, experiment with substances, threaten to drop out of school, or all of the above. Some may even become openly defiant or delinquent. Such behaviors, although creatively nontraditional, are of course very upsetting and frightening to parents and grandparents, who may see the child hurting his own future more than those against whom he is rebelling. However, it is important that parents or grandparents not react too quickly or too strongly. A too strong reaction may encourage the child to rebel even more.

Think back to your own years of teenage rebellion or those of your friends. As Mark Twain said, "When I was a boy of fourteen, my father was so ignorant I could hardly stand to have the old man around. But when I got to be twenty-one, I was astonished at how much the old man had learned in seven years." The teen years are typically ones of experimentation and tradition breaking—at least the traditions that we grew up with. Sometimes teens and young adults will try something just to see what the reaction will be.

The teen years are a time when it is especially helpful for gifted children to have someone other than their parents to talk to. They are searching for what kind of person they want to be. They have begun to see that their parents are not perfect and are looking for other role models to follow. They will likely come back later to valuing the rules, beliefs, and traditions of their parents. But for a period of time, it seems that all teens are critical of their parents and eager to break away.

As grandparents, if you have had a good relationship with your grandchild all along, it is possible that you will be able to maintain communication and a relationship with the gifted teen even in times when the parents cannot. Everything we know about gifted children tells us that communication and a good, trusting relationship are of paramount importance. By maintaining a caring relationship with your teenage grandchildren, you can help them feel connected to society as well as to family, and you can also nurture their creative spirit. You may be able to help them understand the importance of traditions and rituals they may discount, such as celebrating family birthdays and holidays.

Risk-Taking and Resiliency

Some gifted children are comfortable with taking risks; others are not. Perfectionists generally do not like to take risks, while tradition-breakers are eager to do so. Risks are an important part of living a fulfilled life, but risks must be taken with some forethought and care. Life is an adventure and, as every grandparent knows, a journey that is not altogether predictable. Resiliency is needed when things don't go according to plan. But having a plan of some sort, even if it needs modification later for contingencies, can help. We can take our grandchildren on wilderness camping trips or introduce them to other settings where we must plan ahead with care and flexibility because of the potential risks or other conditions involved. When hiking or camping, one needs extra food and water for the possibility that something unexpected might happen. In *Adventures and Challenges: Real Life Stories by Girls and Young Women*,[51] Karnes and Bean describe the importance of helping girls and young women learn to plan thoughtfully prior to an adventure. What steps can you take to ensure that you don't get lost or get hurt? What safety equipment will you take along in case of injury or disorientation? The Boy Scout motto, "Be prepared," is one that can be useful in many situations.

Sometimes gifted children will take a risk, experience failure, and then not take another risk for months or years. But progress is seldom made without taking some risks. As the saying goes, "Ships are safe in a harbor, but that is not what ships were built for." There are risks when we sign up for a job, when we go out on a date, when we go back to school, when we commit to a relationship. Some risks turn out to be mistakes. But if we learn from our mistakes, we can go back and take other risks, possibly gathering more key information. Then we are more prepared to minimize the risk, and we can plan for better success.

Some of the earlier suggestions about perfectionism may help develop appropriate risk-taking. Grandparents can talk about risks they took, large and small, and how there were times when taking a risk led to a life-changing event or experience. They can also share stories of times when they took risks that did not end successfully. The important thing is how the child or young adult interprets the "failure" and how he can make use of it for future endeavors.

Gifted children, like all children, need to learn the art and skills of resiliency. The more situations you expose your grandchild to, the more equipped she will be to handle future situations. Encourage her to try new things. If she doesn't like them, that's fine; at least she tried them. She may be curious about the scary roller coaster ride, learning to swim, ice-skating, rock climbing, or quieter pursuits like sewing, photography, or playing a musical instrument. As the supportive grandparent, you don't need to necessarily do these activities with her, but if you can arrange to help her try them out once, or for a short period of time, that is a great gift to a child. A child who has taken small risks to try new things will have more experience and confidence when planning for college or a future career or when choosing a life-mate. And a child with a variety of life experiences will have more information about interests, preferences, and values on which to base important future life and lifestyle decisions.

Resilience can also be gained from reading and discussing books about people who have been resilient. Novels in the *Harry Potter* or *Anne of Green Gables* series, or classics like *Tom Sawyer*, *Huckleberry Finn*, *The Hardy Boys*, or *Nancy Drew* all contain characters who are resilient. Biographies of Eleanor Roosevelt, Christopher Reeve, Coretta Scott King, Mohammed Ali, Steven Hawking, Maya Angelou, and countless others come to mind. As a grandparent, you may well know real people who have shown resilience in the face of hardship or trauma. It is helpful to gifted children to learn about people who have had difficulties but have gone on to achieve.

Judgment versus Intellect

Still another complicating factor in guiding gifted children is that their judgment so often trails behind their intellect. Intelligence is not the same as wisdom. Nowhere is this more obvious than with gifted children. Gifted children are advanced in that they have a wealth of information, talent, and problem-solving abilities, but their judgment is far behind. Because they are children, they simply do not have enough life experiences yet to have good judgment. You have probably heard this reflected in the phrase, "She may be smart in her schoolwork, but she has not one grain of common sense."

Young gifted children often fail to understand the judgment involved in certain social situations; they seldom possess that social behavior we call tact. Nine-year-old Alex, for example, may start to ask all of the people in the elevator how much they weigh, all the while totally unaware of and insensitive to their discomfort with the question. He has read the notice posted in the elevator stating the "maximum allowable weight," and he wants to know whether the group is approaching that weight. Six-year-old Jorge asks his slightly overweight teacher if she is married, and then asks if she has a baby in her tummy. His mother is pregnant, so he is especially curious about this, and he doesn't understand that this is a rather delicate question that is usually not asked until the person is ready to share or until the pregnancy becomes obvious. Dennis the Menace, in the cartoon strip, is often less than tactful. In one particular instance, he blurts out to visitors, "Can I see the skeletons my dad says you have in your closet?"

As gifted children get older, they understand social and moral issues at an intellectual level, but they have difficulty coping with them at an emotional level. Many young gifted children become emotionally distraught at social injustices. They have little patience for long-term solutions or gradual change. Seeing the thick haze of pollution hanging over a city, they may remark, "We have known for years that car emissions and CFCs cause air pollution. I first learned about it in the fourth grade. So why hasn't our government banished CFCs and gasoline engines entirely by now?" A grandparent may be able to begin to explain at least some of the complexities of various economic forces and other factors that prevent a rapid solution.

As the gifted child matures, the gap between intellect and judgment narrows. Wisdom and judgment cannot be learned in a brief period. A child must simply live long enough to develop the sense of perspective needed to attain them. And judgment and maturity do not usually develop in a smooth, linear fashion, but rather in a way that can be quite perplexing. For example, one might see an eight-year-old gifted child thoughtfully discussing the difficulties involved in an ongoing conflict between two countries, yet five minutes later childishly accuse his brother of taking "his place" in the front seat of the car on the way to the grocery store.

In cases in which the child does show poor judgment or makes an inappropriate comment, it is important not to immediately criticize her or put her down, but rather talk to her privately afterward about what was said and how it might have been said another way, with more tact or care for the other person's feelings. In this way, we help the child understand what went wrong rather than embarrass her in front of others. Saying to the child, "You're supposed to be so smart, and yet you say such dumb things," is not very helpful. The child learns nothing from it except that she has been somehow "bad" and a disappointment to you, but without knowing how to change her behavior to act or speak more appropriately the next time.

Many adults do not understand the simple fact that the gifted child's intellectual development and emotional maturity seldom keep pace with each other. Grandparents can be helpful by reminding others, when appropriate, of the difference between intellect and wisdom, perhaps providing a sense of perspective by reminiscing about some of the actions of the parents when they were younger which demonstrated poor judgment.

Stress and Depression

Some gifted children experience stress and depression, particularly if they have not learned resiliency. Even children as young as six years of age can be depressed. A few gifted children, as teens or young adults, are depressed enough to resort to suicide, leaving their family and others to wonder how such a bright, promising, and talented person could be so desperately unhappy. Suicides like these often surprise parents and teachers, who did not know that there was a problem because gifted children can be very good at camouflaging their depression. A parent will ask, "Are you all right, son?" The son answers, "Sure, Mom. I'll be home after play practice," then suicides during the night. The tragedy leaves scars on the family for years.

How do tragic events like this come about? With their intellect, sensitivity, and intensity, gifted children may feel too different, too alienated and alone in a world that seems to have shallow views and values These feelings are almost always a problem at some point in time for children who are highly or profoundly gifted. From their point of view, the people around them seem to think only superficially—teachers, parents, politicians, or others in positions of authority. The gifted child envisions how the world might be, or how it ought to be, and is distressed that so few people share his idealism or vision. The solutions to some of the world's problems seem so obvious; why don't those in power see them and do something? From his point of view, others seem simple-minded, slow, irrational, materialistic, hypocritical, or just downright foolish. The world appears to be in the hands of adults who sometimes seem only marginally competent to run it.

It is the gifted child's idealism that, in a world of ordinariness, can lead to cynicism and depression. The child or young adult feels very alone in a world that seems to value "going through the motions" or, as Woody Allen reportedly said, where "90% of life is just showing up." Thirteen-year-old Clarissa may seriously question whether life is worth living in a world in which she so clearly does not fit. She may be plagued by feelings of sadness, anger, depression, and anxiety. If, on top of this, she believes that, because of her abilities and talents, she must personally assume responsibility for improving the lot of mankind, the difficulty of the task seems overwhelming. Though certainly not all gifted children experience this type of depression, some do, and those who do need particular understanding from significant adults in their lives.

Grandparents often are in a unique position to understand the idealism, cynicism, disappointment, and depression felt by some gifted children. There is much that is wrong with the world that needs to be made right. Grandparents have the long view, the bigger perspective. They have lived long enough to know that the world will always need improvement and that the best way to work on that is probably to join forces with other idealists.

Grandparents can also easily understand how one can be angry at the world or at fate; surely if you live long enough, you know that the world is not always fair and kind. Bad things do happen. Some people do bad things. Perhaps this can be an opportunity to help your grandchild learn that it is better to light a candle than to curse the darkness, and to reassure your grandchild that there are people who understand his feelings. It might be good for a depressed and disillusioned gifted child to talk to a professional, someone who can help him through his angst and suffering. Sometimes medication is helpful. Grandparents can simply be supportive of such options if parents are concerned that the child is depressed. It is vitally important for gifted children to feel connected to others who understand them.

Not every gifted child is doomed to depression. However, we do need to recognize that the incidence of depression in all ages and walks of life is increasing and has increased for at least the last 75 years throughout the world. The reasons are not clear; perhaps it is has something to do with splintered families and the faster pace of modern life. In gifted children, we know that their intensity and sensitivity makes them more prone to stress, particularly if they are perfectionistic. And their idealism, if not shared by others, may lead them to feel bitterly disappointed. They are even more likely to feel depressed if they are at odds with their peers or their families and if they disagree with attitudes and traditions at school or in society. Many describe themselves as feeling like an alien or a "stranger in a strange world."

We hope that you can see now why it is so important for gifted children to have strong, trusting, positive relationships with family and friends. Because it may be easier for a depressed child to confide in a grandparent than a parent, your role as a confidante is especially important.

Nurturing the Emotions

The very elements that are a positive part of being a gifted child can also be a cause for concern, particularly if the traits are not understood or nurtured by significant adults in the child's life. Strip and Hirsch[52] published an interesting list of intellectual and emotional strengths of gifted children—along with potential problems that might stem directly from each strength. They call this list "The Ups and Downs of Giftedness."

Table 1
The Ups and Downs of Giftedness

Strength	The Flip Side	Possible Consequences
Comprehension is much greater than that of age mates.	Finds age mates' reasoning comprehension silly—and says so.	Other children avoid the child; adults find him or her "mouthy."
Language abilities are advanced for his or her age.	Talks "above" age mates, who don't understand what the child is talking about. The child talks too much, not allowing others their turns.	Other children perceive the child as snooty and superior and exclude him or her. The child is lonely.
Creative in thinking.	Solves problems his or her own way, rather than the way prescribed by the teacher.	Teacher can feel threatened, view the child as disrespectful of authority, and decide to "clamp down," which sets the stage for rebellion.

Quick in thinking.	Easily bored with routine work and may not complete it. On the other hand, may zip through the work and bounce around the classroom, looking for something to do.	The teacher may decide the child is inattentive, negative, or a behavior problem who has a bad influence on other children.
High energy level.	May be very distractible, into everything and finishing nothing.	The child can also be worn out by trying to take on too many projects at once. High energy may also be mistaken for attention deficit hyperactivity disorder (ADHD). Medication may be suggested to "calm the child down."

Great powers of concentration.	Sometimes stays too long on one project; gets lost in detail and misses deadlines.	Poor grades, because assigned work is not completed, causing frustration for the child, parents, and teachers.
Adult-level thinking.	Adult-level thinking not accompanied by adult-level social skills, such as tact. May say rude or embarrassing things.	Both children and adults may think the child is rude and avoid him or her altogether.

Looking at this chart, one can see how a positive trait can also sometimes be a negative when others don't understand. If adults in the child's life focus on the negatives, then the child's advanced interests, abilities, and intense emotions become liabilities rather than assets. This ultimately turns her greatest strengths against her, which only sets the stage for later power struggles, emotional withdrawal, added stress, insecurity, and poor self-esteem. Instead, we hope that you will accept and appreciate your gifted grandchild's strength areas, and help her to do the same. We are not suggesting that gifted children should go around bragging that they are smarter than others. We recommend that they learn that everyone has things to contribute to the world and that individuals have many differences. They can understand that all children have educational needs. They can begin to comprehend their own abilities and needs. They can learn that bragging is just not necessary.

Gifted children simply have higher potential in certain areas, and as a result, they have specific needs. They should accept themselves as unique individuals with strengths, weaknesses, and differences—just like everyone else.

Life affords no greater responsibility, no greater privilege, than the raising of the next generation.
~ C. Everett Koop

One of the greatest gifts adults can give—to their offspring and to their society—is to read to children.
~ Carl Sagan

Being grandparents sufficiently removes us from the responsibilities so that we can be friends.
~ Allan Frome

Chapter 4

Expanding the World for Gifted Children

All children are born with curiosity, and gifted children come into this world with greater curiosity than most children Even as infants, they are excited by the world around them. Some parents have told us that their four-year-old child fights going to sleep as though he doesn't want to miss anything, and he's been like this since infancy. Finally, unable to resist sleep any longer, he just "conks out." As we have said earlier, these children are intense. They look, touch, taste, smell, and listen, and they incorporate all manner of experiences in their preschool years. They truly act like sponges as they absorb information.

Gifted children learn more quickly than most other children, and their excitement for learning is more intense. Some theorists[53] have suggested that the term "overexcitability" should be used to describe the eagerness that many gifted children show for new learning and experiences. This eagerness, particularly when gifted children are young, makes it great fun to be around them. Grandparents can help foster curiosity and excitement in their grandchildren so that they will continue to love learning throughout their lives.

Experiences to Open the Mind

From birth onward, a child needs stimulation if the mind is to develop its potential. And gifted children do require (and greatly benefit from) a lot of stimulation—even as infants and toddlers. As grandparents, we can provide opportunities for stimulating experiences that will enhance their learning. How much stimulation should you provide for your grandchildren? Is there such a thing as too much early stimulation? Should I purchase those Baby Einstein™ or Baby Mozart™ tapes? Should I read to my grandchildren even before they can sit up on their own? Should I try to teach them things? Or should I just let them lead the way with their own curiosity?

We have know for decades the importance of providing a variety of learning experiences to newborn babies and infants, and some professionals even believe that stimulation for a child *in utero* can promote mental development. Parents who talk and sing to their unborn babies find that the babies respond to their voices immediately after birth. This new young human being—your grandchild—needs to be held, talked to, and sung to. There is much evidence to suggest that exposing children at an early age—even as infants—to colors, shapes, sounds, patterns, movement, and touch can stimulate intellectual development. There is also evidence that a rich and stimulating environment, such as colorful mobiles hanging over the crib and varieties of music played to them, actually encourages the physical development of the brain and its interconnections.[54]

Though stimulation will promote development, it is important to keep in mind the overexcitability of some gifted children, even as infants. Many parents have commented to friends, family, pediatricians, psychologists, and their child's teachers about how they have noticed an unusual intensity of focus and of behavior in the child, even at the age of six or eight weeks. The emotions and physical feelings of some of these infants simply seem stronger than for other infants. Whatever they feel, they seem to feel intensely. When they smile, their whole body smiles. When they are angry, they are *really* angry. As a result, children who are gifted can be particularly challenging—even difficult—as infants because they react so intensely to stimulation.

Some experts[55] have noted that gifted infants, particularly those who later turn out to be highly gifted, are for some unknown reason more prone to ear infections and to food allergies. Other experts suggest that some gifted children are more likely to be the colicky babies that can be so frustrating to parents who can't seem to find a solution to their crying and discomfort. Regrettably, few pediatricians or nurses are aware of this connection between giftedness and allergies, or giftedness and colic.

Sometimes this extreme physical and emotional sensitivity shows itself in older gifted children, but it may also be present in infants. Some young gifted children are extraordinarily sensitive to touch; they may be greatly bothered by a bed sheet that is made of rough fabric. Or they are unusually sensitive to sounds or smells. The noise made by fluorescent lights bothers them; they are repulsed by ordinary perfumes or aftershave lotions; or it may be necessary to remove the tags from all of their shirts.

Grandparents who know this can raise the possibility that the colicky behavior could be due to something like allergies or tactile sensitivity. Trial and error may uncover the source of the irritation. As a grandparent, you can offer reassurance that it is okay to cut the tags from shirts, or that there is nothing abnormal about a child who dislikes the textures of certain foods. What we are saying, then, is that stimulation for infants and toddlers is good, even necessary. However, do be aware that some gifted youngsters can receive too much stimulation because of their particular sensitivity and intensity.

Games and Play

During your grandchild's first year of life, you will start to play interactive games—activities that are very important. A simple game of peek-a-boo helps provide a variety of experiences that are just as important as exposing the child to different colors and textures. When the child reacts to a "boo" or a sing-song "I love you," the child is learning to respond as one individual to another. In fact, the games we play with our grandchildren help the children develop a sense of themselves as independent and competent persons, besides providing intellectual stimulation.

As children grow older, continued exposure to different situations and experiences prompts their brains to develop and promotes other kinds of development, too. We know that large-motor skills, such as those used for climbing a jungle gym or swinging on a swing, are important in helping the brain develop its coordination of thought patterns. (Thus, playing on a swing or slide helps reading and other academic skills.) Practice with gross and small-motor skills by helping to set the table, for example, also helps children develop the fine-motor skills that they will need in school to manipulate crayons, scissors, and pencils.

Don't worry about providing the proper "educational" toys. Toddlers are just as happy—and learn just as much—when they bang wooden spoons against cooking pots or stack measuring cups one inside the other. Playing with objects of different sizes helps children distinguish between large and small. Playing with plastic containers in the tub or sink helps them refine skills necessary for pouring and mixing. Colors, music, faces, touch, even smells and tastes—all of these experiences help the developing child. From ordinary everyday activities such as these, as well as your interactions with them, your grandchildren will learn how their behaviors influence the world around them. They will gain a sense of independence and an understanding of what happens when they have the freedom to experiment. Experiences like these can be provided by grandparents and parents both. Scientific support of the importance of early stimulation is so broad that it is now summarized in the general media, such as in the February 2, 1997 article in *Time* magazine entitled "Fertile Mind" and the Oregon Public Television Online Newshour show, "Brain Development in Babies," which aired on May 29, 1997.

The games and play described above may seem like rather simple and unimportant activities for grandparents. Not at all. These activities are very important, particularly in today's fast-paced world in which working parents may have less time to engage in these activities. Grandparents have the time and the patience and also an eagerness to pursue activities such as these with their grandchildren.

The importance of play in gifted children was emphasized by the findings of Benjamin Bloom in his classic book, *Developing Talent in Young People.*[56] Bloom and his colleagues studied adults who were world-class in their various fields (music, art, architecture, etc.) to ascertain what key elements had helped them attain the extraordinary development of their talents. These adults repeatedly said that they first became exposed to their particular talent area through play or through a brief, often chance exposure.

Many successful musicians tell of learning melody and harmony at a very young age when their mothers sang or hummed lullabies or folk songs to them. Similarly, writers tell of being exposed to literature from being read to when very young. This does not mean that by deliberately playing classical music, you can expect your grandchild to become a classical musician. However, there is plenty of evidence to show that exposure (or no exposure) to varying aspects of life does have a lasting effect.

Children who are not given opportunities for active play may not develop a sense of their own bodies or muscles and thus may be developmentally behind other children in that area. Watching too much television can lead to a child not knowing how to run, jump, and play. For preschool children, there is little difference between play and education, and in fact, preschoolers learn primarily through experiences with objects and materials. As grandparents, we can expose our grandchildren to the rhythms of music, to blocks, finger paints, and outdoor activities. We can help develop their imaginations by having them tell us stories and encouraging them to portray characters through make-believe in dress-up clothes. One resource containing suggestions for preschool gifted is the book *Your Gifted Child*[57] by Joan Franklin Smutny, Kathleen Veenker, and Stephen Veenker.

Books and Reading

Most gifted children are highly verbal and start to speak at an early age. One mother, whose ears were tired from the constant chatter and questions, said of her preschooler, "I think she's ready for a million word checkup!" Curiosity and advanced verbal abilities prompt young gifted children to want to hear stories and to have books read to them. Most of us have warm memories of sitting in the lap of a grown-up while we were being read to. Reading is one of the simplest and yet one of the most important activities you can do with a grandchild, and yet it appears that only about a third of grandparents regularly read to their grandchildren.[58] Not only will reading familiarize your grandchild with basic letters and words, and classic rhymes and stories, it will set the stage for reading as a source of enjoyment now and in the future.

Where will you find books to read to your grandchildren? Begin with the books you grew up with, such as Mother Goose rhymes, and go from there. Most bookstores have a children's section, and some stores specialize in children's literature. Perhaps you can take your grandchild to the library to get books, whether general children's books or books about a specific area of interest, such as space exploration. The children's librarian can be a wonderful resource.

Most gifted children, though not all, learn to read and write earlier than other children. Perhaps you will help your grandchildren learn how to read. We are not advocating that you pressure the children to learn. They will let you know when they are ready. It will be sufficient if you just respond to the child's curiosity and readiness. With simple picture books and in learning to turn pages right to left, your grandchild is already taking the first steps toward breaking the code that we call language and reading.

Number Games

Some gifted children are attracted to numbers the way other children are to words, and in our modern world, numbers are in many ways as important as words. The world of mathematics can be exciting. Learning to count, add, subtract, multiply, and divide opens up new horizons and also develops brain functions.

In your role as caring grandparent, you may begin by simply emulating the counting activities of Count Dracula from Sesame Street. Later, you can introduce the concepts of addition and subtraction by using buttons, checkers, dried beans, or other ordinary household objects as "counters." You can put aside three and ask the child to now add two, then count how many, and so on. As the grandchildren get older, games of adding can become a pastime to help make car trips more enjoyable. For example, you can ask the child to add the numbers on the license plate of the car ahead to see if the sum will be an odd or an even number, or a prime number, etc.

Cooking together using a recipe is a good way to introduce measuring and fractions, as well as to spend some fun time together. The game of cribbage is a good way to practice rapid adding skills. Several board games emphasize math skills, as well as the rules of chance. One grandparent used the card game of draw poker to teach the rudiments of probability theory to his 10-year-old grandson. Another grandparent introduced the basics of mathematical scale, the fulcrum, and the algebraic equation in the woodshop using rulers and a teeter-totter board. Real-life opportunities to learn and practice math are everywhere, and they are sometimes more interesting than the paper and pencil math problems in school.

Cultural Events and Travel

One of the most time-honored ways for grandparents to provide diverse stimulating experiences is through cultural events and travel. When grandchildren and grandparents go on special outings to museums or art galleries, or when they travel together, they can explore geography, history, sciences, and the arts as they also get to know each other better.

One partially retired grandparent, who traveled frequently to other cities, found that she was able to take one of her grandchildren with her on most of these trips. During her business meetings, the grandchild quietly read a book. Meanwhile, the grandmother explained to her client that it was a family tradition for a grandchild to accompany her. When business was finished, grandmother and grandchild would then visit a museum, art gallery, or science exhibit, and the child obtained a wealth of experiences relating to business, travel, and culture. And of course, there was special time with the grandparent traveling to and from the events that was also memorable to the grandchild. This grandmother offered travel opportunities to all of her grandchildren, rotating through each of them and then starting over again.

Travel is intellectually and socially broadening for your grandchildren. Children come home from trips to other states or other countries with a new understanding of history, geography, and different cultures. Grandparents may have more money and time than parents to take vacations with the children, and such experiences provide educational enrichment far beyond anything learned in school. There is no better way for a child to develop an appreciation for the size of our country, or the world, or for different climates, terrain, customs, and culture than through travel.

Increasingly, there are programs for grandparents and grandchildren to vacation together. The Elderhostel program features trips specifically for grandparents and grandchildren that are called "Intergenerational." In one such program, grandparents and grandchildren ride horses; in another, they navigate rafts down a portion of the Colorado River at the bottom of the Grand Canyon. The AARP has some excellent suggestions on its website concerning traveling with grandchildren (www.aarp.org/confacts/money/grandtrav.html).

Even if your grandchildren do not accompany you, you can still use your trips to help them learn. Picture postcards from distant places let your grandchild know that he is loved. If parents get out a map and point to the place where the card is from, the child learns a little more about geography.

Although about 17% of grandparents have taken a grandchild on a trip somewhere,[59] not every grandparent is able to travel, and some are simply not interested in taking trips. There are always learning opportunities right in our own communities. It is surprising how often people will travel long distances to visit museums and art galleries without ever visiting the ones in their own city or state. Perhaps you can make a date with a grandchild to attend a live performance at a local theatre or a jazz concert, or to visit the science museum or the zoo. There are always people and places to visit and things to see, even in a small community. Whatever the activity, remember to look at it from a child's point of view. Adults who pay admission to a museum often want to "get their money's worth" and stay for three hours, forgetting that a child gets tired more quickly than an adult. It is more enriching for the child to spend less time and have fun rather than more time and end in tears and fatigue.

In these activities, you should expect your gifted grandchild to ask lots of questions. In fact, encourage her to do so. She'll learn best this way, as it will give her an active part in learning things that she will take home with her.

Many communities offer organized weekend activities for children of various ages; some may be designed for gifted children. Don't assume that the parents will know about these activities. Sometimes they are not well publicized. To find these activities, you can all the state department of education or the department of education at your local university, ask your local librarian, or contact your local or state association for parents and educators of gifted children. All of these sources are likely to have activities for children and can give you a schedule. Or ask other grandparents who are actively involved in their grandchildren's lives. You may learn of a computer camp, chess tournament, creative writing workshop, or model airplane club. These are places where your grandchildren can share the excitement of their interests with other children who are similarly advanced in their skills, as well as wonderful opportunities for you to show your support of the importance of learning. If your grandchild's community is smaller, there will be 4-H Clubs, Future Farmers of America, Boy Scouts, Girl Scouts, religious youth groups, and other organized opportunities for young people. Any of these groups offer a place for children to interact with other children and adults and to learn new skills, including leadership.

Projects

Home projects can be wonderful learning opportunities. Many grandchildren learn important mechanical and engineering skills while helping their grandparent construct a birdhouse, make curtains, or build an addition to the house. The cooperation that is typically needed for such projects provides opportunities for conversation while helping the child learn important interpersonal skills.

One grandfather with a mechanically inclined granddaughter arranged a monthly outing during which they would go to the local junkyard and find mechanical things for her to take apart in the coming weeks. Of course, the grandfather did not want the pieces scattered everywhere throughout the house, so they marked a rectangle on the floor of the basement with masking tape and placed the newly acquired "prizes" there. The granddaughter (with grandfather's help) would disassemble the machines, radios, clocks, etc. to ascertain how they worked and why they likely did not work now. Then they would put the pieces into a box to be taken back to the junkyard to be traded in for a new piece of junk.

Home is a place to learn and practice creativity as well. As grandparents, you may finally have the time to indulge in activities you enjoy, such as painting or sketching. Perhaps you have always known that you had a little creativity in your bones, and now you have decided to take a beginning drawing course at the local community college. What a role model you are for your gifted grandchild! Not only are you developing a setting to enhance creativity, but you are also modeling the fun and excitement of life-long learning.

Television and Computer Games

With the busy pace of modern life, it can be tempting to use television and computer games as sources of stimulation. In our opinion, television and electronic games should be used sparingly, if at all. Some television shows may have appropriate content, but most do not. What is most worrisome about television and other electronic media, however, is the extent to which a child learns to be passively entertained rather than to use and develop his own finger dexterity, imagination, and creativity.

Some experts[60] are now even concerned that the fast-paced but passive entertainment through television and video games has decreased the ability of children to listen, pay attention, and engage in independent problem-solving. TV and computer games may well have increased the incidence of ADD (Attention Deficit Disorder). Recent research published in the prestigious journal *Pediatrics*[61] showed that the more children watched television, the more likely they were to have problems with attention.

Television and other electronic media deprive children of opportunities to learn sustained mental and creative effort. Children who watch television extensively come to passively expect that they will get results quickly and with minimal effort. Things on TV happen that way. Not having learned that some things take effort, children who are TV junkies have trouble with sustained effort and with failure. If success does not come quickly and easily, then their attention wanders to a new activity. In this way, television may be helping to create an increase in the number of children with attention problems.

This difficulty with attention may later affect not only school performance, but also the overall level of initiative put forth in daily activities such as simple household chores, piano practice, and homework, because these activities do not have brightly colored, attractive pictures with digital sound and scenes that change every few minutes or even seconds. Making cookies from scratch takes more time than the TV cooking show suggests. Children need the experience of something like making cookies from scratch in order to learn that most tasks in life require time and patience.

We know some families who have six or more television sets in their home, with one in every room, including one in each child's bedroom. We know other families who have ruled out television entirely and don't have a single one in their home. Still other families limit television programs to educational ones and, within that framework, limit viewing to one hour or less per day. We think the latter approach is wise. In fact, the American Academy of Pediatrics[62] recommends that parents not let children under the age of two years watch television at all, and no more than one to two hours per day of quality television and video for older children. Very young children are developing language skills and learning how to read facial cues by interacting with their adult caretakers. Television is not a good substitute for human interaction. It takes children away from many activities that provide important learning opportunities.

Mary Pipher, in her powerful book *The Shelter of Each Other: Rebuilding Our Families,*[63] points out that various media with buttons and screens are so integrated into today's families that our society is now an "electronic village," where we flood children with stimulation, but in ways that "often erode our sense of community" (p.88). She highlights how "TV isolates people in their leisure time" (p. 90) with all family members watching the big screen together, but without talking or interacting with each other. The behaviors and values played out in today's electronic games are not ones that most of us respect;

yet we and our children and grandchildren allow them to be an integral part of our lives. We suggest that grandparents do what they can to minimize the role of electronic games in your family and, whenever possible, to substitute real life for virtual simulation.

Learning How to Think

In today's world, we are often provided with prepackaged chunks of information and predigested opinions, and we are encouraged to accept them blindly. Our children are often not given the opportunity or the training to learn how to think critically, even though our modern world is faced with numerous problems that require such thinking. Most schools at least give lip service to what they call "higher-order thinking skills." But we fear that if you were to spend a week in a school, you wouldn't see much of this kind of thinking encouraged in the classroom.

Fortunately, gifted children frequently ask probing questions. They want to know how, why, and when, and they are seldom satisfied with superficial answers. As grandparents, we can support higher-order thinking skills. Higher-level thinking is needed to solve everyday problems, as well as for large, global problems. How can we improve the learning atmosphere of our classroom? What would happen if there were no teachers? How can we solve the problem of increasing obesity in our country? How can we solve the problem of higher levels of mercury in fish? The ability to visualize, analyze, anticipate, measure, synthesize, evaluate—all are critical thinking skills that transfer from the immediate problem at hand to future problems. These skills will not develop in children if they are not supported and nurtured. Schools can do much more in this area, but parents and grandparents can do a great deal to make up for what schools lack by asking higher-level questions like the samples above. We can ask deeper questions when our grandchildren give pat answers unthinkingly.

Higher-order thinking skills are often required in everyday tasks around the home. Problem-solving is inherent in such activities as sewing, cooking and canning, designing and building an addition to the house or the landscaping, or planning a trip—all of these can involve a child's mental abilities in ways that will demand some higher-order thinking skills. Thinking skills are developed only with practice. There are valuable learning projects all around us if we take the time to involve our children in making them so.

Learning to Compete

We live in a world that is competitive. Societies compete with each other, groups compete among themselves, and we even compete with ourselves. Competition is a healthy thing because it stretches us to reach beyond our usual performance. However, gifted children, with their intensity, can easily take competition to an unhealthy extreme. This is particularly the case with a gifted child who is a perfectionist and for whom everything has to the best, the greatest, or the most recognized. This child can truly take it too far, to the point where other children don't want to be around him. At the other extreme are gifted children who, unless they become involved in competition, do not learn how to win—or lose—graciously, or how to maintain the sustained effort needed for an endeavor, or how to learn from outcomes that don't turn out the way they hoped.

Winning and Losing

Sports, games, spelling bees, and geography bees all come to mind when we think of competitions.

All can be extremely fun and rewarding, and all result in winners and losers. Since they are so often highly competitive, some gifted children intensely dislike losing. Team sports and board games with family are good ways for children to learn important life skills, such as how to take turns, play fair, respect the rights of other players, and win and lose graciously. It is through sports and games that gifted children can also learn the importance of the sustained effort that is required if one is to master a skill.

Don't be surprised, however, if your gifted grandchild does not enjoy team sports. Many gifted children will prefer small group or individual sports such as gymnastics, fencing, tennis, golf, or swimming—activities that emphasize the effort of an individual rather than a group or team effort. This is more than likely for three related reasons: (1) gifted children like to compete against themselves, (2) they have often had unsatisfactory experiences in trying to play with, organize, or lead other children in the past, and (3) they frequently don't like to depend upon others who may not perform as well as they.

Competing for Yourself

In the long run, we want our grandchildren to compete against themselves, not just to compare their skills and abilities to others. But learning to compete against oneself (instead of others) can be particularly difficult for gifted children. The child must develop his own goals and strategies and then evaluate himself. A task such as this is difficult for most adults; it will be even more difficult for children.

Many gifted children, especially those who have perfectionistic tendencies, are particularly at risk for "goal-vaulting." That is, they will set a goal, but then when they have almost achieved it, they mentally vault over it and set a new, much harder goal. Then, when they are almost able to achieve this new goal, they mentally vault over it and set yet another, more difficult goal. Sometimes gifted children goal-vault so much that they end up with such difficult final goals that they never achieve to their satisfaction and are left feeling quite disappointed in themselves. Grandparents can help by encouraging the child to write down her final goal and her subgoals, including how she will know when she has achieved them, and then post this "goal statement" so that she can mark off her progress. Knowing how to affirm oneself even for smaller goals is a skill that will be helpful in successes and disappointments throughout life.

Activities such as learning to play a musical instrument or learning to paint provide excellent opportunities for children to become skilled at how to compete with themselves. Grandparents can help by encouraging the patience and sustained effort that are required to set appropriate goals and to master new skills within reasonable expectations.

Competing in the Family

Competition often occurs within the family, not just on the playground or with oneself, and with gifted children, these are sometimes the most intense competitions. Sibling rivalry is quite common in families with gifted children. Here, the siblings are usually competing for attention from their parents or grandparents. The first-born child, according to research, is typically the most adult-like—responsible, organized, assertive toward others, and high-achieving. The last-born child usually has the role of the "baby" of the family, the one who expects special privileges, manipulates others, and depends upon others for guidance. The middle-born child is sometimes described as the "lost" child; he is neither the first to get privileges, nor the one who is given special consideration. The middle child may be a relatively quiet child who tries to avoid bringing attention to himself, or he may be a troublemaker in an attempt to carve out a special place for himself in the family.

Birth order is not the only reason for sibling rivalry. Parents and grandparents may unknowingly foster sibling competition in ways that are not helpful. They may openly or privately compare the achievements of one child with another, thereby increasing the competition. On some occasions, they may emphasize achievements so much that the message communicated to the grandchild is: "My parents and grandparents like me only when I am achieving."

Sometimes parents and grandparents may make comparisons among the children by remarking on their particular skills. For example, they may say, "Marcia is our academic grandchild; Ronnie is the comedian in the family." On the one hand, such comments recognize a child's particular ability. On the other hand, comments like these may make some children come to think of themselves as limited to only one special talent, and thus they limit their possibilities for growth in other areas. Or if they detect that their grandparents or parents value a particular talent area in a sibling, then often the sibling rivalry will be especially intense in an effort to gain similar recognition. To avoid these problems, we suggest that you resist comparing children altogether and that you not talk about their strengths and weaknesses to others if the child can overhear the conversation. "Little pitchers have big ears," as the saying goes.

Academic Competitions

Academic competitions can be fun ways for your grandchild to explore and develop interests and gain self-confidence. Some of these are offered through schools, but others are not. Nearly all of these academic competitions can be found by a search on the Internet. An excellent guide to competitions in academic areas, as well as in visual and performing arts and leadership, is the book *Competitions: Maximizing Your Abilities through Academic and Other Competitions*, by Karnes and Riley.[64] Additional information is available through Talent Identification programs, such as the Duke

Talent Identification Program, which annually publishes a book of enrichment opportunities for gifted youth. Two additional resources that list contests and other activities for gifted children are *Re-Forming Gifted Education: Matching the Program to the Child*[65] and *Creative Home Schooling: A Resource Guide for Smart Families*[66]

Learning One's Place in Culture and the World

Probably the single most important learning task for the gifted child (or gifted adult) is figuring out one's place in the culture and in the world. Though this is a task for any child, the gifted child has a particular need to figure out "Where do I fit in a world that seems to value mediocrity, conformity, and fitting in more than it values innovation, creativity, and excellence?"

Gifted children, by the very nature of their intellect, sensitivity, intensity, and idealism, are a small minority group. Yet they will need to learn how to live in this world. How and where will they fit in our education systems? In our culture? In a job or career? In the world? In their extended family? In their own family, when they create one?

Values

A key aspect to figuring out one's place in the culture and in the world has to do with values. Values are important for all children, including gifted children. Perhaps they are even more important for gifted children precisely because of their high potential. Dr. Barbara Kerr and Dr. Sanford Cohn, in their award-winning book *Smart Boys: Talent, Manhood, and the Search for Meaning,*[67] point out that gifted children who do not find a satisfactory place in their culture end up feeling extremely angry, and many of them actually engage in quite antisocial behaviors.

Grandparents are often the primary keepers of the family traditions, including values. It is important for families to talk about what they value, what is important to them, and to explain why. Traditions are the taproots for a family; they provide predictability and a feeling of belonging, as well as reaffirming the importance of certain values. Sometimes, though, traditions become stifling or simply outdated. If this happens, grandparents can help to model how a family can create new traditions.

For example, especially in blended families where there are several sets of grandparents, even a simple holiday like Thanksgiving can become an exercise in stress management. Each grandparent expects, by tradition, that the children and grandchildren will eat with them on that day. Yet it is impossible to be in all of these places simultaneously. One particularly creative family has developed a new tradition; they gather the week before Thanksgiving with one set of grandparents, Thanksgiving day with another set, and Thanksgiving weekend with yet another set. The family closeness is maintained, and the stress is reduced.

Leadership and Service

Not every child of high potential needs to become a leader. However, most gifted children are idealists and care deeply about the world, and many will want to become leaders. Our world will always need persons who care about making it better, and our brightest children have the potential to be leaders in some aspect of that. Leadership and community service projects can help gifted children understand that what they think and care about is important, and that they can contribute to making the world a better place. Involvement in community service or community projects give gifted children a sense of hope that something can be done, versus — despair that the world is beyond fixing.

There are many possibilities for introducing gifted children to community service. Perhaps your family already has one or more traditions that are service projects where the child could occasionally volunteer along with you. Maybe you make regular donations to the homeless shelter, or you help cook and serve meals for the needy, or you help raise money for a charity. Perhaps you assist in a reforestation project or have adopted a section of road to keep free of litter. Include your grandchild in one or more of these as you are able. All such activities provide gifted children with meaningful lessons about humankind and about their place in humanity.

The simplest toy, one which even the youngest child can operate, is called a grandparent.
~Sam Levenson

Nobody can do for little children what grandparents do. Grandparents sort of sprinkle stardust over the lives of little children.
~ Alex Haley

Our grandchildren accept us for ourselves, without rebuke or effort to change us, as no one in our entire lives has ever done, not our parents, siblings, spouses, friends—and hardly ever our own grown children.
~ Ruth Goode

Chapter 5
Maximizing Grandparenting

When grandparents look into the face of a newborn grandchild, they are looking at the continuity of life. This grandchild represents a new generation—the future of your family, your experiences, your culture, your genes— everything you have worked so hard to achieve in life. You want the best for your grandchild. The hope is exhilarating.

Making the most of grandparenting involves more than just providing grandchildren with educational, enrichment, and learning activities. You also hope your grandchildren will learn to value many of the same things you value—honesty, hard work, education, their environment, art, music, life-long learning, and more.[68] You want them to respect you, listen to you, and in later years, after you are gone, to remember times you spent together. In short, you want to have the best relationship possible with each of your grandchildren.

Whether you are just beginning this journey or have been a grandparent for several years, below are some guidelines that may be useful. Some of these we learned from our own experiences, some we learned from our parents and grandparents, and some we learned from other grandparents like you. We hope they are helpful.

Team with Parents

Earlier in this book, we spoke about how society in this new century has lost much of its connectedness. Extended families simply do not have the daily contact that was typical of earlier generations. With some effort, we think you can re-establish some of that connectedness which is so important to families. Of course, this will depend upon how close or far you live from your grandchildren and also on the extent to which the child's parents want you to participate in the child's life. Remember that your role in the family unit began even before the birth of your grandchild.

Don Schmitz, in his excellent book *The New Face of Grandparenting*,[69] says that grandparents generally come in three varieties. The first group he calls the "Been There, Done That Grand-parents," who are finished raising children and have had enough. They feel that their job is over, and they want a rest.

The second kind are the "Help When Asked Grandparents," who are willing to help out with grandchildren, but only if the parents request it. These grandparents often raised their children in ways that are different from those the parents are using, and they may have differing opinions about key aspects of parenting. These grandparents don't want to interfere, so they remain mostly uninvolved.

The third type are the "Parents Forever Grandparents," who actively participate in the lives of their grandchildren, want to stay connected to their adult children, and believe that all adults in a family share the responsibility of raising the youngest generation.

You may wish to consider which type of grandparent you are, because it will have implications for how you will be able to team with the parents. Then too, the type of grandparent you are now could change over time. Depending on how you and your children work together, you may decide to become more, or perhaps less, active in your involvement. We hope that your involvement will increase.

When you hear the news that a new grandchild is on the way, you automatically become part of the team that is planning and preparing for the coming event. You offer emotional and possibly financial support for the parents of the baby-to-be. You share with them your own experiences with pregnancy and childbirth; or if your new grandchild is adopted, you may reassure the parents that you enthusiastically support the decision to adopt. You purchase things for the nursery, or you help organize a baby shower.

You may even decide to set aside some money for a college or savings account for the new grandchild.

If you live nearby and if your children request it, you may be present for the birth or get to hold the baby shortly after birth; several family members may come to show love and support at this special time. Following the birth, you may help the new parents with cooking and other household chores for a week or two while they recover and bond with the new baby. You may be able to help give baby his first bath or burp him after feeding. With your experience, you may able to calm the baby when he is fussy. You will be supportive of this new family in whatever way is needed, either hands-on or from afar. You can tell the parents what a fine job they are doing and how you admire their patience with the new baby. You can tell them you feel sure that they are going to be wonderful parents. Reassurances like these help the new parents feel accepted and loved, and they help the new three-generation bond.

As your grandchild grows—and they do grow quickly—you can offer support in many other ways. Grandparents, as well as parents, can share and support a child's interest area, whether it is music lessons, art, reading, or baseball. If your five-year-old grandchild wants to learn chess or the piano, a supportive grandparent can encourage the interest, even facilitate it to the extent possible. If the parent doesn't have the background to teach the skill, grandparents can help find a teacher who does. If there are no funds for a piano, perhaps the parents and grandparents together can find a less expensive, small electronic keyboard to try. It is often wise to rent an instrument until you know that the child's interest is a lasting one.

Throughout the child's life, grandparents can support efforts made by parents and the school to help the child learn and progress. Working as a team with the child's parents, grandparents can provide enrichment outside of school through books, games, and other activities. Sometimes a gifted child will be placed in a classroom with age mates who learn more slowly than she. Grandparents can provide the child with perspective about the importance of patience and of understanding that others may not be as skilled or quick, thus teaching respect and tolerance for slower learners. Grandparents can also help the child learn ways to entertain and enrich herself while waiting for others to catch up, or how to negotiate with the teacher for challenging work while others practice the basics. Most importantly, grandparents can watch for the child's learning strengths and areas of interest, and find creative ways to support and encourage those.

Parents need the assistance of grandparents. Some of you have had the gratifying experience of hearing your children finally express appreciation for the things you did for them when they were growing up—things they did not appreciate at the time, or perhaps even resented. We hope that your children—now that they have children of their own—will be eager to work as a team. They still may not want advice (unless they ask for it), but they do want your involvement.

Remember that being a member of the team as a grandparent is different from being the parent. As a parent, you were the captain of the team. You set the family rules and expectations; you upheld or created the rituals and traditions within the family. Now, however, your children are adults, and they are the captains. Perhaps your children have married or remarried, and they have melded their background with their partner's. They have taken some of your traditions and some traditions from their partner's family; they have modified these to fit their lifestyle and beliefs, and they have created new traditions.

In some families, grandparents may strongly disagree with how their adult children have chosen to live their lives or how they have decided to raise their children. But the new generation is different from the ones before it. Looking back, your parents may have felt the same way. In fact, you yourself may have sworn, "I'll never be like them when I'm a parent!"

So how can you be a team with your children when you have different views on so many things? The key is in the simple word *respect* Respecting others does not mean that you always agree with them. You may disagree, for example, with the way the parents discipline the children, or with how much time they leave the children with babysitters. You may disagree with how the parents seem to put off planning financially for the child's college education. But even with these disagreements, you can still respect them as the parents who are in charge. You know that they love their child and want to do what is best for him, and that is the most important thing.

Small gifts from the grandparents convey caring. They also can facilitate grandparents becoming a part of the team in which the best interests of the grandchild are the focus. Gifts to the parents can be informative as well as beneficial to your grandchild's development. For example, you may have read an article which summarizes research showing that babies who are breast-fed have IQ scores that are, on average, five to eight points higher than babies who are not breast-fed.[70] Rather than offering this information directly to the parents, you might ask them if they've seen this article, and if not, you could volunteer to send them a copy. Or you might give the parents a book on child development that explains what to expect at each stage of your grandchild's growth. You don't want to be intrusive, so generally, an indirect approach is better. You may also decide to purchase something for the baby—a particularly colorful mobile for the crib or a music box—or perhaps contribute in a more substantial way by offering to purchase a crib or car seat, after asking the parents which items they need and prefer.

Once the baby is born, the greatest gift you can give the parents is your time. Grandparents often have more time, and less stress, than parents, particularly parents of a newborn. An offer by grandparents to babysit for an evening will be a welcome relief to parents who have not had any time to themselves to go out to dinner or a movie. Parents who have more than one child are usually quite eager for the grandparents to be involved, because it gives them a break, if only for a few hours. Your adult children need time for themselves as a couple in order to be good parents. The stresses of parenting, particularly those of a first-time parent, can place a major strain on the marriage relationship. With a baby and later a young child demanding a huge percentage of their time each day, parents find that their conversations with each other are constantly interrupted, that they are too tired to think, and that each may suddenly feel neglected because all of the attention goes to the baby (or babies in the case of twins or multiple births).

In past generations, one parent often stayed home as the homemaker. This often made it easier to juggle work, home, childcare, marital relationships, and parenting responsibilities all at the same time. Today's families, however, face many more challenges and have a greater need of support from grandparents and other family members.

When Parents Are Overprotective

Some parents, particularly with a first child, will be overly protective despite your best efforts to reassure them. They can be reluctant to allow anyone—even the grandparents—to hold the child, much less change a diaper or babysit. They may resist all comments, ideas, and suggestions. If this is the case for you, be patient. Although you may have a great deal of help and advice to offer, it will be best to wait until those things are asked for. These parents will relax with time.

While you are waiting, you can provide a model of how a parent can have a relaxed attitude. After all, you have the perspective and practice that comes with years of life experience in raising kids. You have also watched friends raise their children, and you have seen how families change. You know the value of patience. You know that family bonds are strong and that sooner or later your children will come to you for advice. They will also one day come to value what you have to offer to your grandchildren.

If you do begin to give advice, we suggest a gentle approach. Initially, you might try to offer your suggestions through the use of questions. For example: "Do you think that some quiet music might help the baby feel more calm?" "Do you think the baby would like a gentle back massage?" "Do you think he'd like to sit in his bouncy chair out here where he can watch all of us?" "I've seen some mothers in the store now with a shoulder strap baby-carrier that lets the baby look out rather than facing in toward the mother. Do you think your baby might like that?"

Prior to the baby's birth, you might ask the parents if they would like a subscription to a parenting magazine or a copy of one of the popular child rearing books. Ask them to browse in the bookstores and to suggest to you the title of the book or books they would like. Perhaps you might purchase one copy each of several magazines on the newsstand and then ask them to choose the one they'd like a subscription to. It's important that they do the choosing so that they don't think you are pushing a particular book or magazine or parenting style onto them.

Some first-time parents are understandably concerned that harm may come to the baby or that the baby is fragile and needs protection. Once they realize that the baby won't break and can trust others to hold her without dropping her, they can be more relaxed. And once the parents are more relaxed and comfortable, everyone, including the baby, will be more relaxed, and your grandparenting becomes easier.

Avoid Being a Pushy Grandparent

Unless there is a real danger to the well-being of your grandchildren, you will want to avoid being a pushy grandparent. How much advice can you give before you are seen as bossy or controlling? How do your offer suggestions to your grown children? Are you over-involved with them or with your grandchildren? Disagreements are going to happen. Can you disagree with respect? Do you know when you need to back away from the disagreement? Do you know how to keep a disagreement from escalating to the point that your relationship with your children and grandchildren is in jeopardy?

We have seen some grandparents push relentlessly in their attempts to resolve disagreements in their favor. They are usually free with their advice, not because they are being mean-spirited, but because they care. They want the best for their children and for their grandchildren.

We understand that you care, but you must avoid being a pushy grandparent. Dr. Lillian Carson, author of *The Essential Grandparent*,[71] states that "We must earn the right to voice our opinion," and that we do this "by establishing a supportive relationship with praise, encouragement and assistance." It is indeed the job of the parents—your children—to raise their own children, and they will have the responsibility long after you are gone.

Just as when your children were young, it is important that you pick your battles. If you disagree with your children on too many parenting issues, they will become defensive in anticipation that you will find fault with whatever they are doing. You will also run the risk of losing credibility with them because they will feel that you are not listening to their viewpoint or valuing what they do.

Certainly it is alright to offer suggestions. It is important, though, to look at *how* you give suggestions. Do the suggestions imply a criticism that the parent is not doing a good enough job? Do they imply that you know better? Sometimes grandparents may feel that they are "just making an observation" about how things are or what the parent is doing, but too many "observations" imply that the grandparents are keenly watching—and evaluating—how the parents are raising their children. This is called "observational poison." That is, the grandparent states things that he notices about the parent—comments that are often critical—but then justifies them by claiming that he was just making a harmless observation.

For instance, a mother might remark to her adult daughter-in-law, "I'd be happy to watch the boys this afternoon. What with you working all of the time, it's good to get them away from the babysitter for a change." Or, "I don't mind cooking every Sunday for our family dinner. It's good for the kids to enjoy a home-cooked meal once in a while." These backhanded compliments start out as empathy, consolation, or offers for help, but they end with the grandparent not-so-subtly pointing out their opinions of the parents' shortcomings. Many times, these observations are well-intentioned, but they hurt communication nonetheless and poison the relationship. Other family members quickly learn to be guarded about what they say or do lest they reveal something that might provoke an observation.

You may want to consider offering your suggestions through "anticipatory praise."[72] This is a very powerful technique in which you praise the behavior you hope might occur. By praising it in advance, you make it more likely that it will occur. In this way, you give the other person the benefit of the doubt regarding what you hope they might be thinking about doing, and you plant a suggestion about what they might then do. For example, you might say to your daughter, "I really admire how you are trying so many different foods with Ariel to help her develop a wide range of tastes." Perhaps your daughter has only done a little of this and hasn't even thought about it from the viewpoint you just offered. But you have suggested the idea in a way that is not likely to cause her to feel that you are offering advice that was not asked for.

So how do you know if you are pushing too hard? The test is to look at your relationship with your children. If, by offering suggestions or criticizing with your observations, you think you may be seriously damaging your relationship with your children or grandchildren, then

the price is far too high. The single most important thing you have with your children and your
grandchildren is your bond with them. Without
a strong relationship, your suggestions will fall
on deaf ears, and you will not likely be invited to
spend much time with them. Not only would
that be a tragic loss of relationship for you and
for them, but you would also lose the opportunity to possibly have some influence in the
future when they do want your advice or
suggestions.

Establish Some House Rules

You want to be a team with the parents, but
does that mean that the rules in your house have
to be exactly the same as the rules that the parents have in their house? Probably not. Other
than universal rules for safety and health, the
rules for child rearing and behavior at your
home can be quite different from those your
children follow at their home. In fact, there are
advantages to the child being able to experience
that there are a variety of acceptable ways for
people to organize and live their lives.

One of the most frequent concerns we hear
from grandparents is that they feel their children

are being far too harsh on the grandchildren. Particularly with a first-born child, parents may have overly high expectations regarding the child's behaviors, and they may want to the child act more mature than is reasonable. They reason, "She's very smart; so she should show better judgment and be more mature!" Grandparents, on the other hand, may think, "Don't be so hard on her! She's only five years old! She has her whole life to be responsible!"

You are probably correct in thinking that your grandchild does not need to be overly mature in all behaviors at such a young age. Grandparents generally have more patience than parents; they know that if adults are reasonably consistent in enforcing basic rules, and if they provide models of the behaviors they expect, then most children will gradually learn mature behaviors. It helps to know, too, that many gifted children have an intellect that does not match their judgment. Judgment can often lag behind, and so the children may do things that seem like big mistakes. Your very bright grandchild may download a formula for model rocket fuel from the Internet and then decide to manufacture a version of it in the basement. We hope that the guardian angels are nearby. Fortunately, the judgment of gifted children does catch up with their intellect with each passing year.

For further variance in house rules, grandparents on the mother's side of the family may have different rules and guidelines from grandparents on the father's side of the family. Some parents will worry that this is confusing to the child. But our experience tells us that gifted children quickly learn the different rules of different houses, whether they are visiting grandparents or neighbors. They know, for example, that at the Jensen house, they are expected to leave their shoes at the door and are not allowed in the living room except by special invitation. At the Baker house, however, they have the run of the house and can bring the dog upstairs as well.

Though we are very accepting of most house rules, there are a few that we would encourage you to consider adopting as your own. The first is to understand that you have a right to set the rules in your home, and that gifted grandchildren—like all other children—do need rules or limits. If there are no limits to guide their behavior, children will not learn how to control themselves or how to interact appropriately with others.

They will be uncivilized little ruffians in social situations and could be embarrassed by the reaction they get from others. It is helpful to teach children appropriate behaviors for a variety of situations they may encounter. This is what we do at a concert; this is how we act in a restaurant; this is how to respond to adults who speak to you, etc.

A second suggestion is to place a limit in your home on TV and computer games, as we mentioned earlier in this book. You are perfectly within your rights to restrict the amount of time that your grandchildren spend in front of the television, or to turn off the TV when certain shows come on. You may even say, "No TV or computer games while you are at Grandma's. Period!" The child can then begin to associate time at Grandma's with Scrabble® or chess or drawing or reading or making things.

A third suggestion is that you consider establishing "special time" as a tradition in your home. You can create new traditions within the family—or at least in your house—that will promote relationships and enhance communication. Special time, as discussed earlier in this book, is one of the most powerful of all of these traditions.

Blended, Single, and/or Divorced Families

It's a rare family in today's society that has not experienced some aspect of divorce. The number of single parents and blended families has dramatically increased. More than a quarter of grandparents have at least one step-grandchild.[73] When a family splits or is experiencing serious difficulties with the parents' relationship, the role of grandparents as a stabilizing factor often becomes more important. Grandparents can, without taking sides, offer some consistency through giving extra time and attention to the children.

When divorce leads to single parent situations, there may be tension between the two sets of grandparents, as well as when ex-spouses find themselves together again. Grandparents may find that they must work together to provide both emotional and financial support for their children, as well as for their grandchildren.

When previously divorced individuals marry and start a new family, the blended family creates a new and expanded extended family. A grandchild in a blended family may now have four sets of grandparents. In any of these situations, the relation-ship and quality of communication between you and your grandchildren become even more important. You and your home may truly become a refuge and sanctuary for your grandchildren. If the parents are quarreling, or if there is separa-tion or divorce, or if a single parent is exhausted, you may need to reach out actively to invite your grandchildren to spend more time at your home than you had at first anticipated.

Grandparents as Daycare Providers

Sometimes, parents leave the grandchildren with you more often than you would like. Some adult children expect their parents to be their own personal daycare center. If the parents are struggling financially, this is certainly understand-able. We remember times in our own childhoods when our parents, grandparents, or aunts and uncles took in children who were ill or destitute or suddenly without parents to care for them. In earlier generations, it was a frequent practice, and perhaps it should not be so unexpected now.

Some grandparents, though, are taken advan-tage of by their children. The children seem to have the attitude that "Since our parents are retired and have nothing better to do, we can leave the kids with them several days a week." The children simply do not realize that although grandparents love their grandchildren dearly, this doesn't necessarily mean that they want to be parents all over again.

Please know that you do not have to be either a "Super Grandparent" or a "Daily/ Weekly/ Monthly Daycare Center" for your grandchildren. We want you to spend time with your grandchildren, but we also want you to know that it's okay for you to set limits on the amount of time you will spend with them.

You and the parents may wish to consider enrolling the child in a daycare center. We know parents worry that their child will catch colds and other illnesses from other children, or that the workers will not give their child the proper care or attention. We also know that there are many helpful books and articles that describe how to select a daycare or preschool program that is safe, warm, and supportive, as well as enriching. Preschool programs offer opportunities to socialize and interact with other children, in addition to exploring materials such as beads, blocks, numbers, clay, sand, music, and storybooks, and they can be an excellent environment for gifted children who are so eager for new experiences and learning. These programs can often provide opportunities beyond those the parents can offer, at the same time giving parents a welcome breather from their child's intensity. Perhaps the child can attend daycare or preschool four days a week and go to Grandma's on Fridays. A quality daycare or preschool program can be an excellent resource for the family.

Helping Parents Cope with Peer Pressure

Young children aren't the only ones who experience peer pressure. Adults, even grandparents, experience peer pressure as well. There is an expectation within our communities as to what "good parenting" or "good grandparenting" should be and how children "should act." Parents of gifted children often get peer pressure from other parents. For example, others may say, "Why are you putting so much pressure on your child to learn to read?" The parents of the gifted child know that they are not teaching their son to read; the child is learning on his own from asking, "What is this word?" and so on. But the parent feels somehow put down and certainly unfairly judged by the other parent.

Characteristics of gifted children often make them stand out as different when compared to age mates. When parents of gifted children talk to other parents, they are often met with questioning, disbelief, or criticism. Other parents may say, "*My* child isn't that sensitive. What have you done to make your child so thin-skinned?" Or, "Why do you let your child act in such a rude manner and ask adults so many questions?" Or, "Why doesn't your child want to play with children her own age?" Or, "Why is he so bossy?" Or, "Don't you think you're spoiling her when you cut the tags out of the back of all of her shirts and give her a blanket with a satin binding?" These comments from other parents cut deeply. The other parents seem to be blaming the parent of the gifted child for things that are inherent in the child's nature. The parent feels isolated; she has no one she can talk to about her children.

Parenting gifted children can be a very lonely experience. These parents seldom have other parents with whom they can share their child's unusual accomplishments or their unique

parenting experiences that often are quite different from the experiences of other parents. This is
another reason why parents of gifted children need
their own parents—the child's grandparents—for
emotional support and encouragement. They
need someone to listen and believe and accept
that this is the parent's true experience.

Grandparents who know which characteristics and behaviors are common for gifted children
can provide a sense of understanding and comfort for parents. Chances are that the parents
showed some of these same characteristics when
they were children, and the grandparents may
remind them of this. Parents are interested to
know that their children are bright, but they
aren't always so willing to accept some of the
negative aspects that go along with giftedness.
One or both parents may often just want their
children to be "normal" or "average," or at least
not so different from other children. They may
even criticize their children for some of their
"gifted" behaviors when this is actually who the
child is. The child isn't asking "Twenty Questions" about everything on earth to make life
difficult for the parent. The child is simply being
true to who she is—someone who has a need to

know. Grandparents can reassure the parents that they are doing the right thing in accepting their children as they are, they can help them resist peer pressure from other parents, and they can encourage them to continue to support their children's interests and intensities, whatever those may be.

How It "Used to Be"

As a grandparent, you have a reasonable perspective on life. You have likely lived through many different periods of change in society. You have known many types of people; you have seen what life has to offer—both good and bad—and you have a wealth of experiences and wisdom to share. You may be tempted to talk about how it used to be with your children and your grandchildren as an expression of your wisdom. This can be an asset and is something only you can offer the child. But use it sparingly. Don't reminisce so much that your children and grandchildren would rather not spend time with you.

In American Indian culture, grandparents are expected to tell tales of olden times and pass on the stories, legends, and traditions of their people. Navajo children often spend entire summers with their grandparents living in a hogan and helping with the sheep herding and other chores, giving them several months to absorb the grandparents' language and traditions. Likewise, in Hispanic culture, the grandparents are valued for what they can teach their grandchildren. Anglo culture could learn much from these other cultures.

How much should you talk about the past? That will depend on how interested the listener is and on your personal relationship with the listener. Your grandchildren may become interested if you make an occasional comparison between them and you when you were their age. "My mother used to fix me peanut butter and banana sandwiches for my school lunch. She usually put in an apple and some animal crackers, too." In this way, you can build an interest for the child to ask you about when you were a young girl or boy.

If your grandchildren are interested in your experiences during Civil Rights or Women's Rights days, or in your career or travel experiences, feel free to share with them until the interest diminishes. Sometimes, teachers give assignments in which children must interview older adults about how they celebrated Christmas, or how it was when they grew up on the farm. Grandparents are important resources for such assignments. Eventually, your grandchildren may want to know about the family tree or how and when the family came to this country. There are some fine software programs and Internet resources that can help grandparents with the family genealogy. A child may want only a simple family tree at first, maybe going back two generations. But gifted children, with their intense need to know more, may ask questions that take you back to the 1700s or before.

Sometimes you will want to share certain memories even though your listener hasn't expressed an interest in them. Your children, for example, may be fretting excessively because your teenage grandchild wants to get his head shaved for the summer or his ear pierced. If you have a reasonable relationship, you can, with a sense of humor, remind them of their own teenage years when they wore extremely long or spiked or brightly colored hair. You can even mention the "ducktails" and "pompadours" that were fashionable in your day as a way of reminding parents that the child's wish is probably not worth a family war.

Grandchild as a Teacher

At the end of every yoga class, the instructor usually finishes by saying "Namaste" or "Thank you for allowing me to teach you today." What a powerful statement that is. It implies that it is an honor to be able to teach a student, any student, and that the teacher should be humble. We feel that way about parenting and grandparenting. The student often does teach the instructor, and similarly, grandchildren often teach the parents and grandparents.

What if your grandchild asks questions you can't answer or wants to explore projects that are beyond your capabilities? One of the wonderful things about being a grandparent is that you don't have to have all the answers, and you don't have to be able to do everything. Will Rogers spoke the truth when he said, "You know everybody is ignorant, only on different subjects."[74]

Grandchildren are sometimes amazed that grandparents don't know everything. They may be even more amazed to encounter an adult who is willing to admit that fact and who then shows an openness to learning from a child or learning jointly with a child. Many grandparents have found that exploring a project jointly with a grandchild can be a truly exciting adventure. Not only is it fun to watch a grandchild go through the process of discovery, but it also is important for grandchildren to see that learning is never finished and that adults can still be excited about learning new information and starting new projects.

Long Distance Connections

Some grandparents live physically near enough to visit their grandchildren weekly or monthly, while others live much farther than over the river and through the woods—sometimes several states away. Because grandparents have an average of five grandchildren or great grandchildren, it is not surprising that many of them have at least one grandchild who lives more than an hour's drive away. For 26% of grandparents, all of their grandchildren live at least that far away.[75]

Grandparents who live far away need not give up being important in their grandchild's life. You can make time to listen to your children tell about the grandchildren through weekly or twice weekly phone calls, write encouraging letters or e-mail messages, or request snapshots or digital photos via the Internet. Grandchildren can fax you samples of their school projects or artwork. Some families these days have created websites for keeping in touch with each other, posting events, newsworthy items, and photos.

With all of these methods of communication, staying in touch is easier than ever. A full 45% of grandparents talk to their grandchildren on the phone each week (about three-quarters talk to them at least each month), while half say that they have sent a greeting card to a grandchild in the past month, and 30% have sent a letter or postcard. And 22% of grandparents are now using the Internet, which is another terrific form of communication because of the speed in which messages are delivered and its low cost as compared with long-distance phone bills.[76] Staying connected, even in this busy, mobile society, is clearly prevalent among grandparents and grandchildren. The AARP has some wonderful suggestions for long distance grandparenting on its website at www.aarp.org/ Articles/ a2004-01-16-longdistance.html.

Even from a distance, you can continue to learn about your grandchild's interests and abilities through frequent talks with the child's parents. You can support these interests by sending related books or magazines or other items, or mailing out letters or postcards, or having short phone conversations with the child. Gifts need not be lavish. Correspondence need not be lengthy. Let the child be the guide on length of e-mails or letters. The frequency and regularity of short notes or phone calls will be more important than their length. A postcard every month or so will be a reminder to the child that she is special to you and that you have taken the time to remember her.

There are some children's science and literary magazines designed for a variety of age groups that are very educational. A subscription to one of these could be a nice, regular reminder that Grandma and Grandpa support the child's interests. Here is a list of possibilities from Karen Rogers' book, *Re-Forming Gifted Education: How Parents and Teachers Can Match the Program to the Child.*[77]

Table 2
Gifted Children's Magazines

Magazine	Publication Address	Contents/ Interest Areas
3-2-1 Contact	P.O. Box 53051 Boulder, CO 80322	Science/technology in projects, experiments
Calliope: World History for Young People	30 Grove Street, Suite C Peterborough, NH 03458	Five issues per year each focus on different themes in history
Chickadee	25 Boxwood Lane Buffalo, NY 14225	Nature and environmental study with some features on other sciences
Cobblestone	30 Grove Street, Suite C Peterborough, NH 03458	U.S. history features
Cricket	315 Fifth St., P.O. Box 300 Peru, IL 61354	Variety of literary genres for children
Current Science	3001 Cindel Drive Delran, NJ 08370	Latest advances in technology and science
Faces: The Magazine About People	30 Grove Street, Suite C Peterborough, NH 03458	Articles, projects on anthropology from the American Museum of Natural History

Imagination	Johns Hopkins Press/CTY 3400 N. Charles Street Baltimore, MD 21218	School-age challenges, articles, stories for highly gifted children
Kid City Magazine	200 Watt Street P.O. Box 53349 Boulder, CO 80322	School-age challenges, stories, articles for Sesame Street graduates
Ladybug: The Magazine for Young Children	315 Fifth St. P.O. Box 300 Peru, IL 61354	Version of *Cricket* for children ages 2-6
Let's Find Out	Scholastic 730 Broadway New York, NY 10003	Features on all academic areas for older children who can read well
Merlyn's Pen: The National Magazine of Student Writing	Merlyn's Pen, Inc. P.O. Box 910 East Greenwich, RI 02818	Publishes written works and art created by children; middle school or high school editions
Muse	Cricket Magazine, Inc. 315 Fifth St. P.O. Box 300 Peru, IL 61354	Science and arts features for 8- to 14-year-olds in conjunction with *Smithsonian/Cricket*
National Geographic World	17th & M Streets NW Washington, DC 20036	Science, hobbies, and sports features

asp-num*Odyssey*	30 Grove Street, Suite C Peterborough, NH 03458	Space and astro-nomy features
OWL: The Dis-covery Maga-zine for Children	25 Boxwood Lane Buffalo, NY 14225	Nature magazine published by Young Naturalist Founda-tion for ages 9-12
Que'tal? or *Das Rad* or *Bonjour*	Scholastic 730 Broadway New York, NY 10003	Introductory lan-guage learning through games, stories, pictures
Ranger Rick	National Wildlife Federa-tion 8925 Leesburg Pike Vienna, VA 22184	Nature study for graduates of Your Big Backyard
Scholastic DynaMath	730 Broadway New York, NY 10003	Real world math through activities and games
Sesame Street Magazine	P.O. Box 55518 Boulder, CO 80322	Pre-school challen-ges, games, pro-jects in math, reading, thinking
Sports Illustra-ted for Kids	P.O. Box 60001 Tampa, FL 33660-0001	Sports magazine for ages 8-13
Stone Stoup	P.O. Box 83 Santa Cruz, CA 95063	Art and writings from children ages 5-12
Story Art Magazine	National Story League 984 Roelofs Road Yardley, PA 19067	Short story maga-zine for children and adults

Your Big Backyard	National Wildlife Federation 8925 Leesburg Pike Vienna, VA 22184	Nature study through stories, puzzles, and games
Zillions	Consumers Union/Reports P.O. Box 2015 New York, NY 10703	*Consumer Reports* for kids by Consumers Union, for ages 8-14
Zoobooks	P.O. Box 85384 San Diego, CA 92186	Animal studies

Many of these periodicals can be found in the public library if you would like to check their content and reading level. Many of them can also be ordered on the Internet.

Belongingness

Families are the first and the best place for a child to learn a sense of belongingness. This is true for all children. The family is also important as a "safe haven," a place where a child feels understood and accepted for who he is. Since gifted children feel different from other children almost from the beginning, this safe haven is particularly important to a gifted child. Family is also where the child—any child—forms his concept of self. A child looks around at other family members, sees his relationship to them, and forms a first view of the world based on his family. This is where he learns to trust or mistrust, to cooperate and work as a team or not, and to identify his likes and dislikes. It is where he learns independence and interdependence. And best of all for a gifted child, in his family, he does not need to feel different. He fits in, even if he has a hard time doing so in school.

Gifted children are often impatient and judgmental with others, as well as with themselves, and their feelings of differentness can lead to feelings of estrangement. They may start off liking and being excited about school, but then, when the teacher tells them they ask too many questions or they need to keep their hand down more of the time to give others a chance, they gradually learns that they are not as accepted at school as they would like to be. They begin to compensate by holding back, and they feel estranged.

It is important that gifted children learn to be content within themselves, even if they feel discontent with much of the world around them. Though they may be impatient with others, they can also learn to accept and enjoy others, a skill that they may need to continue to re-learn throughout their lives.[78] For example, they may not want to attend a social event with their parents. But by going and talking with others, they might learn that the gentleman in the brown suit has a fascinating past as an archeologist, and that the older businesswoman sitting in the corner has traveled to every continent of the world. They get practice at accepting others. Or a gifted child might learn by talking to a handicapped child at school that the child has a delightful sense of humor and loves to tell jokes. Situations such as these give gifted children practice at accepting others. In addition, through grandparents' role modeling, gifted children can learn to appreciate differences and enjoy all kinds of people.

How can we help gifted children learn to reach a place of contentment? Mental giftedness is valuable, but it is even more important to live with oneself and others. We live in a world where interdependence and cooperation are important. One's attitude—how one views the world—is the key to helping gifted children who are impatient with others learn tolerance and acceptance. Gifted children who are given loving guidance and thoughtful mentoring can usually turn waiting time, or times when they are frustrated, into creative opportunities for detailed observations or for finding new ideas. They can also learn the value of conversation with others as a way to pass the time instead of relying on video games or music headsets. This turns waiting time to a focus on others rather than entertainment of oneself. Reading and being read to—and particularly reading biographies of well-known people—will offer extra stimulation, as well as information about how other thoughtful children and adults found their place in the world.

A grandparent's nurturance and guidance can help a child come to understand that human beings who are not as bright or as quick as they nevertheless do have value. Gifted children can be taught to realize that traits other than intelligence—such as kindness, love, courage, loyalty, generosity, a sense of humor, a caring spirit, and a willingness to work—are important also. You might, for example, help your gifted grandchildren understand the value of all individuals by learning about all the thousands of careers it takes to make a society. Some careers require sharp minds and the ability to do complex math, while others require the ability to operate heavy equipment or do a routine, repetitive task. All jobs are valuable because we need all of them to make our society, our towns and cities, work. Simply by taking the time to acknowledge the human presence of all the people we meet during the day—crossing guards, bus drivers, waitresses, librarians, grocery clerks—we show our grandchildren that equity can be practiced as well as preached. By the little things they say and do every day, grandparents can set an example for healthy attitudes that will help grandchildren interact with others around them as they progress through school and later enter careers of their own.

If you have a gifted grandchild who is significantly out of step with the surrounding world, your emotional support is particularly important. Such a child especially needs grandparents to be a haven—a place where there are loving family members who can help her understand, untangle, and accept (not necessarily agree with) the existence of the many peculiar behaviors of people in our world. Because communication with grandparents is sometimes different from and often of better quality than it is with parents, especially in the teen years, a grandchild may find a grandparent to be that kind of haven.

Life lessons you teach your grandchildren can provide the inner strength that they will need to withstand the pressures they will encounter in their future, whether that future is junior high school, high school, college, a career, or married life. If you establish a strong relationship with your grandchildren while they are young, they will continue to come to you for affirmation and understanding throughout their life.

*The test of the morality of a society is
what it does for its children.*
~ Dietrich Bonhoeffer

*You can learn many things from children.
How much patience you have, for instance.*
~ Franklin P. Jones

*In the final analysis it is not what you do for your
children but what you have taught them to do for
themselves that will make them successful human beings.*
~ Ann Landers

Chapter 6

When a Grandparent Becomes the Parent

According to the 2000 U.S. Census, more than one out of every 20 children under the age of 18 is permanently living in a home where a grandparent is the head of the family. For some grandparents, the situation is temporary, such as when adult children are shipped overseas for Armed Services duty, or when a parent has to travel due to a special work assignment. In other situations, the arrangement is temporary but longer term, as, for example, when a child's parent is seriously ill. And sometimes a grandparent may become the parent due to sad or tragic circumstances, such as death, incarceration, divorce, serious accident, or disability of one of the adult children.

Whether short-term or long-term, life for a grandparent becomes suddenly quite different when assigned the role of parent again. Although you are still a grandparent, you must now assume a more active and assertive role in *all* areas of the child's life to meet the needs of your gifted grandchild (or grandchildren). You are now both the parent and the grandparent.

In this situation, it has probably been quite some time since you were a parent of young children, and it's likely that your parenting skills are a little rusty. Many things have changed in this modern world in the past 20 or 30 years that make parenting, particularly parenting gifted children, a bit different. Much of what we talked about in previous chapters, however, such as ways to nurture the relationship and support the child's interests, still applies when a grandparent is a parent.

In this chapter, we will highlight three important areas—discipline, praise, and communication—to help you brush up on some key parenting skills. This is not meant to be an encyclopedia of parenting; you will want to seek out other sources as well, particularly if specific problems are evident or suspected either in the grandchild or the child's parents, for instance drug, alcohol, or other substance abuse, or serious psychological or behavioral problems. Such issues require additional intervention and knowledge to achieve a positive outcome for the child and the family. Nevertheless, this chapter should provide a solid beginning. And many of the ideas here will be helpful even if you are not a grandparent who is also the parent.

Discipline

Grandparents who also act as parents of their grandchildren bear a far heavier burden than do ordinary grandparents. Certainly, they can enjoy their grandchildren, but they must also assert consistent and effective discipline. In Chapter 3, we briefly stated that discipline of gifted children can result in power struggles.

One question you should ask yourself when you impose discipline on the child is simply this: "How effective is this method of discipline?" (i.e., grounding the child for two days, or refusing to budge or compromise on an issue). Often, adults will try to assert discipline or values in the same way repeatedly. But if it hasn't worked so far, what makes you think it would work if you tried it one more time? Maybe you can find different approach that is not so adversarial—such as negotiating some points with the child, but staying firm on others.

When we use the word "discipline," we are talking about self-discipline—how to help the child learn from his behaviors in ways that will allow him to achieve self-regulation and responsibility. We do not mean punishment. Discipline is far more than punishment. Punishment, because it is a negative consequence, often does not help with discipline because punishment only tells a child what *not* to do; it does not direct him toward what we *want* him to do. In fact, punishment, particularly if it is harsh and administered in an inconsistent manner, can lead to problems such as power struggles, rebellion, and even juvenile delinquency.[79]

This advice against punishment may be different from the style your parents used in raising you. Perhaps they believed in taking you out to the woodshed and using a stick or a belt on you now and then. That was a different time; the theory on child discipline back then was "spare the rod; spoil the child." Likewise, in the schools of earlier times, the principal used a paddle for infractions. But today, any sort of corporal punishment in schools, even a teacher grabbing a student's arm, can result in that teacher losing his or her job.

Instead, discipline focuses on more positive ways to teach a child self-control so that she can learn to interact responsibly with others in predictable, mutually satisfying ways. Today's thinking on discipline focuses on teaching a child to depend upon her own ability to think and act rather than acting out of fear of consequences or punishment, or behaving simply because of the prevailing pressures of the moment.

The goal of discipline, then, is self-direction, which is quite different from that of punishment, which imposes direction and rules from the outside. For gifted children, self-direction is vital. Why? Because gifted children, by their very nature, are different from others, and throughout life, they will need to rely on their own judgment rather than that of others. Learning self-direction and self-discipline is essential if gifted children are to become autonomous, lifelong learners.[80]

Of course, discipline with gifted children can be challenging for parents and others because of one particular characteristic that we noted earlier—their intensity. This intensity by itself can lead to discipline problems. For example, sometimes gifted children's exuberance causes them to act without thinking, while at other times, their intensity causes them to passionately defend their actions or to actively engage in power struggles with an adult in an attempt to "save face." Although their intensity is a great strength, it also makes it more difficult for them to learn self-discipline and self-control when they are in an intense, passionate disagreement with an adult authority figure.

Since most behaviors are learned, they can also be unlearned or modified. To achieve this, gifted children, like all other children, need appropriate and suitable information and feedback, as well as limits and reinforcements for progress. Almost everything a person does is motivated by a consequence, reward, or pay-off that serves to maintain or support the behavior. For example, sibling rivalry is not just behavior that occurs randomly; siblings are rivaling for something—usually attention from the adults around them. Because gifted children are so adept at learning, they can modify their actions if they see good reasons for doing so.

So how can you, as a grandparent acting as the parent, help your very intense, very bright child learn self-control? In the classic book, *Guiding the Gifted Child*,[81] you will find some fundamental guidelines for parents, grandparents, and others that will help promote effective self-discipline in gifted children. The key points, which follow, are summarized mostly from that book.

Setting Limits

All children need limits. Some adults incorrectly believe that limits stifle creativity or that limits for smart children are not needed because they can handle themselves with good judgment. But even a gifted child lacks the experience that provides the basis for good judgment. With young gifted children, bedtime is one time when limits can be an issue. A parent wishing to help the child learn to self-regulate can say,

"Well, your bedtime is 8:00 P.M, but you may read with the light on as long as you are quiet and not bothering anyone. When we say it's time for lights out, then you need to turn the light off. If you are grouchy tomorrow, then we'll know you need the lights turned off earlier." This helps the child gain experience in setting his own limits.

Gifted children are likely to need fewer rules and boundaries than other children. They are usually able to see the reasons for limits and learn very rapidly to anticipate consequences. We can best help children learn to monitor and control their own actions if we can avoid the temptation to impose too much control from the outside. For example, children who spend their allowances frivolously tend ultimately to learn how to budget their finances better on their own than if we carefully dole the money out piecemeal. With practice, these children can learn skills that they will genuinely need when they get older. We know of one high school junior who became the designated driver in her crowd of friends because she chose not to drink beer when the others did. She observed what happened to her friends' judgment when they had too much to drink, and she resisted the pressure to follow suit. Her parents trusted her to be a safe driver, and her friends appreciated that she could drive them home safely as well. She was not teased for her abstinence; her simple statement, "I don't like the way it tastes," took care of the question of teen drinking for her.

Although limits are certainly needed, our advice is to set the fewest limits necessary and then to allow some freedom within them. The boundaries should allow room for growth and experimentation, and as the child matures, these boundaries can be expanded. If you attempt to set too many rules and limits, the result will likely be inconsistencies and frustration. Similarly, if you suddenly begin to apply limits to an older child who has not had rules or limits before, there is a strong likelihood that the child will rebel or will simply not comply. It is best if children get used to limits at a younger age, which then allows parents to reduce the number of limits more comfortably as the child matures. We used an example above about allowing flexibility on the limits concerning bedtime for a younger child. An older child might be trusted to set his own bedtime; he knows from experience how much sleep he needs. When the child goes off to college, he will surely be setting his own bedtime, as well as managing other behaviors on his own.

The most important guideline is to set (and enforce) limits as consistently as possible. Of course, a gifted child, like any other child, will test the limits on occasion—sometimes just to try out new behaviors, sometimes to see how strong your reaction will be, and sometimes to get reassurance that the limits really are still there. Children are actually more comfortable when they know they have limits and are clear on what the limits are. Limits, rules, and expectations for conduct that are clearly stated and mutually understood give the child a sense of security, stability, and predictability that are especially important for children from ages 18 months to the teenage years.

Children with older siblings will most often develop their own values, limits, and expectations, drawn largely from earlier limits set by parents for the older children. Whether a child is younger or older, guidelines, rules, and limits help her to be in control of herself, as well as to make sense of the world around her. A child learns that there are rules in society, as well as at home. A red light means stop; yellow means caution; green means go. People who don't obey traffic rules get a ticket. No running is allowed at the pool. If you run at the pool, you will not be allowed to swim, and you may be sent home. Rules and laws help to ensure that people live together safely and cooperatively.

Developing Rules

We believe that gifted children should participate in developing family rules. Although this may sound unreasonable or even unwise to some, a family meeting to discuss rules can actually be a wonderful learning experience for the whole family. This will be particularly important for grandparents acting as parents, since your grandchildren may have already spent a good portion of their lives living with their parents' rules, which might be different from the ones you would like to establish. We are not saying that your grandchildren should be allowed to set the rules. However, it will help the transition if grandchildren can join in the discussion about the rules and feel that they have a chance to offer some input. By participating in the discussions about household rules and limits, gifted children see the importance of limits and eventually learn to set their own. As they subsequently encounter the consequences of their actions, they will accumulate valuable experience—the very experience needed to form a basis for good judgment. A good resource for facilitating a family meeting for discussion of rules, or for any other purpose, is the classic book *Children: The Challenge*,[82] which we refer to again later in this chapter when we talk about consequences.

Specific rules will vary depending upon your grandchild's age, experience, and maturity. How do you know how much you can reasonably expect from this very bright child who is now living with you? Gifted children show a wide variation in behaviors, and it is easy to fall into the trap of expecting too much from them. Because they may show a great amount of maturity in some areas, you may be tempted to expect that same level of maturity in all areas, but that is simply not realistic. Remember what we said earlier—that although their high verbal ability may make them sometimes sound adult, their experience and maturity are still more like that of someone their own age.

You may find it helpful to observe other children of the same chronological age to remind yourself what is "normal" behavior for children that age, or you may wish to consult a book or other source outlining normal stages of child development. Certainly it is unreasonable to punish a six-year-old for being a six-year-old, even if most of the time the child seems more like a 10-year-old. This is probably one of the hardest things for parents of gifted children—to remember that their children are still children, even though their intellect is high. Remind yourself that intellect is not the same thing as wisdom, and that in many ways, your grandchildren will simply act their age. Because of this complexity, you will probably want to develop your rules conservatively and then revisit them periodically.

Enforcing Rules

So what will you do when the rules are broken? Wherever possible, we recommend that you enforce your limits by allowing natural and logical consequences to occur, rather than enforcing a consequence that *you* create for the child.

For example, if your grandchild refuses to practice his piano or his karate skills according to an agreed-upon schedule, he will have to face the teacher's displeasure as well as his own failure to perform as well as he had hoped. A "natural consequences" approach such as this will reduce the likelihood of power struggles with the child, and it generally provides a better opportunity for the child to learn important self-management skills. If the child continues to "forget" to practice, you might ask him what he can do to remind himself. Perhaps he can put a reminder sign on his bathroom mirror, or maybe he'll ask you to remind him. If the failure to practice continues, he may ask to drop the lessons. At this point, you might negotiate something like continuing the lessons for a four- to six-week trial period to see if he still wants to quit; or you may have a three-way discussion with the teacher or instructor. If the teacher has noticed talent, he or she may be able to encourage the child to try a little longer.

If you must impose your own disciplinary consequences for your grandchild's misbehavior, let the consequences be logical ones, rather than ones that are unrelated to the child's behavior and that come only out of your anger. If the child leaves a toy in the driveway and it is stolen, there is no need to lecture the child or say, "I told you so!" or, "Okay, now you're grounded for a whole week!" The logical consequence is that you don't go out and buy another toy.

The key to enforcing the rules—whether they are natural, logical, or simply your rules—is that you be firm, consistent, and provide a clear understanding of the reasons for the consequences. For example, let's say that the child is not allowed to take a shortcut through the alley when walking home from school. The reason is that it is dangerous; there are harmful objects and substances in the alley, and the child is less visible to others. The consequence for taking the shortcut is that you will pick up the child after school, and there will be a loss of after-school playtime with friends.

We are not advocating a lengthy explanation or lecture concerning the reason for every consequence. In fact, explanations should be brief so that you lessen the risk of getting caught up in a debate. Our reasoning is simply that gifted children are usually more willing to comply with rules (and consequences) when they see valid reasons for them; conversely, they are less likely to comply with rules they see as arbitrary or as exhibitions of adult power. In fact, in enforcing limits, you should not rigidly apply a consequence without regard for the situation. Do listen to your grandchildren's reasons; sometimes their reasons are valid. Though this approach is probably not how we were raised, it does make sense if we want our grandchildren to learn and attain thoughtful self-discipline. Parenting wisdom over the years has changed. Methods and strategies these days tend to be far more democratic and less authoritarian than in years past.

We also need to consider the possibility that our expectations simply may not be appropriate for a young child in today's world. Do we really need to *insist* on a particular behavior? Is it imperative that the child makes her bed every day? Or that she finish everything on her plate? Brushing teeth every day is certainly important for dental health, but eating every single thing on one's plate at every single meal may be actually be encouraging unhealthy eating. Look at the reasons behind your insistence. How much are you replaying messages that you heard in your own childhood? Are you trying to establish control? Too much control can lead to an unnecessary power struggle. Are you afraid that if you give in, the child will take over? Have you left your grandchild a face-saving way out? Were there any rules that did not work with you as a child or with your children? If so, they probably will not work for your grandchildren.

Regarding consequences, it is easy to overreact to a broken rule, and you may attempt—at least initially—to set consequences that are out of proportion to the offense or that you cannot really enforce. Be careful not to set limits you either can't enforce or later don't want to, or that really are punishments for you. Take this statement: "You're grounded! You're not allowed outside of your room for the entire weekend!" This is an unreasonable consequence. Why? It's unrealistic and unenforceable. Meals and bathroom trips alone will all require the child to leave his room. And now that you have set a limit that you cannot reasonably enforce, your credibility is weakened and you have undermined the seriousness of the consequence. You have also made it more likely that your limits will be tested again, unless the child understands the reasons why you withdrew the consequence or did not enforce it.

If you find yourself in such a situation, it would be wise to renegotiate the consequence like this, "You know, I've been re-thinking yesterday's discussion about staying in your room, and I think I need to make some changes in what I said. You will be restricted to your room for two hours before soccer practice and two hours after lunch. I realize that you need to eat and go to your team practice."

It is particularly important to avoid harsh and inconsistent punishment. By harsh punishment, we mean more than just spanking a child; we are also including angry tirades and verbal abuse. And by inconsistent punishment, we mean punishing a child sometimes for a certain behavior, but then not punishing her other times for the same behavior. Harsh and inconsistent punishments are not only ineffective in changing most behaviors, but they are also one of the most damaging approaches to the child and to your relationship with her. Harsh and inconsistent punishment results in anger, distrust, and disrespect for authority, as well as disrespect for you, and the gifted child will then come to believe that the world is unpredictable and unsafe. Children raised in such an environment rarely have a healthy self-concept or positive view of themselves, and excessive use of harsh and inconsistent punishment can lead to delinquency or even criminal behavior.[83]

Ridicule and sarcasm are also not helpful and often quite harmful. Gifted children, with their sensitivity, are deeply hurt by ridicule and sarcasm. We have seen gifted children ask to drop classes when the instructor uses sarcasm to "have a little fun." A teacher who says to the class, "I doubt if many of you will be able to do well on this test," is using ridicule. Gifted children seldom see humor in it, only criticism and hurt. If gifted children have sarcasm and ridicule inflicted upon them, they may begin using these same behaviors as weapons against others—often with sad results. Sarcasm is not something we want to model for gifted children.

What about arguments? Since gifted children are highly verbal, they will often argue and try logically to defend their behaviors, reasoning, or viewpoint. Parents and grandparents should expect this. Try not to view it as a threat to your authority, but as a potential strength for the child. Keep your sense of humor as you deal with the refutation of your points. This young person might be a great attorney or business leader in a few more years.

With some argumentative, "Philadelphia lawyer" types of gifted children, it may help to draw up a behavioral contract, particularly for complex disciplinary situations involving older gifted children. Ask the child to help you draw up a behavioral contract or agreement that spells out expectancies and consequences under various conditions. Here is a sample contract:

I will not take a shortcut through the alley, even if my friends do.

If I should forget and do it, one of the following will happen:

(1) I will not be allowed to play with friends after school for two days, or

(2) I will have to pull weeds in the garden for one hour.

Signed:_____Witnessed:_____

Date: _____Date:_____

A draft of a contract may then become the starting point for discussions, which we hope can lead to an agreement. The experience of drawing up a contract that is fair to all parties places direct responsibility upon the child for his behavior. Such a contract, tucked away in a drawer, also helps protect against lapses in memory concerning the terms of the agreement.

We do want you to consider the child's situation, and we would like for you to listen to her arguments and perhaps to her opinions about the fairness of the consequences. In the last analysis, however, you, in your role as a parent, must make the final decision as to the rule and how it should be enforced or what consequences will be for infractions. Do remember, though, that you and your grandchild will need to periodically re-evaluate the limits you have set. As your grandchild develops, she will become better able to manage her own limits, and you will gradually be able to pull back the safety net.

When you set and enforce limits, be careful to choose your battles. Not every problem is worth an angry confrontation. Sometimes the price of compliance is too expensive. For example, we may be able to force our grandchildren to do as we wish, but the resulting resentment might be so great that we could seriously damage our relationship with the child. We need to ask ourselves whether obedience in this instance is really that important, or whether we perhaps should focus on larger, more important issues. For example, if a limit of 10:00 P.M. has been set for the child to be home from a junior high party at a friend's house, and the child arrives home at 10:15 P.M., it is not worth arguing over the 15 minutes. The child will probably have an explanation, and you can accept his reason for being a little late by acknowledging that there was a valid reason; his friend's parents were late bringing him home.

Let's say that you have set the limit that your 11-year-old grandchild will have no video games for a whole week because she has not been completing her homework. But then you are out at a social function one evening and are not there to see whether she played a video game or not. It's probably better not to make an issue of it. Just monitor the nights you are home.

Shooing Flies and Nagging

If you doubt that you can set a limit that is enforceable in a given situation, it may be better for you "not to notice" the infraction. Whenever we set a limit that we cannot, or do not, enforce, we diminish our credibility. However, in not enforcing limits, we must be careful that we are not just "shooing flies." When a fly bothers us, we shoo it away, only to have it come back again and again. Sometimes we do this with our children as well. We say, "Joe, stop drumming on your desk with your pencil." In another minute, we say, "Joe, stop!" Then a minute or so later, "Hey, Joe! I said stop!" We set limits over and over, but our words have no effect. We must either try to do something effective about the behaviors to change them, or we must change our attitude and ignore the behaviors until they stop or go away. But we must not just continue to nag and shoo flies.

Sometimes we want a child to do something different, or better, or to stop doing something that is wasteful or ineffective or annoying. We are persistent about it. We keep after the child. We nag.

Nagging is not good communication. When we nag, we teach our child to stop listening to us. We also give the message that we are continually evaluating her, and that nagging is an acceptable behavior for us.

Gifted children can also nag, and they can be incredibly persistent and verbal in their demands.

Their unrelenting requests or demands for attention or pushiness can prompt adults around them to drift into a tolerance for the nagging. Dreikurs[84] describes an effective technique called "taking the sail out of the wind" that can reduce or extinguish nagging behaviors. If you are being nagged (or catch yourself nagging), stop the negative communication by turning away without comment or explanation. This "takes the sail out of the wind," as you are no longer available to be "blown" about by the person who is nagging. Dreikurs suggests going directly into the bathroom (or to some other private place) and locking the door. Stock the bathroom with reading material or a CD player with soothing music to calm you, and enjoy your reading or music until the nagging (or pounding at the door) has stopped. If the nagging begins again when you emerge, go back, once again without comment, to the bathroom. Repeating this a few times is usually effective in reducing nagging, useless bickering, and even fighting among siblings.

In addition to consequences being consistent and enforceable, their frequency is also important. That is, a five-minute time-out in the green chair enforced calmly and consistently on three separate occasions is far more effective than one longer time-out of 30 minutes. Time-outs are very effective for younger children, particularly when a kitchen timer is used so that the adult can avoid giving the child any attention during the time-out. Some experts recommend matching the length of the time-out to the child's age. Thus, a six-year-old would have a six-minute time-out. Make sure that the time-out really is not a secretly pleasurable event. Sending a gifted child to his room—with all of the books and toys there—is not such an effective consequence. For adolescents, another limit besides a time-out must be found—perhaps loss of certain privileges—but the key elements here are also *frequency, enforceability,* and *consistency.*

Sometimes you may feel bad about setting limits, and you may end up enforcing them tentatively or even apologetically. You may give your grandchild a hug as she goes into time-out or, more commonly, as she comes out. If you do this, you are unwittingly giving the child mixed messages because you are communicating, "I really don't mean what I say about limits." Please avoid sending these mixed messages about limits. You want to send the message that limits are important and need to be respected and obeyed. Limits are not arbitrary; they are assigned for good reasons. If setting limits is a particular area of difficulty for you or others in your family, you may wish to read more about their importance and effectiveness in some of the popular books about them, such as those by Barkley,[85] Ginott,[86] MacKenzie,[87] and Schwarzchild.[88]

Natural Consequences

Natural consequences are very important for children. They are really the best way for children to learn, but this model of parenting and discipline can be difficult for parents and grandparents to use unless they learn how it works. As we noted in the beginning of this chapter, natural consequences are generally more effective than discipline that is imposed artificially or arbitrarily, and natural consequences allow you to preserve your relationship with your child. For example, if 10-year-old John forgets to bring in his toy, the natural consequence is that he cannot find it the next day or it gets rained on or perhaps even stolen—all consequences far more effective and meaningful than if you bring his toy inside for him and give him a lecture. One of the hardest aspects of parenting is to allow natural consequences to occur (and withhold the lecture), particularly if this involves standing back to allow your child to fall. Let's say you notice that your grandchild is forgetting his homework, but you don't remind him; after all, it is his responsibility. You let it stay there on the kitchen table, knowing that there will be a consequence—he will lose points or get in trouble with his teacher.

Letting natural consequences occur allows your grandchild to discover consequences on her own. It allows you to be a supporter, encourager, and commentator in a positive fashion, rather than an angry punisher. Using natural consequences helps you avoid power struggles and saves your relationship with the child because you can't be blamed. Instead, you can be supportive and say, "I'm sorry that happened. Let's see if we can think of a way to keep it from happening again."

So when Tyler forgets his homework, stop yourself before you agree to rush over to the school office with it. Instead, let Tyler suffer the consequences so that he can learn that his parents or grandparents will not rescue him when he forgets things. When he comes home and says he lost five points off his weekly grade, you can say, "I'm sure that was hard to think about." But you convey the idea that you are sure he knows just what to do in the future.

The same principle applies if the child forgets her lunch. If she puts pressure on you to bring it to her, your response can simply be, "I'm sorry. I don't have time to bring it to school. I wonder what you can do to make sure you don't forget again?" Such an approach is less likely to jeopardize you relationship with the child than if you scold her for being forgetful. It puts the responsibility back on the child to figure out ways to manage her own behavior, and it sends a message that you feel confident that she can come up with a plan. In this way, you are helping the child to become independent and responsible; she doesn't need to rely on you. The natural consequence of forgetting her lunch is that she does not have a lunch to eat that day. Perhaps she will get a donation of half a sandwich or another snack from a friend.

With natural consequences, you are also able to avoid being caught in conflicts that are really not *yours*. For example, if your grandson decides that a school project is "dumb," it is neither appropriate nor helpful for you to attempt to "rescue" him by talking to his teacher. You may discuss alternatives that he might wish to consider, but you should not intervene on his behalf except in extreme situations.

Using natural consequences as your approach to guiding your grandchildren will, in our opinion, help you preserve and nurture your relationship with them, chiefly because you are in a position to be genuinely sympathetic about the consequences. Natural consequences will also help your grandchildren learn self-managements skills. You can be sympathetic; you can even say, "I remember how my baseball bat got stolen once because I left it out, and I still remember how sad and angry I felt. I never left a toy outside again after that."

For more information on how to use this approach, you may wish to read *Children: The Challenge*[89] and other books by Rudolph Dreikurs and his colleagues: *How to Behave So Your Children Will, Too!*, by Sal Severe,[90] or *Setting Limits with Your Strong-Willed Child: Eliminating Conflict by Establishing Clear, Firm, and Respectful Boundaries*, by R. J. MacKenzie.[91] All of these authors give examples of how to use natural consequences.

Praise, Encouragement, and Motivation

It is helpful to remember that the long-term goal both in discipline and in motivation is for your grandchildren to learn self-regulation and self-direction. Part of learning self-regulation comes from limits and, perhaps, from occasional appropriate punishment or time-outs. But a far larger part of guiding children toward positive self-direction and motivation comes from more positive interventions like praise, encouragement, and other forms of positive reinforcement from others. Behavioral psychology has shown quite clearly that rewards are much more powerful than punishment in helping a person learn new behaviors. Rewards also enhance one's desire to do a task. Rewards are therefore a key part of discipline and motivation. But we aren't talking about monetary rewards. We don't generally advocate giving children money or toys as rewards.

When we are grandparents in the parent role, we may forget what behavioral psychology has shown us. Praise, for example, is a particularly powerful reward, yet it is used far too seldom in our relationships with children. Because we want our grandchild to do her best, we often do not notice or compliment her for what she does well; instead, we seem to focus on, or at least talk the most about, what she did incorrectly or poorly. For example, when a child shows us her report card with seven A's and one B, we often say, "What happened here?"—even if in a joking way—rather than praising the child for the other seven outstanding marks.

Children need us to notice their efforts and positive behaviors. Do we remember to "admire" the way a child attempted a task? Do we remember to say we appreciate how the child is helping us cook or set the table or get the house ready for company? As grandparents, we would be likely to say something like that. Now that we are in the role of parents, we may find ourselves less likely to communicate such respect, appreciation, and admiration because we now think of ourselves as trainers and disciplinarians. For the sake of the child's self-image and our relationship with the child, it is important that we still provide plenty of positive messages.

Praise and statements of appreciation will be more effective if they are connected to a specific behavior of the child. Praising a child's general giftedness or ability is not very effective in enhancing self-esteem, while praising a child's efforts in a *specific* task is more helpful.[92] Thus, instead of saying, "You are so talented at the piano," or "You are so smart at math!" you might say, "I admire how you keep practicing that same part until you get it the way you want it," or, "I'm proud that you try different ways of solving your math problems until you find the way that works best." Or, "I can see that you are trying different ways to arch the ball to make baskets." Or, "Being able to stick with things and keep trying and practicing is a trait that will help you in many areas in the future."

Likewise, we need to remember not to praise poor or mediocre efforts to the same degree that we praise outstanding ones. Bright children know whether or not they really tried and how hard they tried, and they will value your praise more when they know that you are aware of their level of effort.

Of course, excessive of praise can be too much of a good thing. We are *not* saying that you should continually praise your child. Children can become addicted to praise.[93] Try to keep in mind that what we want in the long run is for the child to be self-motivated and eventually to learn to praise himself or feel proud when he's accomplished something. Even so, we should remember that even very competent children (and adults) need at least occasional validation from others, and we should try to find at least one or two things we can praise about a child.

Please keep in mind that change and growth and positive self-esteem happen steadily over time. It is important both in motivation and in discipline to encourage very gradual steps. Remember that self-discipline and self-motivation are learned skills. Whenever people learn new skills, they are usually clumsy in the beginning, and then, with practice, they improve. Whether it is playing the piano, hitting a tennis ball, or learning self-motivation or discipline, a new skill takes lots of practice. Gifted children are sometimes discouraged when they have difficulty, and when they are discouraged, they sometimes put forth very little effort. But these are the children who need us to notice their efforts and their positive qualities the most. They need our encouragement.

You may want to set up some situations in which your gifted grandchild is likely to experience success, thus allowing you to "catch her doing it right." You can use this gradual step-by-step approach with specific tasks such as learning to play the piano or ride a bicycle; you can also use it to help your grandchild learn self-management skills such as persistence, neatness, reading, or remembering to obey the rules. When planning for success, think of some beginning steps that the child could try where she will almost certainly succeed. In piano, teach a simple tune first, such as "Twinkle, Twinkle Little Star." For tennis, set up a bounce to be right where the child will swing the racquet. For riding a two-wheeler, at first hold the back of the seat, running along while the child pedals. Or use training wheels. For neatness, show the child how to put socks all in one place in the drawer and undershirts in another. When she has success with that, introduce the next step. Encouraging *gradual* changes in which the child will surely succeed and can then be praised for her success is the primary way for her to learn both self-discipline and self-motivation.

A powerful technique, described in *Guiding the Gifted Child*,[94] is "anticipatory praise." You simply praise what you hope the child may be about to do. For example, when Tyrone is just beginning to push back his chair from the table so that he can dash out the door to play, you can say, "Thank you for taking your plate to the kitchen. I really appreciate your remembering to do that!" You may suspect that Ty never had that thought in mind, but your anticipatory praise does three things. First, it conveys to him your expectation that he will behave in a that way; second, it reminds him what he is supposed to do and praises him for doing it; and third, it avoids the negative situation of you having to scold him for forgetting to clear his dishes.

If he says, "I wasn't planning to take my plate to the kitchen," you still can say, "Oh, sorry. I thought you were. Well, at any rate, would you please do it now?" Sometimes a gifted child will realize exactly what you have just done, and the two of you may have a good laugh at how it worked out. It's possible, however, that some bright children, particularly if they read this section of the book, will see you as being manipulative. They may even say, "Oh, you're just using that anticipatory praise thing on me, aren't you?" It will help if you respond openly and say, "Yes, but I sure like it better than just nagging all the time. Don't you?" Most children will then, at least grudgingly, admit that they do prefer being given the benefit of the doubt as to what they might be about to do—and certainly children do live up, or down, to our expectations of them.

We are not saying here that you should never punish your child. Punishment may help your grandchild understand the consequence of breaking an important rule or limit. But in the long run, praise will be far more influential in helping your grandchild learn self-management and self-direction, because the message you convey with praise is that your grandchild is competent. The child who believes that she is competent is able to begin taking responsibility for her behavior.

Offering Choices

Giving children choices provides them with opportunities to learn from the consequences of their behaviors and to develop self-esteem and a sense of competency. We encourage you to allow your grandchild to make his own choices in as many situations as possible. Too often, we make decisions for our children that they are quite capable of making themselves, and so we deprive them of learning opportunities. Starting very young, children can make simple food choices—for example, whether they would like instant oatmeal or a toasted frozen waffle for breakfast.

They can choose between the red and the blue polo shirt. Or at a restaurant, they can choose from several items on the children's menu. Allowing the child to make choices shows that we respect him as an individual, and it gives him practice in speaking up for himself with confidence.

We also need to respect the child's use of her time. We have seen some adults act like dictators, making authoritative and inconsiderate demands for immediate action by the child. Sometimes adults will say, almost screaming, "I don't care what you're involved in! We have to leave right *now!*" We would never speak like that to an adult whose respect and admiration we wanted, particularly since we know that most people are busy with something that is meaningful to them at any given point in time. It is better to give the child a choice and some advance notice about *when* you wish to leave. This will give her fair warning and allow her to find a stopping point. For example, you might say, "We need to leave for the dentist in about 10 minutes. Can you finish by then, or can you find a good place to stop?" The respect comes in the parent acknowledging that the child is busy, and the choice offered is also respectful—you may choose to finish, or if not, find a stopping point.

You will encourage your child to take responsibility for himself and his actions by pointing out options and by giving him choices. Just be sure that they *are* real choices. For example, do not ask your child whether or not he wants to take his antibiotic medicine. That is not a real choice, since not getting it could endanger his health. Instead, ask him, "Would you like to take your medicine before we read a story or after?" This is a real choice that gives the child some sense of control. Similarly, instead of asking if he would like to clean up his room, say, "Would you like to clean up your room before or after you eat your snack?"

The key is to give choices that are acceptable to you, rather than giving what superficially sounds like a choice. By emphasizing real choices, you can prevent confrontations that might result in win–lose conflicts or power struggles, while simultaneously promoting healthy independence and self-discipline.

Promoting Good Communication

Without good communication with your grandchildren, you may find that you are groping in the dark or guessing about issues, whereas when you have good communication, family matters are likely to go much more smoothly. As gifted children get older, particularly as they reach adolescence, communication can be more difficult, especially if you have not established good communication in the child's younger years. Communication can be even more challenging if your grandchildren are living with you as a result of a major crisis or trauma in the family, such as a serious illness, divorce, death, substance abuse, or even arrest and incarceration of their parents.

Here are some guidelines that may help enhance good communication with your grandchildren, as well as promote a healthier relationship with them.

Expressing Feelings and Emotions

When we talk about communication, we mean more than just communicating information. We are talking particularly about communication of feelings. The authors of *Guiding the Gifted Child* said it well when they wrote:

> *Communication of feelings is the most important psychological lifeline available to any person, especially to a child. While a negative attitude toward feelings can be*

harmful to any child, the gifted child may be especially vulnerable because so much of the activity surrounding him, so much of the attention focused on him, prizes only achievement and emphasizes only cognitive skills. It is particularly important that we develop methods for ensuring safe, non-threatening, and valid expression of feelings for the gifted child.[95]

Gifted children have unusual abilities for abstract and divergent thinking. Even at an early age, their behaviors and ways of thinking are different from what is considered "normal." Their curiosity, intensity, sensitivity, and advanced skill levels are strengths, but they also make these children appear different from others and can interfere with communication with others. People around them—at school, in the neighborhood, and even at home—often respond negatively to these differences with anger, sarcasm, or criticism. The gifted child may react, in turn, by choosing to keep her feelings and opinions to herself. She may come to believe that it is not acceptable to think or feel differently; she may even think that something is fundamentally wrong with her as a person. Because of the strong reactions from others, gifted children often shut down the honest and open communication that is otherwise natural to them.

You can see, then, why communication of feelings is very important psychologically for your gifted grandchildren, and why it is so important that your home become a sanctuary where honest and safe communication is honored and becomes the norm.

Communication with your grandchild is literally a lifeline for him. In our experience, if the child has even one adult with whom he can communicate freely and by whom he feels accepted and valued, he can withstand a great deal of negativity, frustration, or dissatisfaction from the larger world outside the home. You, as his grandparent, might be this key person—the one who provides a place of emotional safety and acceptance, which then allows your gifted grandchild to withstand criticisms, put-downs, and unfair situations. If it is not you, then perhaps you can find someone else—a teacher or neighbor, mentor or friend—who will validate your gifted grandchild as a person and who can assure him that what he feels and believes in is reasonable and worthwhile.

Creating a Climate for Communication

You cannot force communication with someone. That would be like banging on a turtle's shell to try to force it to stick its head out. We have some tips, however, that will help you create an atmosphere that will encourage communication.

First, realize that every communication has an emotional component to it, and that what you are trying to communicate will be colored by that emotional component. Your tone of voice, inflection, loudness, posture, and gestures all convey feelings that influence the emotional "climate." Interestingly, you may be less aware of these things than others. You may want to ask a friend or family member you trust to give you feedback on your tone of voice or body language and the feelings and emotions that you convey through these means.

Many people are unaware that their voice sounds angry, critical, or judgmental, or that they seem uninterested in others. They would be horrified to know that they come across as critical and judgmental to their children, for example. Many bright, gifted individuals are unaware of the effects of their voice or mannerisms. If your grandchildren are bossy or judgmental with other children, they might benefit from some fictional role-play situations exploring how different voices and mannerisms look or feel to others. Gifted children sometimes need to be taught how to make eye contact and speak in a friendly manner. Role-play practice of these skills can help them in their interactions with their friends.

Listening as Communication

Listening is the single most important element of communicating. When you really listen, you convey to the child that her ideas, feelings, and values are worth listening to. Often, children just want you to listen, and nothing more. They do not want comments, opinions, or evaluations—just a chance to share their feelings. You may find it helpful to ask, "Do you want any comments from me on this, or do you just want me to listen?" The child will know that you have opinions, but that you will keep them to yourself if she asks you to. This fosters mutual respect and trust. Listening without giving advice or opinions is usually very hard for parents and grandparents to do.

When you listen, accept your grandchild's feelings and thoughts. This does *not* mean that you agree with them; feelings belong only to the person who has them. Psychologist Haim Ginott[96] pointed out that if a person has a right to anything, it's to his feelings. It makes no sense to tell someone that he "shouldn't" feel a particular way or "has no right" to a certain feeling. Feelings are not "right" or "wrong." They are simply an expression of a person's state of mind at the time.

Be very careful about saying, "You shouldn't feel angry. Your brother didn't mean to hit you," because the child *does* feel angry for that moment and has a right to feel anger. If you tell her that her feelings are wrong or that she is incorrect in feeling that way, she becomes confused. She may think, "I must be a bad person for having such strong feelings." Repeated messages like this might cause the child to have trouble expressing or dealing with her feelings all of her life as she grows and matures, because she'll hear the message in her head, "I shouldn't be feeling this way. There must be something wrong with me." Such a person may have low self-esteem and could be more likely to be taken advantage of by others later in life.

In some families, children learn that feelings are dangerous territory and that talking about them can result in unpleasant yelling and fighting. Children in these families may learn that it is simply better not to express their feelings—that the resulting emotional chaos is not worth it—and so they keep their feelings bottled up inside.

Our advice is to encourage your grandchild to express how he feels, and do so frequently. You will be communicating to your grandchild that his feelings, opinions, and attitudes are important, and you will also be more likely to find out if something is troubling him. Also, if feelings are held inside or not communicated freely, you run the risk that problems can accumulate for long periods and then suddenly erupt, creating a crisis.

There are many gifted children who are reluctant to talk about their feelings, particularly if they are not in the habit of doing so. When this is the case, you might consider introducing a shorthand way of communicating, one in which the child doesn't have to reveal much. It would be a sort of "emotional temperature reading." You might say, for example, "On a scale of 1 to 10, with 10 being absolute happiness, what is your emotional temperature today?" The child might say 8 or 2 and then no more, but at least some information has been shared. Interestingly, if the grandparent does not pry, the child almost always asks, "Don't you want to know why I'm a 2?" and so opens the door a little more. Since young children often don't have an extensive vocabulary for feelings and use primarily simple words like "sad," "mad," "angry," and "happy," you can help further by offering additional words for feelings like "frustrated," "annoyed," "irritated," "proud," "ashamed," etc. New words for feelings will be found in children's literature, in the books you may read aloud to them, as well. A feelings poster is available from Free Spirit Press with names for more than 60 feelings (www.Freespirit.com).

Communication is always a two-way street; as a role model to your grandchild, you should make a point to express and talk about your feelings in various situations—whether you are encouraged or discouraged, proud or dismayed. You may also want to announce your own emotional temperature. Although it seems amazing to adults, some children seem to believe that adults don't have feelings.

When you are about to discipline a child, it is important to explain how you feel, rather than to convey a judgment of your grandchild's behavior from your superior position as an adult. Saying, "I feel very surprised and disappointed when you do not listen to other people who are talking to you," is far more effective than saying, "You were inconsiderate, rude, and irritating." The latter statement accuses the child of rudeness and puts her on the defensive. The statement using "I feel"—the "I-statement"—places no blame, but rather stresses how the behavior affected you, the one who observed it. Without blaming the child, it says, "This is how I feel when you do this," and it opens the door for the child to respond by saying, "I'm sorry. I didn't mean to disappoint you," or, "I'm sorry I didn't listen." The child can more easily save face in the situation. This is important for gifted children who tend to be hard on themselves anyway.

You can also recognize accomplishments in similar fashion by expressing how *you* feel and how *you* interpret the child's feelings, rather than by labeling or evaluating or criticizing him. For example, you might say, "I feel happy when I see you mastering a difficult project, and I expect that you feel good about yourself also," rather than saying, "You are so smart and good at so many things!" The latter statement puts out an expectation and pressure that the child will continue to be good at many things, or even that the child is valued primarily for being smart and good at many things. There is a danger that the child will think that he is valued only when he achieves, rather than for himself, for just being the person he is.

Remember also in your "I-statements" to praise or punish the behavior rather than the child. "I admire how you completed that difficult project on time," is generally more meaningful than, "You really have a knack for things." In the same way, if you have to disapprove of a child's behavior, do it without broad attacks that criticize the child as a person. Instead of saying, "You never remember the rules, and I have just had it with you!" try saying instead simply, "Behaviors like that are not allowed here." The reason this is so important for communication is that the behaviors are separated from the person. Communication is more effective when it is directed to a *behavior*, not the child as a person.

Touching as Communication

Another important and often-overlooked technique to promote communication is the simple act of touching. Our society has moved away from touching, even within families, yet there is good evidence that touching is important in feeling connected to others. Touch your young grandchild when you talk with her by putting your hand gently around her shoulder. Your touch helps to focus her attention and ensure that she really hears what you are saying.

Touching through hugs, kisses on the cheek, pats on the back, or even "high fives" can help foster a climate of better communication because these touches convey connectedness and caring. Some families are more demonstrative with hugs, so families that are reserved may need to consciously add touching to their interactions. Teenagers sometimes behave as though such touching is "baby-stuff," and they may resist hugs. In these situations, you might say, "I know you don't need a hug, but I do. I'm your grand-mother; so give a hug!" Even a reluctant hug from a teenager conveys a very important message—that there is a family love connection. Hugging that starts when the child is very young is easy to keep up as the child grows, though he will no longer be sitting on your lap.

Avoiding Gossip

One behavior that is particularly harmful to good communication is gossiping. As adults, we are usually careful to avoid gossiping about other adults, but we are far less careful to avoid gossiping about children—we often do it right in front of them. Dr. Sylvia Rimm calls this kind of talk "referential speaking," in which parents and teachers talk about (or refer to) a child's behaviors within easy earshot of the child, but as though the child is not listening or cannot hear. Sometimes this "gossip" is about good things the child has done and can thus be positive for the child to overhear. For example, "Moira got an A on her biology test this week. She had been so worried about that test." More often, however, this sort of talk goes like this, "Tyler was supposed to be studying for his algebra test last night, but I found him playing a video game in his room, so now I've grounded him for two days. I hope he learns from it."

It is as unfair to a child as it is to an adult to air problems in public, and it might well cause the child to mistrust the adults doing it. With their extra sensitivity and a tendency toward perfectionism, gifted children will be hurt deeply if

266

they overhear you talk with others about their shortcomings or problems. Gifted children understand the conversations they overhear on the phone or with neighbors. Later, they will have difficulty understanding why they are not supposed to talk outside the family about their family's problems! When you talk about your children to others, please do it when the children are not nearby to hear the conversation.

Rewarding Honesty

Gifted children want to do the right thing and do try their best, but like other children, they sometimes forget the rules, particularly if they are in a hurry to do something exciting or the temptation to break the rule is too great. You may notice some cookies missing from the cookie jar, and when you ask, the child admits that yes, she took a few. You may simply say, with a sense of humor, "Well, I definitely appreciate that you like my cookies so much that you took a few on the sly to eat between meals, but I appreciate even more that you are honest about telling me you took them and ate them. I hope you'll always be honest like this with me." This sort of approach, not overly chastising or punishing the child, will have better results than berating the child by saying, "How many times have I told you not to get into the cookie jar between meals? Why don't you obey me! You'd better not do this again! I hope you haven't stolen anything else!" This latter approach tells the child that you don't trust her and that you think she may be turning into a thief.

Sometimes, when you already know that a child has done something against the rules, you are better off letting him know what you know, rather than creating a situation that might encourage him to deny it or lie about it. Otherwise, the child is in a no-win position; he will be punished if he is caught lying, but he will be punished if he is honest with you.

Let's say your grandchild runs outside, leaving the screen door wide open behind her, even though you've repeatedly asked her to close it behind her. Now there are flies in your kitchen, lighting on counters and the food that you are in the midst of preparing. No one else is around who might have left the door open. In this case, rather than asking the child if she left the door open and giving her an opportunity to lie, you can simply say, "I notice you left the screen door open just now. What do you think we should we do to help you remember to close it?" So again, instead of delivering an angry lecture that begins with, "For goodness sake, Alicia, can't you ever remember to shut the screen door behind you when you go outside?" you might say, "I sure hope you'll keep trying to remember to shut the screen door, because I really don't like all these flies in my kitchen. Would you help me go after the flies, now, with the flyswatter?" This reaction to the mistake assumes that the child *wants* to do the right thing, but just forgot and is willing to help make things right by swatting the flies. This is a more positive way to handle the situation than to recite "How many times..." which seems to assume that the child is hopeless and will probably never improve.

If your grandchild tells you the truth about taking the cookies or leaving the door open, don't use the story to punish, tease, or embarrass her later. Don't tell the story of the missing cookies or open screen door all around the family or bring it up weeks or even months later. Doing so will punish the child with embarrassment and will only discourage honesty and communication in the future. One day, when she is older, she may tell the story herself and be able to laugh.

You can encourage honesty with anticipatory praise. Consider this scenario. Some loose change was missing from Grandpa's dresser. Grandma knew that, on a previous visit, Grandpa had given 10-year-old Greg some Mexican coins from the top of his dresser, thinking they would be of interest. So Grandma told Grandpa that she suspected the boy had helped himself; in fact, she was sure of it. Before long, Greg asked Grandpa if he could have the loose change that he saw on the dresser (without saying it was already in his pocket). Grandpa replied, "No, not this time, because I need it for something. But thank you for asking. I really appreciate people who are honest and who don't take things without permission. Now I can be sure my grandson would never take anything that wasn't his." As soon as the boy could slip away to put the money back, he returned the change to the top of the dresser. He had saved face, Grandpa had taught some important values through anticipatory praise, and the boy felt good about himself. The scenario could have played out much differently and in a much more negative way if the grandparents had delivered a lecture. And chances are good that Greg will never take anything without permission again.

Expect Grandchildren to Act Wisely

In discipline, motivation, and all other key aspects of parenting, it is important to convey to your grandchildren your expectation that they will act wisely. Children do, over the long run, live up (or down) to our expectations. It is important to respect and trust them as persons.

Steven Covey, in a chapter in the book by Willard Scott, *If I Knew It Was Going to Be This Much Fun, I Would Have Become a Grandparent First*,[97] shares a very positive message he uses with his grandchildren. He says, "You are not only my grandchild, you are a child of God. You have infinite worth. You have divine potential. You are not to compare yourself with anyone else. You are precious in your own right. I believe in you and love you with all my heart" (p. 58). He says that the grandchildren often ask him to say it again. What grandchild wouldn't want to hear that message?

Indicate clearly to your grandchildren that you believe that they have the capability to learn to control their own behaviors responsibly and to manage their own lives independently, and that at some point, they will be increasingly less dependent upon others, including you, for their lifestyle. They will be in charge of their own discipline and destiny largely by the choices they make.

Avoid Giving Up on Your Approach Too Soon

Some grandparents may find themselves acting as parents to grandchildren who are quite distressed, withdrawn, difficult to communicate with, or who act out with significant behavior problems. The grandparents, and perhaps the parents before them, have tried several different approaches for communicating with these children and feel that all of their efforts have failed.

Many times, parents and grandparents use one approach for a couple of weeks and then give up because it doesn't seem to work. They try a different approach for a few more weeks, and so on. It is important to remember that you can seldom change a relationship or a child's behavior in a matter of just a few weeks. It takes *time* and *consistency* and *patience.*

Don't let temper tantrums, communication problems, testing the limits, or other misbehaviors cause you to give up or react in ways that are self-defeating for you and your grandchildren. This can be difficult. Keep your focus on the ultimate goal. As the saying goes, "When you're up to your knees in alligators, it's difficult to remember that your goal is to drain the swamp." Continue to remind yourself of the need to maintain a sense of perspective about goals that you hope to achieve and the progress you have made.

How Do You Talk about the Parents Who Are Absent?

A particularly touchy subject for grandparents who are acting as parents is: "How do we talk to the grandchildren about their parents?" The very fact that the grandchildren are living with you suggests that something out of the ordinary has happened. The situation may be quite sensitive, such as when a child's parents are in jail, or have died, or the children have been taken away from their parents. Or perhaps it is more benign, with the parents being abroad on a work assignment or in the armed services. How do you talk to the children in these situations, and what should the children to say to their friends?

The most important thing, of course, is to be honest—to tell the truth. We talked earlier about elements of good communication, and you should use those same techniques here. If the parent is in jail or in a hospital in rehab, explain this truthfully to the child, and encourage the child to call, write, visit, or in other ways keep in touch with her parent.

If the parent is deployed in the military, talk to the child about what this means, get out a map to show where the parent is, read about that place, and encourage letters, packages, phone calls, and e-mail communication with notes and photos. Of course, don't emphasize the dangers of military service with comments like "You know, your dad or mom might not come back," but if the child asks about the dangers, be honest.

Support for Grandparents Who Are Parenting

Parenting a gifted child can be a very lonely experience, particularly if one is the grandparent. You wonder if others will understand why and how you came to be the parent. You would like some support, including information and assistance, but are not sure where to turn.

Often the most helpful support comes through talking with other parents of gifted children. A good way to meet other parents is through your grandchild's friends and playmates. Gifted children may want to invite friends to spend after-school free time at their house, and in granting the request, you will, no doubt, be contacting the parents for permission. Gifted children are generally attracted to other gifted children. You can be assured that these parents also worry whether their child's experiences are normal and whether they, as parents, are doing the right things.

Support and information also comes from books written specifically about the social and emotional needs of gifted children. Some excellent resources to guide parents of gifted children include books such as *Guiding the Gifted Child*,[98] *Smart Girls*,[99] *Smart Boys*,[100] or *Some of My Best Friends Are Books, 2nd Edition*,[101] as well as videos like *Is My Child Gifted?*,[102] *Do Gifted Children Need Special Help?*,[103] or *Parenting Successful Children*[104]. Ask other parents, check with your librarian or bookstore, or search the Internet or Amazon.com®.

Schools usually have a parent organization such as PTA (Parent and Teacher Association) or

PTO (Parent Teacher Organization) for sharing information on topics of interest to parents. In addition, some schools with programs for gifted children also have an organization for the parents of gifted and talented children called GATE (Gifted and Talented Education) or some other acronym. These groups often have meetings with speakers or other informative programs that are helpful in raising gifted children. Ask your child's teacher or the coordinator of gifted programs to learn if there is such a group in your area and when the next meeting will be held. Chapter 8 will list more on resources for parents, as well as for grandparents.

Websites such as www.hoagiesgifted.org, www.nagc.org, www.sengifted.org and links from these websites can provide helpful information. Additional resources and organizations are listed in the appendices at the end of this book.

Although there are organizations to support parents of gifted children and there are organizations to assist grandparents, there as yet are no organizations specifically focused on grandparents who are parents of gifted children. It may be that you will need more individualized support, counseling, and guidance, possibly from a family therapist or counselor.

When Counseling Is Helpful

A wise man once said, "There are two kinds of people in this world—those with problems, and those you don't know well enough yet to know what their problems are." Sometimes problems are of a type for which counseling will be helpful. Perhaps you have tried several approaches for some time without success. Or perhaps you are simply out of ideas about what to do. Maybe you would just like someone to help you think through some issues in the family and to give you reassurance. Since the grandparents acting as parents are in new territory where many things have changed since they raised their own children, talking to a professional can result in a smoother and more successful family living situation for both children and grandparents.

In earlier decades, counseling was not nearly as common or as widely used as it is today. People learned to "tough it out," and families kept their problems and worries to themselves. These days, we know that much personal and family pain, worry, and misery can be prevented or certainly helped with counseling. We have finally realized that families can often use a coach much like a basketball or soccer team benefits from a coach. Certainly, many sources, including a well-known 1995 *Consumer Reports* study,[105] have confirmed the effectiveness of counseling.

How will you know when to seek counseling? And how do you find a good counselor? As a general rule, if a problem such as anxiety, sadness, depression, or poor interpersonal relations continues for more than a few weeks, it is probably a good idea to seek professional help. Even if the problems are relatively minor, you will at least have received reassurance and some guidance, which is worth a good deal in terms of your peace of mind.

Some families have a family therapist or a psychologist in the same way that they have a family physician—someone they can go to regularly for checkups or for assistance if things seem not to be going well. We have often recommended a family therapist, particularly to parents and grandparents of highly or profoundly gifted children. We recommend counseling not only because the intensity and sensitivity of highly and pro-foundly gifted children are so much greater than even other gifted children, but also because these children tend to be more asynchronous (out of sync) in their development, and therefore even more of a puzzlement to teachers and others around them. A gifted nine-year-old third grader, for example, may be reading and conversing at a high school or adult level, but socially may act just like all other third graders. This asynchrony is obviously going to create some difficulties and confusion for parents and others who interact with the child. They will need to stop and think to themselves, "What age am I dealing with here?" and then interact appropriately, letting the child give the clues by her behavior which age she is at the moment. When the child reads every book in the children's room of the library and wants to move on to "real books," you may need to remind yourself that you're dealing with an "older" third grader who needs access to older resources. When the child says, "I hate Kari because she wouldn't sit with me at lunch," you will know that she is being like other nine-year-olds.

Some grandparents will be concerned about the cost of counseling. A thorough professional will need to take several hours over two or three appointments to get to know you and your child and to understand your child's environment. The cost of hiring a psychologist who would do some testing of talents and abilities could range anywhere from $400 to $1,000, depending on how many tests are used. This can seem quite high; however, when you consider what you pay for a thorough dental exam that includes x-rays or to have your child's teeth straightened, the cost does not seem so prohibitive. Most parents and grandparents who have contracted for a psychological consultation, including testing, say that it is very helpful, not only because of specific recommendations they receive, but also because the assessment results provide a yardstick with which to gauge the severity of any problem areas, such as a learning disability, and to assess what is reasonable to expect of the child. This consultation and its resulting recommendations will have just as important a lifelong result to the child's mental health and optimal social, emotional, and academic growth as orthodontia will have for dental health and social appearance.

Your health insurance may also cover part of the cost.

Regrettably, it is often difficult to find a counselor or therapist who is knowledgeable about gifted and talented children. Few psychologists, psychiatrists, social workers, and counselors have received training in the particular social and emotional needs of gifted and talented children. Like many others, they often believe that giftedness can only be an asset, and they do not understand that high ability is sometimes associated with serious problems.

So, then, how do you go about finding a good psychologist or counselor? You could start by asking other parents of gifted children for their recommendations. Other parents are usually quite happy to share their information and experiences, and many of them will have looked for professional help somewhere along the way.

If other parents cannot recommend a qualified professional who is already knowledgeable about gifted children, you may be able to find a well-trained counselor or psychologist who is open to learning about gifted children, and that may be sufficient. You should feel free to ask the counselor or therapist about his or her experience and background with gifted children and their families. Then, ascertain if the counselor or therapist is open to learning about the special needs of gifted children by consulting with other professionals or by reading a few publications. You may also want to look at an article titled "Tips for Selecting the Right Counselor or Psychologist for Your Gifted Child" on the Internet at www.giftedbooks.com.

An increasing number of continuing education programs for psychologists and counselors about the social and emotional needs of gifted children and their families are being offered in different parts of the country, and we think that in time, there will be more mental health professionals who are trained in this area and available to help families.

If the professional does not have training in gifted issues, you may have to educate him or her about the characteristics and needs of gifted children by supplying reprints of articles or by suggesting books to read. You may point out to the psychologist, psychiatrist, or pediatrician that the book *Guiding The Gifted Child*[106] received a prestigious award from the American Psychological Association Foundation, or you may give the counselor copies of articles on the social and emotional needs of gifted children, or provide copies of downloads from websites such as www.SENGifted.org, www.hoagiesgifted.org, or www.didt.org.

Once you find a professional, we recommend that you enter counseling on a trial basis to see if the counselor's approach and style fit your needs. Sometimes a very competent psychologist may have a personal style that simply doesn't fit with yours. If you are uncomfortable with the initial findings and recommendations, consider getting a second opinion or switching to another counselor. Second opinions have been accepted for a long time in medicine, and they are equally important in psychology and education.

How do you tell your child that you and he will be going to see a counselor? You can simply describe the consultation as a professional "look see" to help you plan so that family and school experiences can be as productive and enjoyable as possible, and perhaps to get ideas on how to work with the school to provide appropriate challenge. Generally, you will want to suggest to the child that the consultation will be a family endeavor. You might say, "We are going to get some family consultation to help us be better grandparents to you." Of course, you never want to suggest that the child has a "problem" and that the counselor will "fix" the child. You may wish to talk to the professional ahead of time to get suggestions for your particular situation concerning the best way to approach your child.

What can you expect from counseling? Often the counselor or therapist will want the grandparents, as well as the child, to fill out preliminary questionnaires or take brief psychological tests to help the professional understand the family setting. The counselor will probably want to see the grandparents and the child together, then the child alone, and then the grandparents alone. If there are serious problems at school, the counselor may want to talk to the teacher or even visit the school for observation. The counselor or psychologist may wish to talk to the child's pediatrician. A psychologist may also want to do formal testing of intellect, achievement, and emotional functioning, particularly if there is concern about a possible high level of intelligence or a disability mixed with high intelligence.

All of this will take time. The testing alone may take three or four hours. The psychologist will divide testing into two or three sessions to make sure that the child is not fatigued, and also to have the opportunity to see the child on at least two separate occasions to look for any behavior changes. A counselor will do a lot of listening and asking questions. All of this is good and to be expected. You want thoughtful suggestions and advice based on a thorough assessment, not a casual or sloppy approach. Try to be patient, but feel free to ask the professional questions.

When the initial interviews or assessments are finished, you should expect to have a meeting of at least an hour with the counselor, psychologist, or psychiatrist to learn what the findings are and to plan what should happen next. If there is a significant diagnosis, ask about the basis for the diagnosis. Make sure, well ahead of this appointment, that the professional is aware of articles such as *Mis-Diagnosis and Dual Diagnosis of Gifted Children*[107] to try to minimize the likelihood that the child's gifted behaviors are not misdiagnosed. For example, some gifted children, if they are in an environment with few intellectual peers, can be misdiagnosed as suffering from Asperger's Disorder. Other children with intense moods can be misdiagnosed with Bi-Polar Disorder. And some gifted children who are not challenged academically in school can be diagnosed as ADD or ADHD because their frustration comes out in behaviors that can resemble those in children with these disorders. When given appropriate academic challenge, the ADHD behavior disappears.

Conversely, be alert to the possibility that gifted behaviors may mask another, real diagnosis. More than one gifted child has been able to put on a happy face or "mask" to conceal significant depression, and sometimes children suffering from Asperger's Disorder are mistaken as just "really quirky gifted children." From the above examples, it is easy to understand why consulting with a professional with training in gifted traits and behaviors can be especially helpful.

If therapy is needed, insist that the counselor or therapist meet with you, the grandparents, as well as the child—at least once for every three or four times the child is seen. For pre-adolescent youngsters, it is rarely appropriate for a therapist to counsel the child for several sessions without also consulting with the parents or grandparents who are acting as parents. You are a key part of the child's world, and you need to know how to assist the counseling process. Most therapists will suggest specific behaviors for you to try at home, as well as things for teachers to try at school.

Medication for children—including gifted children—should be used only when necessary. Try to ensure that the medication is not being prescribed to treat characteristics that are really traits of giftedness, such as the child's intensity, curiosity, divergent thinking, or boredom in an educationally inappropriate placement. As we have said before, all too many highly gifted children have been misdiagnosed as ADHD or depressed or with Oppositional Defiant Disorder or even Bipolar Disorder and placed on medication, when what really was needed was more understanding, appropriate behavioral guidelines and approaches, or modification to the child's educational program.

If, along with the counselor or psychologist, you conclude that modifications need to be made in the educational setting, talk to the counselor or psychologist about how this might be achieved. Professionals often can provide significant support and assistance in negotiations with school personnel since their assessment information will be highly relevant. Often, the school will convene a Child Study Team meeting, with the child's teacher(s), the school psychologist, and the outside professional to discuss specific strategies that would improve the child's educational program. Ideas from a professional will be important whether your child is in public, private, or charter school[108] or is being home schooled.[109]

As a final word, believe in yourself. As a grandparent acting as parent, you are the one in charge of the family. Professionals are your "hired help." Seeking counseling or therapy may not be easy, but when you have an exceptional child—in this case, a child who is gifted in one or more areas—the benefits to you and the child are well worth it.

*Children are remarkable for their intelligence and ardour,
for their curiosity, their intolerance of shams, the clarity
and ruthlessness of their vision.*
~ Aldous Huxley

*Do not confine your children to your own learning,
for they were born in another time.*
~ Chinese Proverb

*Our progress as a nation can be no swifter than our
progress in education. The human mind is our
fundamental resource.*
~ John Fitzgerald Kennedy

Chapter 7
Educational Planning

Why do you need to know about educational planning for gifted children? Perhaps you are a curious grandparent who wants to know how schools work these days. You want to be actively involved in attaining the best education for your grandchildren. Perhaps you are a school board member or in some other way you can influence how gifted children are educated. Or perhaps you are a grandparent who is now a parent, as we discussed in Chapter 6. Whatever the case, you may find it helpful to know something about the educational options for gifted children because they are probably different now from what they were when your children were in school.

If you are a grandparent who is now the parent, then this chapter will be very important to you. Previously, decisions about your grand-child's education were the responsibility of the parents. Now you are the "parent" making all of these decisions. You probably have many questions. How do schools look for and find or identify gifted children? At what age? Do schools sometimes overlook gifted children? What kind of program is best? Should a child who is gifted be grouped with other children who are gifted or stay in the regular classroom? Should the child ever be grade-skipped? How will I know if she is "bored?" Might she just say that to get attention? Or, how can I get my grandson to achieve better in school? He doesn't seem to care.

Can't I Simply Trust the Schools?

Parents used to trust the schools and stay away, thinking that the schools and teachers knew best. These days, parents are more involved in their children's education. The schools don't always know best. The *parent* usually knows the child best, and in large classrooms, it is difficult for teachers to know everything about every child. Some parents have found that they are not always able to trust the education of their gifted child to the judgment and skill of teachers and the educational system. Likewise, you may not be able to trust that they always recommend the best thing for your grandchild. Many experts in the field[110] have concluded that about half of our gifted children fail to be identified as developmentally advanced or "gifted" by schools.

Although some schools provide adequately for gifted children, the sad fact is that all too many do not. We recommend that parents and grandparents not wait for the schools to identify your grandchild as gifted. Instead, learn as much as you can about traits of gifted children; then you will have a better idea of whether or not your grandchild appears to be gifted, and you can begin to provide opportunities for enrichment and challenge in the home environment as well as request it at school.

From a grandparent's perspective, it is important to understand behavioral characteristics commonly shown by young gifted children such as those we described earlier in this book. Many schools don't begin to look for potential giftedness until the third grade. Gifted children are raring to go at age one or two—long before the third grade. Therefore, you can probably help your grandchild best if you gather some information about education for gifted children before the school normally tests the children or allows them to be "identified gifted."

In this chapter, we are not attempting to make you more of an expert than the professionals. However, a basic familiarity with programs and services commonly offered in schools will be not only helpful, but also important. We will mention resources for further information. We also want to lay some groundwork for you so that you can support the child's parents and encourage them to advocate in the schools for their children. You may find that you or the child's parents will need to get actively involved in the school if your gifted grandchildren are to receive the educational opportunities they need.

At What Age Do Schools Identify Gifted Children?

Schools wait to identify children as gifted until the third grade for several reasons, one of which is that young children are difficult to test with a written test—they aren't used to taking paper and pencil tests—and the school psychologists are too busy testing special education students with disabilities. Schools also believe that some children are just getting lots of enrichment at home and so appear smarter than others, but that later this "smartness" will wash out and they will appear to be more like the other children.

An accurate assessment of younger children, particularly gifted children, is also difficult because they do not develop in a smooth, even fashion. Young children are more likely instead to have developmental growth spurts or lags that can lead others to overestimate, or to underestimate, their potential. Sometimes the growth of gifted children is rapid; other times they seem to reach a plateau or a "resting" period before moving into yet another growth period. A talent seen at one stage of development in a young child may disappear or diminish at another stage. Sometimes the talent disappears because there is no opportunity for learning and practice, or sometimes it diminishes because of other factors or stressors in the family such as marital problems, divorce, separation, substance abuse of a parent or other family member, domestic violence, various kinds of abuse or neglect, or other concerns that take priority over the development of the child's talent or high ability.

The task of accurately identifying gifted children is even more difficult because of the wide areas of difference that exist among gifted children. As a group, gifted children are probably more diverse than any group of average children[111]—that is, their individual traits and behaviors are vastly different. Additionally, gifted children—particularly the more highly gifted—often have wide variations in abilities within themselves—so much so that this phenomenon has been called "asynchronous development."[112] The abilities within the child are "out of sync." Their intellectual skills may be quite advanced, but their motor and social skills may be far behind those of other children their age. Or they may show precocious ability with puzzles or machines, but be average in their verbal or math skills. The more highly gifted the child, the more out of sync they are likely to be within themselves. One can see how this makes accurate assessment difficult, particularly if the person doing the assessment is not very familiar with the developmental patterns of gifted children.

Regrettably, this delay in identifying children as developmentally advanced or gifted often results in the loss of valuable opportunities for enrichment or acceleration. You can help by gathering information and data that will assist the school when your grandchild does reach third grade. Your information and other evidence may also prompt the child's teacher to provide extra challenge or academic enrichment opportunities prior to third grade.

How Do Schools Identify Gifted Children?

You can see how all of these different factors mixed together can make it difficult to accurately identify gifted children. Even so, gifted children do have quite a few characteristics in common, as we described earlier this book, and many of them show abilities that are so advanced that there is no doubt as to their high potential.

How many of the common characteristics are needed in order to call a child gifted? Does a child have to excel in all of these areas or behaviors? Who decides when a child meets enough of these criteria to qualify, and on what basis? And what about the "hidden gifted"—children who are underachieving? Or what about the "twice-exceptional" gifted children whose potential may be hidden by a learning disability? And still another question, are gifted children only those who show high academic performance in school-related tasks? What about children who are unusually creative, for example?

As we noted in an earlier chapter, the concept of "gifted" does not focus just upon intelligence, or on specific academic aptitude, or on creativity; it also includes visual and performing arts and leadership. But as far as school districts are concerned, the gifted child is the child who shows advanced academic achievement. There is little, if any, attention given to other types or aspects of giftedness.

We know that every child is far more than her academic achievement or test scores. But since academic strengths are easier to measure than creativity or sense of humor or moral concerns or emotional sensitivity or sense of justice—all of which are also typically quite advanced in gifted children—the academic strengths alone are what schools usually measure to determine whether a child meets the criteria for a gifted program. This doesn't mean that the child who is creative or advanced in leadership is not gifted; it just means that the school doesn't measure anyone for giftedness in the areas of creativity or leadership.

So for the present, we must live with the fact that most schools identify gifted children by looking at how well the child performs in academics, particularly in mathematics and in language. Some schools are now attempting to broaden their definition of gifted individuals because they recognize that tests and other academic measures are often biased in favor of children who come from home environments where there are books and magazines, where parents read to their children, and where the family watches educational television. These biases admittedly discriminate against children from low socio-economic populations or children who are in other ways disadvantaged. Therefore, since the late 1980s, schools have been searching for methods that are less biased. As a result, some schools now test for non-verbal or visual-spatial ability as well as ability in math or language in order to better discover or identify gifted children who have not had an abundance of cultural opportunities. Some school districts have found success in finding minority and disadvantaged gifted children through interviewing parents of kindergartners. In other school districts, bilingual interviewers, representative of the child's culture, go into the homes and question parents about the child's developmental milestones. And some schools are using a method in which children are observed in problem-solving situations and are rated on their abilities by trained observers. In this way, the schools are able to find children with advanced ability who can then receive enrichment and academic nurturing, so that in later grades, they may qualify for the gifted program on a written test.

Because of all the difficulties with formal assessment described above, the National Association for Gifted Children strongly recommends that multiple criteria be used to identify gifted children, and that multiple sources of input are needed if we are to identify different talents and abilities.[113] Information from parents and grandparents and even neighbors can be a powerful addition to the traditional sources of information gathered by schools. These individuals often know the child's unique talents because they see the child in a non-school setting. Unfortunately, not all schools are using these newer methods. Budget cuts have resulted in a lack of advancement in the area of gifted and talented education.

Teacher Nominations and Group Achievement Tests

The most recent—though actually quite old—national survey of more than one thousand school districts across the country[114] revealed that the most frequently used techniques for identifying gifted children were: teacher nominations (91% of school districts), achievement tests (90%), group or individual ability tests (82%), and grades (50%). In practical terms, then, the actual screening of gifted children is currently performed largely by teachers—based either upon observations of classroom behavior or the score results of group achievement tests. These teacher-identified children make up the majority of most gifted programs.

Searching for and finding gifted children on the basis of teacher nomination overlooks many gifted children. Studies have shown that unless teachers are specifically trained, they often fail to identify many gifted children because they choose primarily the children who do the work and get good grades.[115] They do not identify the non-conformist rebels and the creative intellectuals—those gifted students who may not do the work or get good grades. In all fairness to teachers though, we want to emphasize that teachers who receive training in characteristics and traits of giftedness are then better able to identify children who are gifted, though parents are perhaps better at identifying younger children who are gifted.

Standardized group achievement or ability tests are another tool used to screen students for gifted programs. Some commonly used group achievement tests are the *Iowa Test of Basic Skills*, the *California Achievement Test*, and the *Stanford Achievement Test*. Common group ability tests are the *Cognitive Abilities Test*, *Otis Lennon*, *Matrix Analogies Test*, *Naglieri Nonverbal Ability Test*, and *Raven's Progressive Matrices* School personnel generally use the top 3% to 5% as the criterion for the gifted label, meaning that children who score above the 95th or 97th percentile on these group tests are the ones who are designated as intellectually gifted. To learn which tests are used in your school district and which percentiles are used as cutoff scores, contact the school testing coordinator or your state department of education.

Group tests have their problems, too. Children in the primary grades sometimes score overly high on group tests if they have received unusual early learning opportunities in their homes. Their intellectual ability may be somewhat above average, but not quite in the gifted range. And some gifted children actually score lower than expected on group achievement tests because they are not motivated to show their abilities in such a standardized format. They may even be handicapped if they are creative in their approaches to test questions, or because these tests emphasize verbal skills rather than other skills. And of course, gifted children with learning disabilities or developmental lags are less likely to be identified on standard group tests.

Another factor that makes accurate test scoring difficult is that all of these achievement tests were originally developed primarily to assess children whose scores would fall mid-range and below; therefore, these tests are usually not so good at finding scores that fall in the upper ranges. The tests simply don't have enough items at the upper levels to adequately reflect a child's abilities. At the upper percentile rankings, missing only one or two items can cause a drop of three or even seven percentile points. So these group tests do not discriminate among children at the top. For example, on the *Iowa Test of Basic Skills*, the highest score possible—even if all items are answered correctly—yields only a 99th percentile score. This may tell us that a child is gifted in math or verbal ability, but because the child "topped out" on the test or "hit the ceiling" of the test, we do not know how advanced the child may actually be in this area. He may be even higher; we need to use another test to see how high the child actually is in his achievement.

Some schools are able to compensate for this problem through "above-level-testing" or "out of level testing." What this means is that a bright fifth-grade student may be given the seventh-grade version of a standardized test, such as the *Iowa Test of Basic Skills*, and the fifth grader's scores are then compared with seventh-grade norms. There can be no doubt that a fifth grader who scores above the 75th percentile on a seventh-grade level achievement test is gifted, and now we know how the child compares with children who are two grade levels above what would be expected of a fifth-grade student. This approach can allow more sensitive identification and better possibilities for accurate school placement. We can measure differences in levels of ability in different subject areas. One is more likely to get good and helpful information about a gifted child using above-level testing because the ceiling has been raised high enough to give an accurate measurement.

Rating Scales and Checklists

Rating scales and checklists are also sometimes used in the initial screening process to find gifted children. They ask the teacher to rate common behaviors and traits of gifted students based upon their classroom observations; some rating scales get parent input as well. Schools are most likely to use parent checklists to help find potentially gifted children in primary grades, where testing is difficult because children do not yet have skills for written tests.

These scales and checklists not only focus on school behaviors that may relate to giftedness, but also include behaviors such as sense of humor. Probably the best known of the rating scales are the *Scales for Rating the Behavioral Characteristics of Superior Students.*[116] Although 10 different areas can be rated using these scales, most school districts appear to use only the first four (Learning, Motivation, Creativity, and Leadership) and ignore the other six categories (Visual Arts, Music, Dramatic Art, Communications-Precision, Communications-Expression, and Planning).[117] The emphasis in schools continues to be on the academic or scholastic aspects of giftedness.

It is important that parents and grandparents not give up the idea that their child may be gifted if their own observations seem to detect gifted behaviors. It is helpful to keep records of the child's developmental stages from babyhood on. Knowing that the child sat up, talked, and recognized letters long before most children are able to can help other professionals determine the child's level of giftedness. Parents who have samples of the child's drawing or writing at different ages can use these things as "evidence" of advanced development. Parents or guardians should talk with the child's teachers to share observations and information, or talk with the child's nurse practitioner or pediatrician.

Parents or grandparents acting as parents can certainly request that school personnel do an individual evaluation of their child, or they may arrange for an outside evaluation by a psychologist. Remember, you get to see the child in settings away from school that can provide a very different picture of the child's abilities from what is seen in a structured school setting.

If you are not sure whether your grandchild is just "bright" or whether she is actually "gifted," we recommend that you act as though the child is indeed gifted—at least until the second or third grade in school. We are not suggesting that you put any kind of pressure or undue high expectations on the child, but we do recommend that you support, enrich, and encourage the child's abilities and interests, whatever they are, to develop the child's self-worth and confidence.

If the teacher at school does not support working ahead in math or reading at the level that seems natural for the child, grandparents can encourage the child to read books at home that challenge and interest him. If the child is *very* unhappy in school, parents may wish to request a change of teacher or may decide to change schools. If this is not possible, some parents may even wish to take their child out of school for a year or more to school the child at home, where the child will not be "held back" in progress by teachers who make statements such as, "I can't let your child read ahead because then what will we do with him next year?"

My Grandchild Has Been Identified as Gifted—Now What?

Unfortunately, in most cases, very little will happen once a child has been identified as gifted. In recent decades, it has become evident that many schools are neither sensitive nor responsive to the needs of gifted and talented children. The reasoning seems to be as follows: since the U.S. is governed on democratic principles with equal opportunity for all, that means equal educational opportunity for all, which in turn means the same—or identical—education for all. All six-year-olds will be placed in first-grade classrooms where they will read and study the same books and materials; then all seven-year-olds will be educated in second grade using the same materials, and so on, regardless of a child's ability to do more difficult or challenging work.

It seems that educators have not stopped to think that reading the same books might not be appropriate for all children. To them, what makes the most sense is simply to group children by age, without regard for learning ability or achievement level. Many of these educators think that socialization is more important than academics; they even believe that it is important for brighter children to slow down their learning in order to fit in with others their same age. Grouping children by age is an efficiency model that goes back to the mid-19th Century Industrial Revolution.

Prior to the Industrial Revolution, education occurred in private schools or in one-room country schools, where children were grouped according to how much they had already learned at home or during their often-sporadic attendance at school. Many children did not attend school at all. Education was a privilege, not a right. Following the Industrial Revolution, it became important to educate larger numbers of people, and to do it efficiently. The industrial model of education, however, seems outdated for the competitive world of the 21st Century with its globalization and use of technology. However, schools still practice the model where same age groups are taught the same curriculum at the same pace. Perhaps that is why increasing numbers of families are choosing private schools, charter schools, and home schooling. There is certainly agreement that public schools need to change and improve.

In defense of public schools, many people who aren't educators do not realize the wide span of ability within most classrooms and how difficult this is for the teacher who wants to help all children.

In theory, it is certainly possible for a teacher to modify instruction in the regular classroom for different levels of ability and learning. Let's say, for instance, that every child in second grade would be given reading material appropriate for his reading level. Not all children in the second grade, then, would be reading second-grade books. Some of them would be reading first-grade books, and some would be reading forth-grade or possibly even sixth-grade books, if they were gifted children with high verbal ability. This would require more time and effort from the teacher, as she would need to search for the appropriate books; but otherwise, the strategy seems quite reasonable. In practice, however, very little differentiation of instruction happens for gifted children unless the teacher has had training in the strategies and has done some very careful and thoughtful planning for what the various levels of children will do while she works with one group and then another. She will need to plan for what the gifted readers will be doing while she works with slower readers.

In spite of the teacher's good intentions for challenging the gifted students, what most often happens is that the teacher becomes distracted or busy with the slow or more demanding students, and the gifted students, with little or nothing interesting to do, become disenchanted with school. Over time, these gifted students realize that they must learn just to slow down and wait for the others to catch up. When this happens, they are neither using their potential nor developing good learning and study habits.

Some gifted students who are now adults report that they *never* had to study until they reached high school and took Algebra or Geometry or Calculus. Many of these gifted individuals tell us that they didn't really learn how to study until college or graduate school—and some of them never learned, because in college it was too late to overcome bad habits of just going to class and expecting to get an A on the exam. They suffered when they finally found themselves in challenging classes where the other students knew how to study and organize their time to do hours of homework. They were at a disadvantage compared to the students who had been in schools that challenged them all along.

A gifted child in an inappropriate learning setting is almost certain to underachieve, and regrettably, many—perhaps even most—public and private schools are not currently providing appropriate learning settings. It has been estimated that most gifted children waste one-half to three-quarters of their class time waiting while other children practice concepts and skills that the gifted child already knows and has mastered.[118] Or they are required to "re-learn" things they already know. They are not allowed to move ahead into curriculum areas that are more interesting and appropriate for them.

The simple solution, of course, is for the teacher to be well aware of the knowledge and ability level of each child in the class and to plan lessons to fit various skills of the learners. As we have said, this is much easier said than done when teachers have 24 or more students of varying abilities in their classrooms. It takes training, plus some years of support and coaching, for teachers to become proficient in techniques and strategies of differentiation.[119]

There are, of course, some well-trained and dedicated teachers who have effectively educated gifted students. Children who come in contact with these teachers are fortunate indeed. And some teachers seem to have a good intuitive understanding of gifted children—probably because they were once gifted children themselves with the same drive to ask questions and the same enthusiasm for learning. Children who find these teachers are fortunate as well.

But in our experience, the majority of teachers have not received training in traits of gifted children or how they learn, and they need that training if they are to meet the needs of all of their students. In the meantime, parents and grandparents acting as parents can request a change of teacher if there is one they think would offer more challenge or would be a better "match" for their child.

School Programs for Gifted Children

Schools have tried to solve the problem of providing for gifted children by establishing a designated gifted program. Some schools will offer an "enrichment" or "pull-out" or other program like "Odyssey of the Mind" or "Future Problem Solving" as their gifted-program. Most of these programs are part-time and are offered only one or two hours a week. The gifted student is gifted all day every day. Still, these programs are better than nothing, and gifted students often tell parents, "The day I go to the resource room is the only day I like school."

Once you have read about the many different program options for gifted children, you will be better able to evaluate the type of program your school offers, and also to request additional services or options that may not be currently offered.

Enrichment

Enrichment is the most common provision for gifted children and can take many forms. It can be exposure to new ideas and things not explored before; it can be extension of things in the regular curriculum, or going into ideas further; and it can be concept development, or

exploring a concept more thoroughly.[120] Sometimes enrichment occurs within the regular class
setting. Enrichment refers to curriculum that has
been modified in some fashion—usually by adding
material—that allows students either to explore
related side-issues (sometimes called "horizontal
enrichment") or to work ahead in more
advanced issues ("vertical enrichment").[121]

Some of the so-called enrichment programs
lack academic rigor and substance, clear goals, or
specific teaching strategies.[122] Clark,[123] for example, noted that enrichment in many classrooms is
interpreted as just more work—sometimes more
of the same kind of work. We hope that your
grandchild's school will avoid the "MOTS" or
"More Of The Same" approach, in which children who are gifted are simply given additional
problems to do. For example, instead of the eight
problems assigned, the gifted student is asked to
do 20. Once a gifted student has mastered a concept, there is no need to ask the student to demonstrate the skill 20 times. The MOTS approach
is not a valid educational practice and will quickly
dampen a gifted child's motivation for learning.

Enrichment does not simply add more work; it
adds "breadth" to the curriculum being studied.

It goes beyond the core curriculum and is often in the form of a "parallel curriculum."[124] Thus, if children are studying medieval castles in France or Germany, they might also learn about gradual changes in the construction of castles as new weapons were developed to attack them. The concept of "change" as a topic for a thematic unit or as a question within a unit adds breadth and depth to the study, because change happens everywhere in history. Why did society need castles? How did castles change? What things in our society have changed as new things were invented? Asking some analysis, synthesis, and evaluation questions like these can make learning situations more interesting for gifted children.

Enrichment Programs

If enrichment is included in the gifted program, parents will see greater breadth and/or depth to the curriculum than students in the regular classroom generally get. Some enrichment programs may be separate from regular classroom experiences. For example, following a dance performance given in an assembly for the whole school, gifted students who might like to do further study that area can learn about choreography, the music, the training of the dancers, or can even learn to design or choreograph their own dance, thus exploring the area in greater depth. Other examples of enrichment programs in schools include Saturday or after-school classes, interest clubs.

Pull-Out or Resource Programs

The pull-out program and/or resource room model has traditionally been the most widely used educational option for gifted students,[125] probably because it is visible. The school is thus able to say, "We have a gifted program, and it consists of students going to another area with a special teacher."

In this model, students leave their regular classes for some specified period (typically one to four hours per week) to go to another classroom or building where they meet with other gifted students and a gifted specialist teacher. They work on lessons or projects that encourage higher-level thinking or creativity or independent study. The better of these programs offer enrichment activities that extend what is being taught in the regular classroom. In this model, the gifted child stays with her age peers for most of her instruction, and thus most of the education of the gifted child happens in the regular classroom with a mixed, or heterogeneous, group — of learners.

These pull-out programs/resource rooms are generally popular with parents because parents know that the needs of the gifted are being addressed at least part of the time. They are often popular with the children as well, who sometimes tell their parents, "It's the only thing about school I like. I hate all the rest." However, there are problems with pull-out or resource programs.

Perhaps the biggest problem is that with the pull-out or send-out program in place, the rest of the school staff may assume too readily that the gifted teacher is taking care of all of the needs of the gifted students, and that therefore, they have no responsibility for meeting those needs in their classrooms. They don't stop to think that the gifted student is gifted all of the time, not just when he attends the pull-out program.

Another problem is that classroom teachers complain that the send-out programs cause students to miss things in their regular class, consequently requiring students to make up work. Or sometimes, teachers resent sending their brightest —

t students out because they feel that they can do "as good a job" as the specialist teacher, and besides, they need the gifted students to be there to help the other students. Teachers with these beliefs do not understand the learning needs of gifted students, or that gifted students need to be with other gifted students at least some of the time.

Pull-out programs work best when the teacher is supportive and does not require the student to complete work missed. The teacher can plan a review or skill session for the rest of the class during the time the gifted student is gone, or he can help the gifted student catch up quickly if new concepts have been introduced while the gifted student was gone.

Another concern of pull-out programs is that, due to the brief time that children actually spend in the programs, extended projects are difficult to undertake. As a result, academic rigor can suffer, and instead, the projects are more likely to be brief and superficial ones that can be done within the timeframe allowed.[126]

A final concern with the pull-out program is that what happens in that program often has no connection with what goes on in the student's regular classes, so that if the child is asked what she did in the special class, she might say, "We learned to build rockets, but I'm not sure why." It is always best if the gifted teacher has some connection with the regular teacher and knows the regular classroom curriculum so that she can plan enrichment activities that extend and build on the regular classroom curriculum.

From a financial standpoint, a pull-out program is not as cost effective as other types of gifted program delivery systems. A pull-out program requires hiring an extra teacher for each elementary school where the program will be offered.

Despite their limitations, pull-out programs are still popular. They are relatively easy to administer, and they do offer students at least some opportunity to interact with similar peers and to feel a sense of emotional and interpersonal support. Gifted children need challenge every day, and pull-out programs can provide such stimulation.

We have seen a few pull-out programs in which gifted children are sent out every day for a class in their area of strength. For example, a gifted child in this type of program would go out every day for two classes—reading and math—if his test scores put him in the gifted range in those two areas. This type of send-out program, sometimes called grouping and re-grouping, meets the needs of the gifted student every day, but causes scheduling issues. To offer this type of program, the school will need to schedule all reading classes and math classes at the same time each day in order for the gifted children to be sent out to their appropriate advanced reading and math classes. When scheduling can be worked out, this program allows gifted children to learn with other gifted children on an everyday basis and with an appropriate level of challenge, which of course is better than going to a resource room a once a week for an hour. It also allows the gifted children to be in the regular classroom for a portion of every day and to interact with age peers during social studies, gym, lunch, and the other "specials" that are offered, such as music and art.

Other Options

Here are some of the other popular models for providing challenge for gifted students.

Ability Grouping

Ability grouping is often seen in various formats. The placement of students in high-ability classes, or grouping them within a class according to demonstrated ability levels, usually occurs in middle and high schools. The classes are sometimes called "college prep," "Advanced English," or "AP" (Advanced Placement) courses.

Cluster Grouping

Cluster grouping is another form of ability grouping and is usually found in the elementary or middle grades. It usually refers to an enrichment activity for a group of gifted students within a regular class. Administratively, it makes sense and is cost effective. If there are four second-grade classes in a school and each class has two gifted students, then the eight gifted second graders can be grouped or clustered with the same teacher—the one with the most training in how to work with gifted children. Research shows that gifted students thrive when grouped with other gifted students.[127] They "spark" with one another and feel free to be themselves. When isolated in a class of only one other student like them, they feel isolated and different and may hide or camouflage their abilities to fit in with others. Clustering gifted students with a teacher qualified to work with them is obviously an advantage for these children.

In the last decades of the 20th Century, there was major opposition to ability grouping. These educators believed that: (1) it is unfair to deny all students exposure to a common curriculum, (2) ability grouping discriminates against minority groups who may not have had a sufficiently enriched background to allow them to compete favorably for high-ability classes as compared with children from more enriched backgrounds, and (3) ability grouping does not particularly benefit youngsters of high ability.[128]

Subsequent researchers,[129] however, refuted these arguments regarding the benefits of ability grouping for gifted students. Ability grouping does seem to be quite appropriate and helpful for gifted students despite earlier opposition against it. Evidence continues to accumulate that all children are *not* equivalent in intelligence or academic ability, and that there are some students who are highly intelligent for whom a regular school curriculum would be totally inappropriate.

Certainly, problems of equity still remain. It is generally accepted that youngsters from economically and educationally impoverished backgrounds do have difficulty in demonstrating their academic potential. However, the solution for the lack of equity should not be one of eliminating differentiated educational experiences for the more able students. Rather, the solution lies in more accurately identifying potential in youngsters who are economically disadvantaged and culturally diverse, and in providing specialized experiences to find gifted potential in those populations when children are quite young, then to provide enrichment to allow them work to catch up, particularly in the primary grades.

Academic ability grouping programs are criticized by some as elitist and, therefore, undemocratic. Yet when ability grouping occurs in basketball, football, track, tennis, gymnastics, ice skating, and other sports as selection of the best athletes, such grouping of the top performers is not seen as elitist or undemocratic. Ability grouping is not frowned upon in band or chorus, where auditions take place for first chair seats or solo parts. Why, then, is it seen as elitist in the academic arena? Interestingly, we admire college students who are accepted to the top universities, but we do not seem to want to notice or identify those same individuals as younger students in the primary or elementary grades. There, our society wants everyone to be "equal."

As one might expect, "the evidence is clear that high–aptitude and gifted students benefit academically from programs that provide separate and specialized instruction for them."[130] Individualized programs, such as mentorship programs,[131] though not actually considered "grouping," likewise are helpful and appropriate because they take into consideration the student's ability and performance level.

The National Association for Gifted Children[132] has adopted formal position statements endorsing ability grouping for gifted children, as well as acceleration. Excerpts from their position statements are shown in Table 3.

Table 3
Ability Grouping and Acceleration

➤ "Grouping allows for more appropriate, rapid and advanced instruction, which matches the rapidly developing skills and capabilities of gifted students."

➤ "Strong research evidence supports the effectiveness of ability grouping for gifted students in accelerated classes, enrichment programs, advanced placement programs, etc. Ability and performance grouping has been used extensively in programs for musically and artistically gifted students, and for athletically talented students with little argument. Grouping is a necessary component of every graduate and professional preparation program, such as law, medicine, and the sciences. It is an accepted practice that is used extensively in the education programs in almost every country in the western world."

➤ "The practice of educational acceleration has long been used to match appropriate learning opportunities with student abilities."

➤ "Although instructional adaptations, such as compacting, telescoping, and curriculum revision, which allow more economic use of time are desirable practices for exceptionally talented students, there are situations in which such modifications are insufficient in fulfilling the academic potential of all highly capable children. Personal acceleration is called for in these cases."

➤ "Research documents the academic benefits and positive outcomes of personal acceleration for carefully selected students."

Excerpts of NAGC Position Statements on Ability Grouping and Acceleration (NAGC, 1998)

Acceleration

The term "acceleration" can be used to describe two educational models: (1) acceleration of curriculum—that is, moving the child through a subject more quickly, or (2) acceleration of placement, such as moving a student ahead one or more grade levels, either in one subject only (single-subject acceleration) or by skipping one or more grade levels to place the student in a more advanced but more appropriate curriculum. In either instance, "the goals of acceleration are to adjust (or match) the pace of instruction to the student's capability, to provide an appropriate level of challenge, and to reduce the time period necessary for students to complete traditional schooling."[133]

Acceleration of Student Placement

Acceleration of student placement is one of the options for flexible pacing for gifted children. Examples of acceleration include early entrance to kindergarten (or to high school or college), full grade-skipping, or part-time grade acceleration.[134] Unfortunately, many educators have a personal bias against this kind of acceleration, even though research has shown it to be one of the most viable options for providing appropriate educational experiences for gifted students.[135] Certainly, there are factors that need to be considered in individual cases,[136] but "it must be emphasized that no study to date has shown acceleration to be detrimental to social and emotional development."[137]

The Iowa Acceleration Scale

The *Iowa Acceleration Scale,* a tool used by educators to choose appropriate acceleration, allows families and educators systematically to identify and consider each factor that research has shown to be relevant to early entrance or to whole-grade-skipping.[138] Long-term studies of individuals who have skipped one or more grades show that these people, when compared to persons who were not grade-skipped, were as happily married, as often leaders or presidents of organizations, and just as frequently top students and successful in their careers. In general, they were quite satisfied with the decision that had been made to skip a grade.

Accelerated Curriculum

Some other terms used for other types of acceleration are "curriculum compacting" or "telescoping." In these two methods, material is covered in less time, often using self-paced learning.

Accelerated curriculum is particularly important for rapid learners, because textbooks have dropped two grade levels in difficulty over the past 10 to 15 years.[139] Many bright students spend a large portion of their time in school repeating things that they already know. Accelerating the curriculum can allow students to gain time which they can use for participation in other activities, to work ahead, or to take a college or correspondence course.

Accelerated curriculum approaches are not without their problems. Some students may have difficulties with self-discipline, particularly if a self-paced model is being used. Busy teachers may resist having to spend extra time planning for content acceleration. Teachers at upper elementary levels may be unhappy that the fourth-grade math book is being used by a third grader, for example, because it means that the fourth-grade teacher will need to extend the content acceleration to fifth grade or higher when he gets the student. But most of the problems with acceleration have to do with teacher concerns, rather than with problems relating to the child's learning. Gifted children are easily able to learn material one or more grade levels above the grade they are in.

Accelerated placement will usually encounter resistance. Some educators have strong biases against grade-skipping or any form of acceleration, feeling that all students of the same age should stay together. Thus, if a third-grade student is accelerated to fifth grade, it is important that the receiving teacher be supportive in order to make the grade-skip successful. A child study team approach, such as that used by the *Iowa Acceleration Scale*, in which the principal, the child's parents, and all relevant teachers are involved, helps to facilitate such a transition.[140]

Advanced Placement Programs

Many bright students who plan to attend college choose to participate in the Advanced Placement (AP) program offered through the American College Board. AP classes are available now in many subject areas and offer motivated students an opportunity to study subjects at a college level while still remaining in high school. *Time* magazine reported in its cover story "The Top High Schools"[141] that the best high schools producing the best educated students were the ones that offered a wide selection of AP courses. Over 30 specific course areas are available through the program—everything from American and U.S. History to Physics, English Literature, Calculus, Studio Art, Spanish, and Music Theory.

These are college level courses offered in high school to students who want academic challenge. Teachers receive training through intensive weekend workshops put on by the College Board and taught by master AP teachers. Students taking the courses sit for standardized exams given nationwide on specific dates in May, and depending upon their scores, they may receive college credit, advanced standing, or both.[142] Some advanced students who take and earn credit for several AP courses are able to enter college with one full semester of college credit. There is now a pre-AP program for students in junior high school and the ninth grade leading up to the junior and senior year high school AP classes.

Talent Search Programs

There are several Talent Search Programs now operating through different universities across the country. Intellectually gifted junior high students between 12 and 14 years of age who scored high on the SAT or ACT are invited to participate in radically advanced programs in mathematics (and more recently, in computer applications, psychology, anthropology, science, etc.), usually in residential summer programs held on college campuses, with some talented students being able to complete as much as five years worth of pre-calculus mathematics course work in a single summer of intense work.[143] A listing of these programs can be found in the book *Re-Forming Gifted Education: How Parents and Teachers Can Match the Program to the Child*[144] or through an Internet search.

International Baccalaureate Program

The International Baccalaureate Program is particularly effective for teenagers of high ability.[145] Initially, this program served children of ambassadors and others living abroad. Now, more than 80 high schools in the United States and approximately 35 in Canada are authorized to participate in the International Baccalaureate Program. The curriculum offers subjects arranged in six areas for grades 10 through 12. The high level of expected achievement is integrated with an international slant in social studies courses, along with mastery of a second language.[146] More information may be obtained from: International Baccalaureate North American, 680 Fifth Avenue, New York, NY 10019.

Self-Contained Schools for Gifted Children

In one sense, self-contained schools for gifted young adult students have existed for many decades; they are medical schools or law schools or other graduate schools such as Juilliard School of Music. They are also the many local community private and parochial schools that emphasize and are known for a rigorous college preparatory curriculum. They are the Governor's Schools and other special schools such as the Illinois School for Science and Mathematics and The Bronx School for Science. However, at the pre-college level, such specialized schools have often been considered by some to be elitist.

Recently, schools like the Bronx School of Science have evolved into "magnet schools."

These schools are advertised as focusing on a specialty area in education to try to attract children who are motivated or talented in that area. New York School for the Arts is another example of such a magnet school. In some cities, magnet schools have been set up primarily as a way of desegregating school districts, to attract top students into the inner city, but they also provide advanced educational experiences to youngsters who desire them. Families should recognize that they cannot simply request enrollment in a magnet school; virtually all have entrance requirements or criteria.

Some parents worry that if their child attends such a school, the range of peer relations will not be broad enough to support social development. This does not seem to be the case. In fact, for gifted girls in general[147] and for highly gifted youngsters in particular, there is evidence to show that such programs help academic achievement with little or no handicap in later adult life adjustment.[148]

Charter Schools

Charter schools have sprung up during the 1990s in several states to provide parents with more choices regarding their children's education.

They are not public schools, though they typically receive public money—state funds based on enrollment, just as public schools do. They are not, strictly speaking, private schools, though they are usually incorporated as private entities with their own board of directors and budgetary processes. Charter schools represent an attempt to provide a non-parochial alternative to public education.

Charter schools usually are required to be very broad in their educational philosophy and must accept all students who apply. They cannot be exclusive or turn anyone away, and thus are not really schools for gifted students. The only ones that might qualify as "gifted" schools are the ones that specialize in the arts, because unless a child is interested in music or art or drama, she wouldn't enroll there. Students in these schools have to be bright because they have to study the regular curriculum and take the required classes in addition to their art specialty.

Private Schools

Private schools, including parochial schools, are certainly an alternative, and one that many parents of gifted children have used because of their dissatisfaction with public education. Public schools in the United States are overwhelmed with responsibilities—discipline, feeding, drug education, violence prevention, etc.—and find it difficult to emphasize excellence and the highest development of potential because of the great concerns with creating equity. Although private schools may face the same problems, they often have a larger per-student budget. However, this means that these schools can be very expensive—up to $12,000 or more per year.

It is important for parents to realize that they do not need to send their bright child to a private school in order to receive a sufficiently challenging education. Some public schools offer more challenge than some private schools. It depends upon the academic philosophy of the particular public school and the willingness of individuals within that school system to be flexible and to work with parents. It probably is not worth jeopardizing the entire family financially in order to send a child to a private school, though some of these schools offer financial aid. Other alternatives such as family-based enrichment to compensate for less-than-adequate public education may be an sufficient compromise if private school would create extreme financial hardship.

Home Schooling

Home schooling has become an increasingly common practice in the U.S. in the past two decades. Some parents choose home schooling for religious reasons or because they have concerns about safety or differences in values and moral standards, but now, increasing numbers of families are home schooling because their child has unusual talents or characteristics that do not fit the available public or private schools. Home schooling is permissible in every state, either by law or by court decision.[149] Society as a whole seems to be reluctant to accept home schooling, probably due to the long tradition in this country of sending children to public school. On the other hand, the public is supportive of home schooling or tutoring when it is done for athletes who are Olympic hopefuls or for children of actors or musicians whose careers include extensive travel.

If you know parents who are considering home schooling, we would suggest that you encourage them to gather as much information as possible about home schooling *and* about the alternatives before starting so they will know what to expect. Home schooling is a full-time job and can be difficult to do—it is hard enough just being a parent! Many education professionals are convinced that parents lack the training and patience to handle the responsibility of teaching school curriculum. Others[150] disagree and say it actually brings the family closer. In recent years, there are certainly increasing numbers of home-schooled children being accepted into colleges.

Before parents or grandparents take steps to begin home schooling, we suggest that you look at *Creative Home Schooling: A Resource Guide for Smart Families*, by Lisa Rivero,[151] and consider the following advice adapted from *The Faces of Gifted.*[152]

1. Research all you can about home schooling. Begin at your public library. Then contact local, state, and national organizations.

2. Talk to parents who are presently home schooling their children.

3. Discuss your desire to home school with local school officials to learn the specific steps that need to be taken.

4. Sharpen your own skills through local college courses.

5. Consider whether your child has special needs, such as a learning disability, and how you could meet those needs at home.

6. Gather sample educational materials to review and evaluate.

7. Make a "contract" with your children stating the goals and objectives for home schooling.

8. Think it through, not only for yourself, but also for others involved.

9. Be brave! Do what is best for your children and yourself.

Developing an Educational Plan

We have briefly described some of the most common programs offered for gifted children. Since we cannot explain all of the possible program options offered by schools for the gifted in this chapter, we will list some other sources of information that can help you develop an educational plan. Two excellent books that provide information about various program strategies are *Helping Gifted Children Soar: A Practical Guide for Parents and Teachers*[153] and *Re-Forming Gifted Education: How Parents and Teachers Can Match the Program to the Child.*[154] The first book presents an introduction to gifted children, their behaviors and educational needs, as well as ways to provide for their needs in the regular classroom. The second book gives detailed descriptions of how families can observe and document strengths and weaknesses of a particular gifted child and can then develop an educational plan for that child, including how they can negotiate the new plan with the school. Sometimes negotiation will involve getting the child into a specific type of gifted program offered by the school; other times it will involve advocating for some modification in the academic work currently being offered.

More Important than the Actual Program

A final caution is that even though a school may have one or more specifically designated programs for gifted students, there are issues more important than whether or not a child is included in that program. Dr. Donald Treffinger, a long-respected leader in the field of gifted education, concluded that parents and grandparents should not be satisfied with the simple fact that their child is in a school gifted program. He concluded that there are "25 tough questions more important than 'Is my child in the gifted program?'" (www.creativelearning.com). Here are his 25 questions, reproduced in Table 4 with permission of Dr. Treffinger. Parents and grandparents should search to find the answers to these questions.

Table 4
Questions that Are More Important than "Is My Child in a Gifted Program?"

1. How does my child learn best? How does my child's school program take into account students' personal characteristics and learning styles?

2. In what academic content area(s) or extra-curricular area(s) does my child display strengths, talents, or special interests?

3. What provisions does my child's school make for them to be recognized, valued, and developed?

4. What provisions does my child's school make to ensure that students receive instruction that is well suited to their real instructional needs?

5. What specific provisions are made for students to learn at their own rate or pace, rather than being limited to a rigidly prescribed, "lockstep" curriculum?

6. What resources and materials are available to expose students to the newest ideas and developments in many fields, and to in-depth pursuit of their areas of special interest and abilities?

7. How does my child's school provide students with access to, and experiences with, other students and adults who share their strengths, talents, and interests?

8. How does my child's school use community resources and mentors to extend students' learning in areas of special talents and interests?

9. How does my child's school help students to become aware of their own best talents and interests and to appreciate those of others as well?

10. How does my child's school help students to consider future career possibilities and to cope with rapid change in our world?

11. What provisions are made for advanced content or courses for students whose achievement warrants them?

12. How are the students' needs determined and reviewed?

13. What enrichment opportunities are offered that are not merely "busywork" or "more of the same" assignments?

14. How do teachers provide opportunities for students to learn and apply critical and creative thinking, problem solving, decision making, and teamwork skills? How are these skills taught and used in classes, and through the curriculum?

15. What other activities or programs are offered that focus on these skills? (Future Problem

Solving Program? Destination ImagiNation? Invention Conventions? Others...?)

16. How do the teachers help students learn to plan and investigate everyday (or real-world) problems, and to plan and conduct research, rather than relying on contrived, textbook exercises?

17. How do the teachers help students create and share the products or results of their projects and investigations?

18. What provisions does my child's school make, or what support do the teachers offer, to create opportunities for students to explore a variety of motivating and challenging topics outside the regular curriculum?

19. How do my child's teachers help students learn to set goals, plan projects, locate and use resources, create products, and evaluate their work?

20. What provisions do teachers make to help students feel comfortable and confident in expressing and dealing with their personal and academic goals and concerns?

21. What specific steps do teachers take to ensure that learning is exciting and original rather than boring and repetitious?

22. How do teachers ensure that students are challenged to work toward their full potential ("at the edge of their ability") rather than permitting them to drift along comfortably ("on cruise control")?

23. In what ways do faculty members inspire students to ask probing questions, examine many viewpoints, and use criteria to make and justify decisions?

24. How does the school program help students to learn social or interpersonal skills without sacrificing their individuality?

25. Have teachers asked me about my child, and discussed the insights I have about his or her interests, activities, experiences, relationships, and feelings about school, and in areas outside the school day?

As you can imagine, we are often asked, "What is the best kind of educational program for gifted children?" There is no simple answer—not because research isn't available, but because there are so many factors to be considered. In what area or areas is the child gifted? And how gifted is the child? Is she moderately gifted or highly gifted? What are her interest areas? What are her special skills? Does she have areas of weakness that need strengthening? Every gifted child will have his or her own unique set of needs based on individual strengths and weaknesses.

Grandparent and Parent Involvement

To summarize, it is important to realize that you need not depend solely upon school personnel to determine whether your grandchild is gifted. Your observations and judgment are important, too, and other resources are available outside of the school, including professionals, to help identify whether you grandchild is gifted. Remember, many gifted children do not demonstrate their abilities through their achievement in school.

It is also important to evaluate the appropriateness of the school's programs for your gifted grandchild. Grandparents and parents, as well as educators, must understand the needs and characteristics of individual gifted children in the school setting, and they must monitor whether the child is progressing and being challenged with new material that he does not already know, or whether he is having to sit quietly and patiently while the other children practice with concepts or skills that he has known or been able to perform for some time.

Grandparents and parents should particularly scrutinize school programs that attempt to meet the needs of gifted children within the regular classroom and which emphasize treating all children in the classroom the same—same books, same standards, same expectations. The pace of learning varies tremendously for any group of students who are grouped by age. Equity does not mean the same as equal. Equity for all means the chance for all students to progress. Equal would mean the exact same curriculum for all. Equity should be the word we use. It will take some slow learners a longer time and many repetitions to master two-digit subtraction, for example, while rapid learners may learn subtraction in kindergarten, with no further repetition or drill. Average students will need some practice and some repetition to master the concepts. As Thomas Jefferson said, "There is nothing so unequal as the equal treatment of unequals."

We encourage you to advocate for educational opportunities that are appropriate for your type of gifted grandchild. What represents truly fair and equitable education for all students, including gifted students, is curriculum that will interest and challenge them in ways that fit their individual abilities and needs best.

The foundation of every state is the education of its youth.
~ Diogenes

Imagination is more important than knowledge. Knowledge is limited. Imagination encircles the world.
~ Albert Einstein

If we value the pursuit of knowledge, we must be free to follow wherever that search may lead us. The free mind is not a barking dog, to be tethered on a ten-foot chain.
~ Adlai E. Stevenson, Jr.

Chapter 8

Other Resources for Gifted Children

Gifted children thrive on new information, activities, and challenges, and many families rely on resources outside the family to meet this need. Depending on where your grandchildren live, you may be able to take advantage of several community resources. Classes, programs, activities, lectures, and other outings planned for children of all ages offer different perspectives, new challenges, and opportunities to make friends. Grandparents can take the lead in suggesting these resources and even offering to take the grandchild to some of them.

The best way to learn about good resources and programs in your area is simply to ask other grandparents and parents for recommendations, especially if you know that their children are bright, creative, and intense. You could ask about their experiences with art classes or museum camps or music teachers.

Libraries often have tables or shelves filled with brochures for local classes and camps. Your grandchild's school may also have a list of community resources, perhaps even a list that is particularly suited for gifted children. Also, usually each state's department of education has one or more persons designated as education specialists for gifted students. These specialists and their departments will have information about programs in that state, both in the schools and those offered by agencies or organizations, such as local colleges or universities, Boys and Girls Clubs, Scouting activities, parent organizations, and museums. Phone numbers for state departments of education can be found in the government pages of your phone-book or online.

In addition, most states have a state association for advocacy for gifted students that is made up of dues-paying parents and teachers who support gifted programs. These organizations usually hold at least one educational conference per year at which experts in the field of gifted education are invited to speak, and where teachers and parents can get additional training. Networking with members of these organizations can provide much helpful information, as well as leads on resources for enrichment or summer options for gifted children. Sometimes scholarships are available to camps or other learning opportunities. Contact information for state advocacy groups can usually be found on the Internet using the state name and then "Association for (or of) Gifted." For example, California Association of Gifted, Iowa Association of Gifted, Kentucky Association of Gifted Education, or Arizona Association for Gifted and Talented. There is also a national group under the name "National Association for Gifted Children." This organization, NAGC, lists upcoming state conferences on its website. Most state associations publish a newsletter for members that lists events and programs of interest to parents of gifted children, including a variety of Saturday and summer programs.

Libraries

Libraries are a wonderful yet often overlooked resource for gifted children. Most libraries in sizable cities have ongoing education programs for children. These include puppet shows and other pre-reading programs for preschoolers, story time for new readers, weeknight or weekend book clubs for school-age children, summer reading contests with prizes for readers ages 6-12, and teen book clubs that focus on young adult or classic fiction. Some libraries also have volunteer opportunities for older children. Larger libraries invite famous children's book authors to give readings or lectures. (Local book stores may also host author visits and book signings.) Public library programs are published in the local newspaper, or a schedule may be obtained by calling the library or by going online.

A good children's librarian can be a wonderful resource to parents or grandparents of bright children in guiding the child's reading toward books with appropriate content that are also at the child's correct reading level. Libraries are usually staffed by specialists trained in children's literature as well as in the classics, and many libraries offer reading lists of books good for children to read. If you give the librarian an idea of the child's reading level and titles of some of the books that the child has enjoyed in the past, the librarian can almost always offer suggestions of other books to read that will keep the child interested and challenged. *Some of My Best Friends Are Books: Guiding Gifted Readers from Preschool to High School*[155] is a book that does the same thing. It contains synopses and themes of more than 300 books that will be of interest to gifted students, plus a theme index to help parents, grandparents, and teachers find just the right book for a particular gifted child.

Libraries are also good places simply to "hang out" and relax or browse books with your grandchildren. You may want to set aside a time every week for searching library shelves together for good books, sitting side by side in the reading lounge, or attending a story hour together. You will not only learn more about your grandchild's particular learning style and interests, you will also provide a valuable model of a life-long learner who loves the written word. You may even want to ask your children's librarian about starting a grandparent-grandchild intergenerational book group. Or maybe you and your older grandchild can work as library volunteers together, helping to shelve books, reading to younger children, or answering patrons' questions. Some children's sections use teen volunteers to help younger children select books.

Museums and Zoos

Gifted children usually love to visit museums and zoos. These children and their significant adults often enjoy frequent visits so much that the museum feels like a second home! The popular children's book, *From the Mixed Up Files of Mrs. Basil E. Frankweiler,*[156] tells the fictional story of two children who run away to a famous art museum to escape and are able to live there undetected for several days and nights while they attempt to solve a mystery.

Families who live in urban areas are usually fortunate to have several downtown art and historical museums and perhaps even a wonderful science or natural history museum, all of which feature new exhibits monthly with special tours and hands-on activities for children. Some communities are also fortunate enough to have one of the Challenger Space Centers close by, made possible by a foundation to memorialize the astronauts of the Challenger Mission, that offers weekend classes and simulated space missions. Art museums often have weekend activities for children (for a nominal fee) such as working with clay, painting with tempera, or making masks or puppets. Most larger communities have at least one zoo, and these usually offer classes and tours for school-age children.

If your grandchild lives in an urban area, chances are that you will find many exciting things to explore. If your grandchild lives in a small, rural community far from these kinds of resources, perhaps the child can have an extended visit with relatives in another community for a few weeks in summer or over spring break to take advantage of more extensive resources offered by museums and libraries in a larger city. It could be a special trip with grandparents or with the whole family. We know families who plan years ahead of time to go to Washington, D.C. when their children are junior high or high school age, or to take a trip out West to the Grand Canyon and some of the National Parks as a special, planned family activity. Most families live within a day's driving distance or train trip of a city large enough to have at least one or two museums and galleries. Also, be sure not to overlook smaller, specialized museums that may be in your own backyard. These smaller museums are often connected with a university or industry.

Living history museums such as Old World Wisconsin, Old Sturbridge Village (Massachusetts), Williamsburg or Jamestown (Virginia), or the Pioneer Living History Museum (Arizona) are a wonderful way to explore the past with your grandchildren. Living history museums strive to replicate bygone eras as faithfully as possible, with volunteers dressed in period costumes and taking on the roles of the village blacksmith or farmer or soldier.

Especially if the parents' family budget is tight, grandparents may want to consider purchasing family membership to local museums or zoos either as a gift to the family or as a way to have regular outings with the children. And some museums and zoos have one day of the week set aside when admission is free or reduced for seniors who are city or county residents.

Nature Parks

Most communities have parks, botanical gardens, or nature trails open year around. Children and adults of all ages can enjoy and learn from these outdoor natural "museums." Some of these parks and nature centers offer classes for children on topics such as butterflies, desert animal habitats, bird watching, maple sugaring, vernal ponds, winter habitats, and other aspects of nature. Sometimes the trails offer horseback riding or mountain biking as well as hiking.

You may be surprised to learn that there may be a state park just around the corner from where you live. An Internet search for the name of your state and "state park" will reveal several places where you can take your grandchildren for a day trip or even an overnight visit. You can also search for national parks at the National Park Service website: www.nps.gov/parks.html.

Internet Resources

Appendix A lists many websites for grandparents, though none of them focuses on the particular needs of gifted and talented children. Some of our favorite websites that include information about upcoming events for and about gifted children are:

- ➤ www.nagc.org
- ➤ www.hoagiesgifted.org
- ➤ www.sengifted.org
- ➤ www.ditd.org

Saturday Programs

Several states offer Saturday enrichment programs for children, either through their state and local gifted associations or through high schools, colleges, and universities. For example, children may register for advanced math or computer or language arts classes, and they attend the class on Saturday mornings for six or eight weeks, when the next set of Saturday courses begin. These programs are important to students who are not receiving appropriate challenge in their regular school. They allow students to meet and make friends with other children of similar interests and abilities, and to experience academic challenge; sometimes these classes are the first time the child has been taught and challenged at an appropriate level.

These Saturday enrichment programs often use college or university students or community experts who are willing to teach children in a particular area of expertise. The skill taught could be beginning drawing; it could be learning simple chemistry, or building rockets, or learning something on computers. Families register a child for a nominal fee in a class or workshop area of interest such those listed above, or perhaps digital photography, computer chess, beginning pottery, or some aspect of science. Sometimes the workshop is a half-day or one-day event. Sometimes the program might be an ongoing Saturday class that continues for three weekends or more. The design is up to the organizer. Children generally love these sorts of activities. They allow gifted children to stretch and, in some cases, be challenged far more than they are challenged in their classes in school.

Summer Camps

Summer camps for children are available all across the country. Some of these camps are very general in nature and provide a way for children to simply have some fun and experience sleeping in a cabin with a counselor and interacting with a group of children they have not known previously. Most camps offer a variety of activities like swimming, boating, hiking, making crafts, and singing songs around a campfire in the evenings. Some camps specialize in specific areas of talent or interest such as music, drama, computers, sailing, horseback riding, or wilderness skills. Camps like these are particularly good for gifted children who are strongly interested in a specific area or who cannot satisfy their learning needs in that area throughout the school year.

Interlochen in Michigan is one of many summer camps for students who are musically talented. Some of the children who attend this camp are headed for Juilliard School of Music and, someday, professional musician positions in symphonies and concert halls across the country. Admission to this camp is increasingly competitive, as its reputation has grown over many years.

Concordia Summer Language Camps in Minnesota, sponsored by Concordia College, are known for teaching children through language immersion. In the Spanish Village at this camp, nothing is spoken but Spanish. The same is true in the German, Norwegian, and French Villages. As children live and play and participate in camp activities in their respective villages, they learn about the culture as well as the language. Many children attend for successive summers, thus building their language fluency over several years. This is an excellent program for children interested in other cultures or for children who do not receive foreign language instruction in their local schools.

There are of course computer camps, math and science camps, scout camps, church camps, and camps for every interest and every budget. Check with your local state advocacy organization or gifted association to see if they have a listing of summer camps and other opportunities in your area. These organizations often publish this listing in the spring of all the summer activities for children. Local newspapers usually have a section devoted to summer activities for children, and local schools and libraries may also have listings.

Summer Gifted Residential Programs

Numerous colleges and universities throughout the United States offer summer residential programs for gifted students. Check with your state department of education or call the colleges and universities directly to ask whether they offer summer programs designed for bright and gifted high school students.

A recent ad in *Newsweek*[157] described a Harvard University summer residential program (www.summer.harvard.edu) using these bulleted phrases:

- Open enrollment
- College-level program for high school students
- Study abroad programs
- Study with distinguished faculty
- Earn college credit
- Choose from over 200 courses
- Learn with students from 90 countries
- Participate in extracurricular activities
- Explore Boston and New England

It sounds exciting enough that we grandparents wish we could attend!

Carleton College in Minnesota has a summer writing program for high school juniors. Johns Hopkins, Northwestern University, The University of Southern Mississippi, and Purdue University are examples of other universities with special summer residential programs for high-ability students. Many state universities, as well as some private colleges, offer special summer orientation and "get acquainted" programs for minority students who may be the first in their family to attend college. The summer program is meant to familiarize these students with the campus, with dorm life, and with the format of classes. Students generally give these programs high praise for taking some of the fear and the mystery away from college attendance.

Some colleges offer programs for younger children in addition to high school children. Pacific Lutheran University in Tacoma, Washington, for years has offered a two-week program with several courses at each grade level. In this program, students live in dormitories on the college campus and elect two to four classes. A seventh-grade student might take Creative Writing, Algebra, and Beginning Drama. A fourth-grade student might sign up for Fencing, Botany, and Chess. Students have roommates, and college students act as dormitory advisors. Younger students may choose to stay on campus or go home on weekends.

Northwestern University in Illinois offers both Saturday and summer programs for gifted children through its Center for Talent Development (www.ctd.northwestern.edu). Johns Hopkins University (www.jhu.edu/~gifted), Duke University Talent Identification Program (www.tip.duke.edu), and the University of Denver Rocky Mountain Talent Search (www.du.edu/education), among others, all offer similar programs.

Governor's Schools and Other Special Schools

Thirty-seven of the 50 states now offer what are called Governor's Schools for Gifted. These schools are usually summer residential programs for gifted high school students that allow students to take higher level and challenging classes on a university campus. Classes may be taught by high school Advanced Placement teachers or by college instructors. Students apply for these programs, and admission is somewhat competitive. Tuition at most governor's schools is paid by the state.

In the 1980s in Illinois, a special school for math and science was established called the Illinois Math and Science Academy, located west of Chicago in Aurora. Talented students in Illinois apply for entrance to this school when they are sophomores in high school and enter when they are juniors. Admission is competitive. Students live in dormitories, sometimes far away from home if they are from the southern part of the state. The state pays tuition. This special school was founded by a group of businessmen in the "high-tech corridor" 40 miles west of Chicago that includes executives from companies such as Motorola, IBM, and the Argonne National Laboratory. These businessmen helped raise the money and lobby the Illinois legislature for such a school to encourage more students to enter science and technology.

Travel Abroad

One last idea we have for invaluable summer or year-round learning and enrichment for gifted students is that of travel, either abroad or on the American continent. Families with connections abroad may be able to arrange private exchange programs through friends. There are summer learning opportunities in Mexico where students go to live with a family. Some churches offer goodwill ambassador trips to Europe. There are summer exchange and six-month exchange program opportunities available through Rotary International in which students live with a family, usually with same-age children. (Check with your local Rotary Club: www.rotary.org.) University faculty members who go on sabbatical for six months every six or seven years often take their families with them for the experience of living in another part of the country or the world. They may travel to other cities in the United States, Europe, New Zealand, Australia, and other locations.

A Family Year Abroad[158] is a book written by a father who describes the experiences of his California family as they went to live in Europe for a year. They had no special reason for doing this other than that they wanted the experience for themselves and their children. The parents were dissatisfied with the level of challenge offered by U.S. schools. They decided to take a time-out and try living abroad. Their account of the year relates how they grew closer as a family and how their two young children came home a hundred times more confident in themselves, having learned another language, made new friends, and experienced life in another culture. This same family now hosts an exchange student from another country every year because they feel that the information shared between cultures is so important and valuable.

On a smaller scale, we know one grand-mother who takes her grandchildren on a trip when each grandchild turns 10. One child went with Grandma by Amtrak across Canada. Another went with Grandma to the bottom of the Grand Canyon by mule. Still another went with this Grandmother to London. We think rich memories of these trips with Grandma, as well as many new perspectives on the world, probably result from these travels.

Progress lies not in enhancing what is,
but in advancing toward what will be.
~ Kahlil Gibran

The most important seed I can sow in this life is my
children, and the love and knowledge that I can bestow
upon them and the help I can give them.
~ Steven Seagal

We live in a world in which we need to share
responsibility. It's easy to say "It's not my child, not
my community, not my world, not my problem."
Then there are those who see the need and respond.
I consider those people my heroes.
~ Fred Rogers

Chapter 9

Advocating for Your Gifted Grandchild

Contrary to what some people think, gifted children do not always make it on their own. They often need help in the form of advocates, or people who will work and lobby on their behalf to understand them and to make sure their needs are met.

Grandparents can advocate for their bright, creative, talented grandchildren in many ways. How much you can do and how effective you will be will depend largely on your knowledge about the nature and needs of gifted children. It will also depend, of course, on your relationship with your children and your grandchildren.

There are four types of advocacy that are important for gifted children. They are advocacy with the child's parents, advocacy with the child's school, advocacy in the community, and advocacy through charitable giving to support programs for gifted children.

Advocacy with the Child's Parents

As we have noted previously, the roles and rules of grandparenting are often complex in today's modern world of fractured families, blended families, and one-parent homes. Grandparents' effectiveness depends upon their relationship with the parents and how willing the parents are to have them involved with the grandchildren. Of course, good communication with the parents is important, and it helps if the parents are not defensive, but open to suggestions and assistance by the grandparents. Some parents readily accept information, suggestions, and support; others want little or none of this, and grandparents must wait patiently until the need or the appropriate time is there. Will one or both parents feel threatened or perceive concern and interest as interference? The healthier the relationship between the grandparents and the child's parents, the more likely there will be easy opportunities to promote new insights and sponsor new activities.

Sometimes problems arise just because all parties do not have the same information. For example, the child's father may feel that "he got through school without any special classes or enrichment, and his child will too!" Grandfather, on the other hand, has been reading about gifted persons, and he wants his daughter and her husband to have the child tested for placement in the gifted program. Sometimes differences occur because of differing attitudes toward education. The son-in-law doesn't believe in testing because he says it leads to labeling, and he doesn't want his child to be labeled a "geek." He just wants a "normal" child.

It is important to try to get all of the family members to agree at least on some basic information and issues. For example, does everyone agree that the child is unusually bright? If so, do the parents think that there are some problems at school, with peers, at home, or within the family that might be related to the child's brightness, curiosity, intensity, or sensitivity? Or that the child might benefit from additional learning opportunities?

Grandparents can be advocates within their own family by becoming informed and by supplying information to the parents. Websites such as www.hoagiesgifted.org, www.sengifted.org, www.nagc.org, and www.giftedbooks.com have informative articles that can be printed and shared. Perhaps the grandparents could suggest a complete intellectual and academic evaluation of the grandchild to determine what is reasonable to expect and how best to nurture the grandchild's abilities. Such suggestions may have to be made gently several times and in varying ways. The grandparents may find that they have to back off and wait patiently—sometimes for quite a while— before parents can come to see the wisdom or appropriateness of their suggestions.

The supportive advocacy of grandparents also can occur in less direct ways. Grandparents can offer to babysit so that the parents can attend workshops and conferences. They can obtain information about summer camps, mentors, and other opportunities, as well as help to fund these activities. Or grandparents might take siblings on a special outing so that parents can have extra time with the child who needs more focused attention. Grandparents might give parents a subscription to magazines such as *Parenting for High Potential,* published by the National Association for Gifted Children. Most of all, grandparents can offer a sympathetic ear to listen to the parents' concerns; there will be few other people the parents can trust and rely upon.

Advocacy with Schools

Regrettably, as we noted earlier, many schools will be both uninformed and lukewarm regarding appropriate options and special opportunities for gifted children, even though the need for such opportunities may be quite clear. Families find themselves feeling puzzled, frustrated, or even quite angry that their child's educational needs are not being met and that the child is becoming discouraged about education. Grandparents and parents alike wonder how much they should simply trust the decisions of professional educators or whether they must attempt to intervene and lobby with the schools.

We believe that education should be joint venture between home and school and that parents, and often grandparents, are essential parts of that formula. Perhaps passionate advocacy for gifted children is not how it *should* be, but that is how it *is* in many places. And if your child is exceptional, you have a right to want an exception to the typical educational experiences that are offered to most children.

However, to be an effective advocate, you will have to inform yourself about educational models for gifted children. The Glossary section of this book will help you. You may even find that you have to educate the professionals who work with your grandchildren. If this is the case, we encourage you to be patiently impatient. If you find yourself feeling angry, remind yourself that very few principals, superintendents, or teachers wake up in the morning saying to themselves, "I will try to ruin the educational experiences of every gifted child I see today." These educators simply may not have had the training to know what is appropriate to do with a gifted child. Or they may have the mistaken belief that if a child is gifted, then "she can get what she needs on her own," and they therefore believe that the child doesn't need any extra interventions or curriculum.

How can parents and grandparents help? We encourage you to be informed and positive in dealing with the schools; it is much more effective than storming in angrily. Grandparents can play very special roles in advocating for a gifted child. For example, as a concerned grandparent, you might offer to attend the parent-teacher conference to take notes or to provide an extra set of ears. You may discover that school administrators and teachers will listen to an informed grandparent who accompanies the parents more readily than they will listen to parents. The grandparents have often had years of business experience in negotiating and are thus able to take a calmer, more reasoned approach. Because of this calmer approach, school personnel may offer grandparents more respect than they give to parents. In addition, grandparents can always talk to, listen to, and provide support and encouragement to the child's parents, who are often feeling tired and frustrated in their advocacy efforts with the school.

Grandparents can assist the parents by providing them with information. Two books, *Helping Gifted Children Soar*[159] and *Re-Forming Gifted Education: How Parents and Teachers Can Match the Program to the Child*,[160] contain excellent tips about how to approach the school and how to negotiate for your child's needs. The first book serves as a good introduction to gifted education and the services that schools can and should provide. The second book goes into detail about how to tailor an education to a specific gifted child, and it is useful for parents or grandparents who have an unusually bright or highly gifted child. Still another book, *Creative Home Schooling: Resources for Smart Families*,[161] offers countless resources, websites, and curriculum ideas for young gifted children—and the ideas and materials are useful whether or not the child is home schooled.

Grandparents can be advocates in other important ways as well. Some grandparents, because the parents are so busy, research the published policies of the state and the school district concerning the philosophy and procedures for programs for gifted students. They are then able to give the parents information about the focus, grade levels, entrance requirements, and activities that are typical for certain schools in the area, as well as similar information about local private and charter schools. Other grandparents delve into the appropriate order of persons to approach within the school system. They are able to suggest to the parents that they initially talk to the teacher, then to the principal, the gifted educational coordinator for the district, school psychologist, school board members, and superintendent.

Grandparents can promote and support quality education for gifted students in still other ways. A modest donation of supplies or money earmarked for the education of gifted students will be extremely welcome. Or they could find information about grants that teachers might apply for. Grandparents might offer to provide a special lecture or experience to the class, or to arrange for an artist-in-residence, an assembly speaker, or a mentor. Or perhaps a grandparent could help the school librarian. All of these offers are likely to be well received and can change the attitudes of educators about gifted children and their supposedly "pushy parents and grandparents." And of course, you can attend meetings of the school board and planning committees where you can question and support decisions about programs for gifted students.

As a grandparent, you might volunteer to help in the classroom so that the teacher will have time for special projects or to give individual attention to a student. If you volunteer in your grandchild's classroom, you will be able to observe lessons as they are taught and whether different groups of children sometimes do different assignments or whether all of the children do the same thing all the time. You will see how your grandchild interacts with others and with the teacher. You can see if the work is at the child's ability level. You will be able to talk informally with the teacher and the principal about your grandchild's interests and skills. Perhaps you will even be able to suggest that some children might enjoy being given a more challenging assignment on occasion.

After you've been there awhile and you have seen how the classroom operates, you can ask the teacher or principal if the school has a formal written policy statement or program philosophy about the identification and education of gifted children. Request to see it. Inquire about what educational options are available and whether flexible pacing is offered. If your school has only one educational option, such as a pull-out program or enrichment model available for only a portion of the week, you might wish to remind the educational staff in a gentle way that students are not gifted for just one or four hours per week; they are gifted all day every day and therefore need modifications to curriculum every day. Any student who has unique educational needs should have those needs taken into account every day in school.

If your school does not offer a variety of flexible educational options for gifted learners, you could purchase two or three books about gifted education to donate to the school to get them started thinking about alternatives they might try. Perhaps these might be *Helping Gifted Children Soar* by Carol Strip and Gretchen Hirsch,[162] *Re-forming Gifted Education: How Parents and Teachers Can Match the Program to the Child* by Karen Rogers,[163] and *Teaching Gifted Children in the Regular Classroom* by Susan Winebrenner.[164] In your conversations and school visits, it will also be helpful if you, too, are familiar with some of the educational models and terms used to describe program modifications for gifted children.

The National Association for Gifted Children periodically issues policy statements on important issues and has adopted a position statement that strongly encourages schools to provide "differentiation of curriculum and instruction" for gifted students. Excerpts from this policy statement about appropriate education for gifted students are shown in Table 5. A complete version is available at www.NAGC.org.

Table 5
Differentiation of Curriculum and Instruction

Learning needs of gifted students often differ from those of other students and should be addressed through differentiation, a modification of curriculum and instruction based upon the assessed achievement and interests of individual students.

Differentiation for gifted students consists of carefully planned, coordinated learning experiences that extend beyond the core curriculum to meet the specific learning needs evidenced by the student.

Differentiation may include:

➤ acceleration of instruction

➤ in-depth study

➤ a high degree of complexity

➤ advanced content, and/or variety in content and form

Problems occur when teachers attempt to meet the needs of gifted students by limiting learning experiences to:

➤ offering more of the same level of material or the same kind of problem

➤ providing either enrichment or acceleration alone

➤ focusing only on cognitive growth in isolation from affective, physical or intuitive growth

➤ teaching higher thinking skills (e.g., research or criticism) in isolation from academic content

➤ presenting additional work that is just different from the core curriculum

> ➤ grouping with intellectual peers without differentiating content and instruction
>
> *Excerpts from NAGC Position Statement on Differentiation of Curriculum and Instruction (NAGC, 1998)*

Differentiation strategies like those listed above can be provided through several types of school programs to match the child's readiness and need. Many of these flexibly-paced educational options are ones that school systems can implement with very little administrative difficulty, once the teachers understand learning characteristics and needs of gifted children.[165]

Gifted children are a diverse group, and their educational needs are likewise diverse. It is generally recognized that the curriculum for gifted students should be differentiated according to the characteristics and needs of those students—i.e., the students' academic experiences would be qualitatively different; there would be greater breath and depth to the learning, in addition to the learning being faster-paced.[166]

Parents and Grandparents Have a Voice

When educational alternatives do exist within the school or district, it is important to recognize that families do have a voice in choosing among these alternatives for their children. Parents often are unaware that they have substantial freedom of choice and that they can say yes or no to program options that are offered. For example, they can select not only which school their child attends, but they can also choose which educational opportunities within that school they would like their child to participate in.

Some school districts have alternatives such as open enrollment, in which children may go to a different school or school district than the neighborhood school. This option usually depends upon whether the receiving school has room for additional students; there may be a waiting list. Parents also can choose private, charter, or parochial schools rather than public schools, though of course this option usually costs more; or they can select a different school district and either move as a family or transport their child to the new district. The option of home schooling is also becoming an increasingly popular choice for families of gifted children.[167]

Despite the freedom of choice that actually exists, we also recognize that parents in public school districts, particularly in smaller communities, are often told that they simply have to accept what is offered. Even in these situations, however, there are options if families are willing to advocate for their child.[168] For example, parents may be able to convince the school to allow their child to do more advanced math work based on the child's "testing out" or by otherwise proving that the child has already mastered the concepts that are being covered in the current grade-level math. Perhaps the school is flexible and will allow the child to work with a higher grade level math book, or perhaps the child can move across the hall to a higher level class during math time and then back to the regular classroom for the rest of the day. A flexible option like this does not cost the school much and typically attracts little special attention that otherwise might prompt other children to tease or taunt the child. The key is whether there is philosophical support for gifted children among teachers and administration.

In selecting a school, parents should ascertain the extent to which that school encourages options for flexible pacing—options that will allow students to move ahead educationally as they are ready to do so. Flexible pacing could mean that a first grader might do reading with the third grade, but stay in first grade the rest of the day. It might mean that the first grader would be given reading within the classroom that is of a level that matches the child's reading readiness. A highly gifted sixth or seventh grader might attend high school for science and/or math classes, but return to sixth grade for the rest of the day. Flexible pacing might also mean skipping one grade, or it could mean organizing a group or "cluster" of advanced learners within a classroom. There are many potential education options, and it is important to choose the option that best matches the readiness and needs of the child.[169]

To help parents and grandparents be aware of what is happening in their child's classroom at school, they might wish to ask these questions: Does the teacher really understand and enjoy working with the gifted and talented children? Has the teacher had specific training regarding gifted children? Does she attend conferences, take classes, and keep up on the most recent developments? Do the school administration and the school board genuinely support—not just tolerate—learning for gifted children? Unless you have both administrative support and teacher training, educational programs for gifted children—whether in the regular classroom or in a special classroom—will probably be mediocre at best. On the other hand, where both training and administrative support exist, there can be wonderful educational opportunities for gifted children in a wide variety of educational structures.

What if your neighborhood school offers no special provisions for able learners? Or if the teachers have no training in gifted education or needs of gifted students? A school like this is simply not able to offer an appropriate education for gifted, talented, and creative children, and parents should look elsewhere, if possible. In such a school, every student is exposed to the same material, at the same time, in the same manner, with the same amount of repetition. Brighter students who have already mastered the particular skill or material will be bored and will likely underachieve.

You may try to change the school policies, procedures, or funding, but this is a difficult and lengthy process. Three or more years of planning are usually necessary before a program for gifted education is in place. It simply takes that long to get the necessary training for teachers, and for the administration to grasp the importance of meeting the needs of gifted children. If you decide to advocate for long-term change, and we hope that you will, guidelines such as those written by Dr. Frances Karnes and her coauthors[170] can help you. In states where there is a mandate for gifted education (check with the state department of education), parents can initiate legal action or request mediation. However, this is a time-consuming and tedious process; by the time school practices are changed, the child may have experienced several years of insufficient progress.[171]

Advocacy with schools is a slow process, and sometimes the outcome is simply unsatisfactory. In such situations, it is essential to remember the importance of the education and support within the family, as well as the fact that your advocacy efforts with the school, even though not immediately successful, are providing models for your grandchildren of ways in which one can influence our social system. When children see and hear their parents' and grandparents' efforts to improve social institutions, including schools, they not only develop important values, they also learn how and why one can make an impact. A classic book, *Cradles of Eminence: Childhoods of More Than 700 Famous People*,[172] documented that the extent to which a family emphasizes and supports learning and education is more important than most formal school experiences.

Advocacy in the Community

Community advocacy is a major way that grandparents can advocate for their gifted grandchildren. People are often apathetic about politics of community involvement because they fear that their work will never filter down to their individual concerns. Grandparents, however, often have been involved in leadership roles within their communities. They know how communities evolve, and they often know the influential people who help shape the community's priorities, including educational priorities. Because of your knowledge and your connections with others, you—as a grandparent of a gifted child—have the potential to become a very effective advocate within your community, and you can educate other grandparents about the needs of gifted and talented youth.

You might decide, for example, to invite some gifted youngsters in your local area to present or perform at a meeting of senior citizens. Perhaps you may arrange special events, such as breakfasts, luncheons, or dinners, where the special needs of gifted youngsters are discussed along with how gifted children and adults are portrayed in today's media.[173] Or you might organize a seminar, a conference, or a book study group concerning these issues.[174]

Grandparents can network with government, business, and education leaders to help them understand the importance of supporting our gifted and talented. They can suggest programs on gifted education for occasions such as Rotary or Kiwanis club meetings. They can talk to business leaders in their community about the importance of having excellent education for our brightest youth. They can request city or state government agencies to support more flexible educational options. Or they can simply write letters to school boards and to the media expressing their opinions.

The elders of our communities will, we hope, become leaders in advocating for fundamental changes regarding the attitudes about gifted and talented children. Our society—at least in the U.S.—seems to be drifting perilously into an anti-intellectual mode in which the emphasis is far more on mediocrity, conformity, and fitting in, rather than on innovation, excellence, and creativity.

Here are a few interesting facts that may help you understand the severity of the problem. Federal and state support for educational programs for talented students is lacking; for example, out of every Federal dollar spent for education, less than two cents goes to fund programs for gifted children.[175] State funding designated for these programs varies, but it generally supports only minimal services.[176]

It is sad to note that the last comprehensive nationwide survey of gifted education programs in U.S. public schools occurred in 1985—20 years ago—and the results of that four-year study were published in *Educating Able Learners*.[177] The survey found that over one-half of the school superintendents surveyed believed that they had no gifted children in any of their schools, and less than 60% of the schools offered enrichment opportunities to gifted students for only three hours per week or less.

Another recent change that has had a negative effect for bright students in public schools is that of mandated standardized testing. Many states now require students to pass written tests at third grade, sixth grade, etc., in order to progress to the next level of schooling. Of course there is no problem with bright students passing these tests. The problem is that with so much emphasis in the daily classroom on meeting basic minimal standards, quick learners are left without suitable enrichment or academic challenge.

Today's teachers are pressured to prepare all students for yearly achievement tests to measure whether or not students have reached "grade level competency." With school ratings and teacher evaluations becoming more dependent upon the results of these standardized tests, teachers spend more time each year "teaching to the test" and therefore less time modifying curriculum for individual students, particularly those students who are advanced.

As *Genius Denied*,[178] by Jan and Bob Davidson, so poignantly describes, our educational system and the attitudes toward gifted children in our society need a major overhaul if we are to nurture the talent in our country. Our brightest minds are getting very little support, and in fact, they often meet not only with apathy and neglect, they also encounter active hostility.

Non-Profit Associations, Private Foundations, and Charitable Giving

One significant but often overlooked advocacy approach is that of charitable giving to provide support for gifted children. Non-profit organizations and foundations play a significant role, yet their efforts are not widely known, and they have received insufficient support, both financially and politically.

Few grandparents, for example, are familiar with the National Association for Gifted Children (www.nagc.org), nor are they aware that almost every state has a non-profit association dedicated to meeting the needs of gifted children. Their conferences, workshops, and publications disseminate information to educators and parents. These associations, particularly at the state and local level, have very small budgets, and they are supported almost solely by the annual dues of parents and teachers; they depend heavily upon volunteers. Even a modest—and tax-deductible—donation to these associations would be most welcome.

Supporting Emotional Needs of the Gifted (www.sengifted.org) is a nationwide non-profit association with the mission of providing information about the social, emotional, and family needs of gifted children and adults. SENG holds an annual conference and also gives modest grants to support research and education of teachers and other professionals. SENG is able to function primarily because of the generosity of one benefactor, Mrs. Eugenie Radney. This organization, like the others, could do much more if it had even modest additional financial support. Perhaps some grandparents who are financially comfortable will be able to assist these dedicated volunteers in their work.

In addition to SENG, only a handful of independent non-profit charitable foundations exist at present for the primary purpose of encouraging, nurturing, and supporting gifted children and their education:

➤ the Davidson Foundation and its Davidson Institute for Talent Development (www.ditd.org)

➤ the Malone Family Foundation (www.malonefamilyfoundation.org)

➤ the Jack Kent Cooke Foundation (www.jackkentcookefoundaiton.org)

➤ the Nicholas Green Foundation (www.nicholasgreen.org)

➤ the Esther Katz Rosen Fund of the American Psychological Association Foundation (www.apa.org/apf/Rosen.html)

➤ the Cottington Trust for Gifted Children of the Hawaii Community Foundation (www.hawaiicommunityfoundation.org).

We hope that grandparents will fund these, or other, foundations so that the currently small number of foundations will increase substantially in the future.

Some grandparents who have been leaders in business and industry know that many businesses have affiliated foundations to support worthy causes that are suggested by management personnel. If you are one of those grandparents, we invite you to encourage these business foundations to offer financial support to programs that will assist gifted children and their families. Advocacy is most powerful when money is given to support its efforts.

As a grandparent of a gifted child, you have a great amount of wisdom and perspective, and perhaps also skills in speaking, writing, creativity, interpersonal communication, organization, and development. You can use your experience and skills to make an important difference in the education, growth, and development of your gifted grandchild and the millions of others across our nation.

The future belongs to those who believe
in the beauty of their dreams.
~ Eleanor Roosevelt

We do not inherit the land from our ancestors;
we borrow it from our children.
~ American Indian Proverb

If a man leaves little children behind him,
it is as if he did not die.
~ Moroccan Proverb

Nothing is certain but death and taxes.
~ Benjamin Franklin, 1789

Chapter 10

Planning for the Future of Your Gifted Grandchild

Estate and Financial Planning for Grandparents

We spend our younger years working, raising and educating our family, and setting aside assets for our own retirement. We plan, hoping our children will grow up to find satisfying careers and start the cycle again. We anticipate that our

ancial obligations to children will miracu-
lously come to an end as they become adults.
Life will then be at its best. We can think about
retirement and travel, or maybe fixing up the
house or buying a cabin on a lake somewhere.
Then we become grandparents. We note with
pride that good looks and intelligence continue
through the generations and that our children, no
matter how difficult they were when they were
younger, have now produced the perfect bright
and talented grandchildren. In some cases, the
grandchildren are almost too perfect. We adore
them; we want to help them grow and develop;
we want to be involved.

But times have changed, as the saying goes.
The days of sandlot baseball, the football games in
the front yard, and a piano lesson or two seem to
be over. Our grandchildren are all engaged in
organized sports. They require uniforms and
equipment. Week-long summer camps, held in
our day in a leaky, hot cabin, are now held in
air-conditioned dormitories where children are
taught the finer points of a backhand or a pitch-
ing wedge. Private lessons are available in everything from art to zoology. Private schooling,
available only to the wealthy two generations

ago, is common. We now live in a world where there is competition to get a three-year-old into pre-kindergarten at an exclusive private school that may cost $10,000 or more per year. The financial obligations imposed on today's parents to see that their children have the best education and opportunities to develop individual talents and skills is unlike anything that we as grandparents ever saw, either as a child or as a parent. For grandchildren with special talents, opportunities to develop those talents abound, but the cost can be overwhelming.

The cost of securing a college education has increased dramatically. One hundred thousand dollars for a college education is no longer the exception. Graduate school is desirable and, in some cases, mandatory if the child is to pursue a chosen career. The financial strain placed on our adult children as parents is beyond anything that we as parents or that our parents ever imagined. It is at this time in our lives when we, the grandparents, are most likely in a position to provide financial assistance to our own children as they try to provide their children with the best possible opportunities.

Assistance from grandparents is appreciated. In some cases, it is expected. What does all of this have to do with estate and financial planning? The answer is simple. The tax laws limit, and in some cases control, what we can do for our children and grandchildren during life and at death. If we spend a lifetime accumulating assets, it is foolish to ignore the tax concerns that affect us as we attempt to move those assets on to our children and especially to our grandchildren.

First, you should understand the basics of gift and estate taxation as they exist today, and then you can choose among strategies that will allow you to transfer assets to, or use assets for, the benefit of your grandchildren.

Historical Perspective of Gift and Estate Tax

In 1862, Congress imposed a temporary inheritance tax to finance the Civil War. In 1898, again during war, an inheritance tax was reintroduced. These taxes were the ancestors of our current estate tax, which was enacted in 1916. Realizing that the estate tax could be avoided by simply giving away everything prior to death, Congress adopted the first gift tax in 1924. The law remained relatively unchanged for the next 50 years, exempting half of an estate from tax when assets passed to a spouse, and providing an exemption of only $60,000 on the balance of the estate. The maximum estate tax rate was 70%. The gift tax law at that time provided an annual exemption of $3,000 per donee per year and a $30,000 lifetime exemption. Gift tax rates were approximately 66% of estate tax rates, making lifetime gifts more advantageous than death transfers.

All of this changed in 1976 when the law was modified to gradually increase the estate tax exemption to $600,000 by 1987 and to increase the gift tax exemption to $10,000 per donee per year. The maximum estate tax rate was reduced to 55%.

In 2001, Congress made sweeping changes to the estate and gift tax laws that currently affect all estate and financial planning for the benefit of the family. The only thing certain about the current law is its uncertainty. We think it highly unlikely that it will remain in place.

In addition to the federal estate and gift tax laws, the individual states have their own inheritance and gift tax laws. Some states have no inheritance tax or gift tax. Thus, in planning, it is imperative that you consult tax professionals who are familiar with the laws of your individual state.

Transferring Assets to Grandchildren

Establishing a plan and setting aside assets for grandchildren during life is a rewarding experience because we are able to observe the fruits of our gifts. There are no legal obligations on the part of a grandparent to support or provide for a grandchild. Therefore, transfers to or for the benefit of a grandchild may be subject to gift tax unless they fall within certain specific exceptions.

Providing for grandchildren upon your death requires special considerations. Transfers to grandchildren at death require one to consider federal estate tax, state inheritance tax, if any, and yet another tax called the Generation Skipping tax. Death transfers cannot be revoked. Given all of the above, it makes much more sense to distribute funds to grandchildren prior to your death.

Federal Taxation of Gifts

Gift tax concerns result from any transaction in which money or assets are transferred to a person without any legal obligation to do so. Parents are obligated to support their children during minority. Money spent by a parent on a minor child is not a gift. Grandparents are not legally obligated to support grandchildren. Therefore, money spent on a grandchild is a gift for gift tax purposes. Gifts are neither income to the recipient nor deductible to the donor for income tax purposes. Other than gift taxes owed by the person making the gift, these gifts are tax free.

The Internal Revenue Code provides that certain gifts can be ignored; they do not count Specifically, the Code provides that gifts in the form of tuition paid for education or training of the grandchild are exempt from gift tax. To qualify, the IRS specifically requires that a payment be made directly to a qualified educational organization. A check cannot be written to the grandchild or to the parent of the grandchild who then pays the tuition. You must make payment directly to the educational institution.

In addition to tuition, direct payments for medical care for the benefit of a grandchild are not considered taxable gifts. This includes glasses, braces, or other medical procedures that might enhance the grandchild's ability to achieve.

All other transfers to or for the benefit of a grandchild, however, regardless of the purpose, constitute taxable gifts. The good news is that the IRS provides two significant exceptions that allow us to avoid actually paying tax: the annual exclusion and the lifetime exclusion.

The Annual Exclusion

The first exclusion, which exempts most gifts from tax, is the annual exclusion. Each of us is granted an annual exclusion from gift tax liability for gifts to a grandchild or other donee that do not collectively exceed $11,000 during a calendar year. The $11,000 exclusion will increase in the future based on inflation. You should check with your tax professional to determine the current exemption.

You and your spouse can each gift $11,000 per year to or for the benefit of each grandchild—for a total of $22,000—without incurring any gift tax concerns. In fact, with the consent of one spouse, the other spouse can gift the entire $22,000 to one grandchild. This is referred to as gift splitting and requires the filing of a gift tax return. You and your spouse can each gift $11,000 to your child, the spouse of your child, and your grandchild. Nothing stops your child and spouse from using those funds for the benefit of the grandchild. Remember, your children are legally obligated to provide for their minor children. Their use of the money for your minor grandchild is not a gift.

Gifts of $11,000 per year do not sound like a lot of money when looking at the future costs of educating a grandchild. However, assuming that the money is invested and earns 6% over 15 years, the value of such gifts will exceed $270,000. In addition, if your estate is large enough to produce federal estate taxes at your death, removing $270,000 from your estate may save more than $120,000 in federal estate tax.

The Lifetime Exclusion

Once a gift to a grandchild exceeds the $11,000 limitation in a calendar year, the excess is applied against your lifetime exclusion. The Code grants you a lifetime exclusion of $1 million, which can be used and allocated at any time during your life to offset what would otherwise be a taxable gift. Each spouse has an exclusion. Unfortunately, for every dollar in lifetime exclusion that is utilized during life, the exclusion available to us at death for estate tax purposes is lost. The advantage of making gifts during life and using the lifetime exclusion today is that your grandchildren can enjoy and benefit from the gifted assets without waiting until your death. In addition, assets gifted today and properly invested will grow. The growth is removed from your estate at death.

Only when gifts exceed the annual exclusion and when the lifetime exclusion is fully utilized are federal gift taxes due. Federal gift tax rates range between 45% and 48%. Before bestowing gifts that exceed your lifetime exclusion, you should consult with a tax professional to verify that your estate either would not be subject to a gift tax or that there is some other exclusion. Otherwise, such gifts may result in state gift taxes.

Federal Estate Taxes

The federal estate tax is proof of the old adage — "You can't take it with you." At death, your estate is valued and subjected to tax if the value of the estate exceeds the federal exemption. Inheritance taxes may also be due depending on applicable state law. Because state laws differ substantially, we will focus our attention on the federal estate tax law.

At death, the assets that you own are valued and taxed as a part of your estate. The Internal Revenue Code states that all assets that you own at death, including some assets gifted away during lifetime, are included in your estate for estate tax purposes. This includes cash in the bank, stocks, bonds, retirement assets, real estate, annuities, and even life insurance. A common misconception is that estate assets are not valued at their true fair market value. This is incorrect. The Code clearly provides that assets are valued at their fair market value at the time of death. Substantial penalties can be assessed for under-valuation of assets.

Between spouses who are U.S. citizens, there is no federal estate tax on transfers at death to a surviving spouse, regardless of the amount. Special rules apply to residents who are not U.S. citizens. No federal estate taxes result from bequests to qualified charitable organizations.

For gifts at death to children, grandchildren, and others, the current federal estate exclusion for estate taxes at death is $1.5 million. The exemption is scheduled to change over the next several years. The exemption will increase to $2 million in 2006 and $3.5 million in 2009. In 2010, the estate tax is repealed. Unfortunately, this repeal only lasts for 12 months, with the exemption returning to $1 million in 2011. Only Congress could pass such insane legislation. We jokingly suggest to grandparents that they avoid their children and grandchildren during 2010; the appeal of inheriting free of estate tax in the year 2010 may produce far too much temptation for family members seeking a larger, tax-free inheritance.

Bills are pending in Congress to either make the repeal permanent in 2010 or to adjust the exclusion to levels between $3.5 million and $15 million. One thing is certain: confusion will exist until Congress acts, and probably thereafter. To properly plan for estate taxes, it is now necessary to know in what year you plan to die, the value of your estate that year, and whether Congress will change the law yet again before then—all of which are, of course, unknown factors. As a part of any estate plan, you should consult an estate planning professional regarding the current status of the law.

What we know for certain is that if your estate exceeds the exemption at death, federal estate tax rates of between 45% and 48% will apply. Careful planning of your estate can substantially reduce these taxes. In the case of a husband and wife, the exemption can be doubled. As stated above, gifts during one's lifetime can also substantially reduce tax liabilities.

Generation Skipping Taxes

Perhaps one of the least understood and most complicated portions of the estate tax law is the Generation Skipping Tax. Originally passed in 1976, then subsequently repealed and reinstated, the law produces a special problem in leaving assets to grandchildren. A discussion of the Generation Skipping Tax Act far exceeds the scope of this chapter. However, it is sufficient to say that the tax law puts limits on the amount that can be given by a grandparent to a grandchild, either during life or at death. The Generation Skipping Tax also limits the amount that can be placed in trust for a child for life without tax at the child's death when the assets pass to grandchildren. In general, the Generation Skipping Tax Act will not have any application unless the amount passing to the grandchild exceeds the amount of the federal estate tax exemption. If that happens, yet another tax is imposed. In those cases in which the amount passing to a grandchild would exceed the exemption, it is imperative that you consult an estate-planning expert.

Planning for Grandchildren

These are the basics of gift and estate taxation, and we can now focus on some techniques that might allow you to transfer assets to, or use assets for the benefit of, grandchildren. These procedures focus on lifetime gifts. However, these techniques may also apply equally well to provisions that you may wish to make in your estate plan and which are effective at death. Before beginning any program to set aside funds for the benefit of a grandchild, you must bear in mind a number of important considerations.

Age of the Grandchild

A minor cannot own assets. Placing assets in a grandchild's name can produce substantial problems, and gifts to minor grandchildren must be made in an approved form. Consider the grandparent who titled his home in the name of his six-year-old grandchild. This was a wonderful thing for the grandparent to do until it became appropriate to sell the home. The grandchild was then only 12 years old. The sale of the home required court approval. The proceeds from the sale were placed in a court-supervised guardianship. The court required the father to post a bond to guarantee that he would not steal the grandchild's money and, worse yet, the funds were delivered to the grandchild when she reached age 18 and became an adult by law. The money lasted 93 days.

Holding and Investing the Funds

Gifts may be made to individuals or financial institutions for the benefit of a minor. The unfortunate truth is that occasionally, individuals holding assets for minors will improperly use the funds. Naming the right person or financial institution to hold and invest the grandchild's assets may be the most important decision you make.

Spending the Grandchild's Funds

Giving complete instructions to the custodian of any funds held for a grandchild is imperative. Although it is an admirable thing to set assets aside for a grandchild, one needs more than the statement, "I'll tell the custodian how to use these assets as we go along." Of course, that statement offers little assistance if you fail to survive to be able to give those instructions.

Age of Distribution

Some grandchildren are capable of making financial decisions for themselves at 18. Others are not capable at 38. Your decision as to when the remaining assets must be given to the grandchild may dictate the type of procedure that you use.

Death of the Grandchild

Your decision as to who should inherit if the grandchild dies is important as well, and it also may dictate the technique that you use to transfer assets to grandchildren.

Uniform Transfers to Minors Act Accounts

A common and simple technique that can be used for gifting to a grandchild is a Uniform Transfers to Minors Act account (UTMA). UTMA accounts are allowed in every state. They are sometimes referred to as Uniform Gift to Minors Act accounts or UGMA accounts. The distinction is based on the version of the law that was adopted in your state. UTMA accounts allow you to transfer assets to a custodian for the benefit of a minor. You, your spouse, your adult child, or a third party may serve as custodian. The transfer is a completed gift. *You cannot change your mind later and take the funds back.* The gift is subject to gift tax if it exceeds the exemptions.

UTMA accounts are generally established by using a financial institution such as a bank or a stock brokerage company. The advantage of UTMA accounts is that they are inexpensive to create. They do not require the immediate services of an attorney or a tax adviser. The financial institution that makes the UMTA account available provides the forms to be executed, and the institution accepts the gift for the grandchild by depositing the assets into the account. Because the transaction is considered a completed gift, the income earned in the account is taxed to the child. The child's tax rate will depend on his age. The "kiddy" tax requires that if the income of a child under age 14 exceeds specified minimum amounts, that income is taxed at the parents' highest marginal rate. If the child is 14 or over, the income is taxed at the child's rates.

Subject to variations in state laws, the UTMA account may invest in any type of property, such as securities, CDs, credit union accounts, life insurance policies, and in some states, real estate. The custodian is required by law to invest the assets as a prudent person dealing with the property of another, typically referred to as the prudent investor rule. The custodian is often required to invest so as to produce reasonable income, taking into account the need to preserve and grow capital.

The custodian is allowed to use the funds for the benefit of the minor, without court order. Generally, the funds may be used for the health, education, and even support of the child, although using funds to provide the basic support of a grandchild may result in the UTMA income being taxed to the parent rather than the child. Typically, UTMA accounts are not protected from creditors.

The UTMA account will terminate according to the provisions of the applicable state law in which the account is established. Some states require termination as early as 18. Other states require termination at 19, 21, or 25. Regardless of the required termination date, once the child reaches the age for termination in your state, the custodian is obligated to turn over the balance of the funds to the grandchild. Once these funds are under the sole control of the grandchild, it is not uncommon to see a disagreement arise between the parents or the grandparents and the grandchild over how these funds are used.

Selection of a custodian is extremely important. As a general rule, if your estate exceeds the amount that can pass tax free for federal estate tax purposes, then you should not name yourself as the custodian. To do so could result in the assets being included in your estate at death even though you gifted them away by establishing the UTMA account. Thus, naming the child's parent or other adult as custodian may be preferable. In naming a custodian, it is important to consider whether you can also name an alternate or successor custodian, in case the custodian dies or is unable or unwilling to continue to serve. Note also that the custodian has absolute control over the UTMA accounts, is not bonded, and is not subject to court control. If the custodian wastes the UTMA assets, they will be lost, and there will be little ability to recover them.

Section 529 Plans

College education of grandchildren is often a particular concern for grandparents, and the cost of college is likely to continue to increase. Fortunately, there are some specific ways to plan for this.

Section 529 Qualified State Tuition Programs were first introduced in 1996. Modifications to the law in 2001 made the use of these plans much more attractive as ways to prepay the college education of a grandchild. The principal advantage of Section 529 plans is that assets contributed to the plan are generally gift-tax free, and the assets grow income that is tax free and are distributed to or for the benefit of the grandchild free of tax so long as the distributions are used for college education.

Qualified State Tuition Programs are established by the state, or by an agency of the state, and there are specific requirements. Contributions to the plan must generally be in cash. The contributor to the plan cannot direct how the contributions are invested and can exercise no control over the investments or the earnings of the plan. There are two basic types of programs. The first is a Prepaid Tuition Program. The second is a College Savings Plan.

Under the law, many states and colleges have adopted Prepaid Tuition Programs that provide for the purchase of "credits" to finance future college educational costs. These plans allow the designated beneficiary to attend a college or university regardless of the impact of inflation on the cost. The plan is funded by the purchase of credits, perhaps a full semester's tuition, based on the cost of tuition at that time. The credits are cashed in when the grandchild enrolls in college, and they are applied against tuition regardless of whether or not the cost has increased.

As a general rule, if the beneficiary does not attend college or goes to a school that is not participating in the prepaid tuition program, the tuition credits are refunded based on a set formula that may result in a loss of the income tax benefits, as well as a portion of the growth of the fund assets. In most states, if one grandchild cannot use the credits, they can be transferred to another grandchild. However, a transfer to someone other than a family member may trigger tax liabilities and penalties on account earnings.

College Savings Plans are investment accounts established under Section 529. They are not tied to a specific college, university, or system, but they are approved by the state. The assets are contributed to the plan and invested, and they are held by the plan administrator—generally a financial institution—until the grandchild is ready for college. Although the individual states have their own approved plans, the funds can be used to attend college in any state. Section 529 plans allow the account owner to change the beneficiary at any time for any reason. Thus, if a grandchild will not be using or needing the funds for college, the funds may be transferred tax free to another beneficiary within the family. If the funds are transferred to a beneficiary outside of the family, the transfer may trigger income tax and penalties.

The benefits of a Section 529 plan are many. First, the income earned by the plan and the appreciation of assets is exempt from income tax. Second, distributions to the beneficiary for qualified higher education expenses are income tax free. Third, no income-threshold test exists that would prohibit or restrict you from contributing to the plan. Additionally, many states exempt 529 earnings from state income tax. The plan owner can control disbursements, change beneficiaries, and in some cases, even revoke the account. Tax consequences of these actions will vary.

Unlike other gift techniques, the donor of a 529 plan can retain control as the custodian of the plan over the account and, at the same time, exclude the account assets from being included in her estate. This is in sharp contrast to the UTMA accounts and trusts, which were described earlier.

The gift tax rules, as they apply to 529 plans, are changed as well. The federal gift tax laws allow you to combine up to five years of gifts ($55,000 under present law) at one time to fund the account. Thus, a husband and wife could fund a grandchild's Section 529 plan with $110,000 without any gift tax obligations. States limit the maximum amount that can be placed in a plan. In most cases, however, the limit exceeds the maximum amount that you could ever desire to place in a college fund.

Qualified higher education expenses, which may be paid under Section 529, include tuition, fees, books, supplies, and equipment required by the educational institution. In addition, reasonable costs for room and board constitute higher education expenses for students residing in housing owned by the educational institution. In the case of a special needs beneficiary, such as a beneficiary with physical disabilities, other expenses necessary for the beneficiary's attendance at a qualifying educational institution may be paid.

As always, there must be some downsides. The plans may be considered assets of the student. Financial aid may be lost as a result of the existence of the account. Some plans have charges that are relatively high, and it is important that you examine the fee structures of the various plans. Since these plans are new, examining their past investment performance will be difficult Worst of all, if the funds are used for anything other than qualified educational purposes, the untaxed income is then taxed, and the IRS imposes a 10% penalty.

Like most current tax laws, Section 529 plans are scheduled to "sunset" in 2011. However, most people believe that Congress will continue this very valuable technique and make it permanent.

Education Savings Account

A Coverdell Education Savings Account, formerly called an Education IRA, is an educational savings account that is exempt from federal income tax. The account is established with a financial institution for the purpose of paying qualified education expenses for a designated beneficiary. Contributions can only be made in cash before a beneficiary turns 18 and in the maximum amount of $2,000 per year. In this regard, it is similar to an IRA. However, contributions are not deductible, although the income earned is tax free if used for education expenses. Assets must be used for qualified education expenses with final distribution to the beneficiary by age 30. The amount that can be gifted into such an account is phased out for taxpayers in the higher income tax brackets. Thus, you should consult with your tax professional to determine whether you can qualify for this type account.

Because of the limitations placed on the amount that can be gifted, few individuals establish these types of Coverdell Education Savings Accounts. The most significant difference between this vehicle and others is that education expenses include qualified elementary and secondary education expenses. Thus, if established early enough to allow growth in the assets, income tax savings may be produced to provide tax-free assistance for elementary, secondary, or college education expenses. Penalties are imposed to the extent that payments are not made for educational purposes. Otherwise, the rules are similar to those for the Section 529 Qualified State Tuition Plans.

Using Trusts to Provide for Grandchildren

Many grandparents will find the UTMA accounts, the Section 529 Qualified State Tuition Programs, and Education Savings Accounts to be sufficient, especially for lifetime gifts. However, the restrictions placed on the use of funds for these types of accounts, and especially the ages for required distribution, may cause one to reject these techniques and seek other opportunities. The most common vehicle selected by most grandparents is a trust. Trusts can be established to take effect during one's lifetime or at death.

Stripped of its legal jargon, a trust is nothing other than an arrangement in which the person creating the trust (the grantor) delivers assets to a custodian (the trustee) to hold under the written terms and conditions of the trust for the benefit of a beneficiary, in this case, a grandchild. The principal advantages of a trust are control. The grantor establishes a trust for the benefit of a beneficiary and names a trustee who will manage and invest the assets and who will distribute the assets to or for the benefit of the grandchild under the directions of the grandparent. As a general rule, trusts established by a grandparent during life must be irrevocable if the goal is to remove the trust assets from the estate of the grantor or to transfer the taxation of the income earned by the assets from the grantor to the trust or the beneficiary.

The grantor directs the investment and management of the assets through language in the trust document. The trustee, perhaps a financial institution or the parent of the child, invests the assets as allowed under the trust instrument. If the grantor is conservative, investments may be restricted to government-insured funds. If the grantor is more liberal, stocks, bonds, or other investments may be purchased.

The most significant advantage of the trust is that it gives the grantor the ability to designate how and when the trust income and principal are to be distributed. The grantor may require distributions upon certain events, such as graduation from college. He may provide for distributions for a wedding or for the purchase of a home. He might even create rewards for a grandchild who performs in an exceptional way. Most important of all, the trust may be structured to give the flexibility to react to the needs and circumstances of the grandchild in ways that cannot be foreseen when the trust is created.

The trust can provide for termination at a given age, and it may also require partial distributions at earlier ages. For instance, the trust may provide that if the child does not obtain a college degree, the trust does not terminate until age 40. If the child obtains a college degree, the trust may terminate at age 35. With a master's degree, the trust may terminate at age 30. The trust may be used as a carrot to provide incentive to the child to make the most of the opportunities that the funds in the trust provide.

In the event that the child fails to survive until termination of the trust, the trust directs who receives the assets. They may pass to the grandchild's children or to the siblings. The grantor makes these decisions in the trust document.

A trust does have disadvantages. Unlike the UTMA account, Section 529 plan, and Education Savings Account, there may be considerable costs in establishing a trust, which include legal and tax advice. If a financial institution is used as a trustee, it will charge a fee for its services.

Income tax issues associated with a trust may add complexity. The trust income can be taxed to the grantor, or it can be taxed to the trust, or it can be taxed to the beneficiary. Because the trust income tax brackets are higher than personal income tax brackets, careful planning of the taxation of income earned by a trust is required. What the trust does do is give flexibility that allows the trust income to be taxed in the most desirable way.

Gift tax issues are more complicated for trusts, particularly the gift tax exemptions discussed above. Gifts to a trust do not automatically qualify for the annual exemptions because the gift is not made to the beneficiary but rather into a trust for the benefit of a beneficiary. The beneficiary may not receive the actual trust assets for years. This causes the trust not to qualify unless the trust meets one of two exemptions. The first exemption, known as a 2503(c) trust, is a trust containing the requirement that it terminate when the beneficiary attains the age of 21 and that all assets be distributed to the beneficiary. This makes the trust much like a UTMA account. Accordingly, this option is rarely acceptable to grantors.

The second exemption is a trust known as a "*Crummey*" trust. *Crummey* trusts evolved from a tax court case decades ago. In general, it requires that when the donor makes a gift, the beneficiary must have a temporary right, perhaps for 30 days, to request that the gift be withdrawn. If the gift is not withdrawn, the funds remain in the trust for the benefit of the beneficiary. As long as the beneficiary is a minor, the parent has the right to make the withdrawal for the grandchild. However, when the grandchild is legally an adult, the grandchild is given the right. It is sometimes necessary to appropriately coach the grandchild on the advisability of not requesting distribution of the gift but rather allowing it to remain in the trust, which will cause the grandparent to remain happy and to continue gifting to the trust.

The most important decision to be made in establishing a trust for a grandchild is to give the trustee clear instructions on the purpose of the trust and how the trust income and principal are to be used and distributed. The trustee can only do that which is directed. Giving the trustee the authority to make distributions to allow the grandchild to achieve her goals is important. Restrictions on how trust funds can be used must be carefully considered.

Just as important as the instructions on investing and distributing assets is the selection of a trustee. A trustee generally operates without court supervision and rarely is required to file inventories or accountings with a court. Since the purpose of the trust is to remove assets from the grandparent's estate, it is generally necessary to name someone other than the grandparent as the trustee. Naming trustees is important, but naming successor trustees is just as important, especially in the case of trusts that are to run for many years. It is rarely desirable to petition the court to appoint a successor trustee. Naming successor trustees, or at least describing a method for appointing successor trustees, is crucial.

Establishing a trust, whether it is created during lifetime or at death, requires thoughtful deliberation and the advice of an estate-planning professional. Not only should the instructions be given to the trustee to cover what you expect to occur, but instructions must also be given to take into account what you hope does not occur. Grandchildren do not necessarily achieve as we might hope. Establishing and funding a trust does, however, provide the resources that give them every opportunity. Once established, these trusts generally cannot be altered by you. Accordingly, careful deliberation should be given to the very important decisions.

Conclusion

Providing for grandchildren is, indeed, a rewarding experience. Providing for grandchildren in a way that maximizes their opportunities but at the same time does not destroy their motivation to achieve can be difficult. If we spend a lifetime accumulating assets, then determining how they can best be used for the benefit of those we love is certainly most important.

Using Your Wealth

Grandparents not only have gained valuable wisdom and perspectives on life that they can share, but they also may have accumulated financial resources they wish to pass along. We hope, frankly, that this book will inspire grandparents to financially support a variety of programs for bright, young, gifted children and their families. There are at present only two or three foundations for gifted and talented children, and all are in need of financial support. Philanthropists Jan and Bob Davidson, who together established the Davidson Institute for Talent Development, wrote an excellent book, *Genius Denied*,[179] which highlights the need for many additional foundations to be established. We hope that those of you who are financially able will also help this cause.

Of course, we hope that you will consider financially supporting your own gifted grandchild's future. The expenses of raising a gifted and talented child can be unusually high. Because of their potential in so many areas, these children need to have a variety of opportunities available to them. Flute lessons, gymnastics classes, summer camps, computer camps, foreign language courses, mathematics, mentorships—all of these cost money, yet all are important in helping children reach their potential.

As grandparents, we face choices. How much do we help with the expenses? Do we pay the full costs of these enrichment opportunities, or only a part? Are we interfering with our children's lives if we contribute money for our grandchildren's adventures? How much should we give for our children's and grandchildren's welfare, and how do we balance that against other worthwhile charities or agencies—and with what we ourselves may need for our own future health or retirement living costs?

Only you can answer these questions. As outlined above, there are a variety of legal trusts and other financial planning tools that can be established to ensure that your grandchildren have the financial resources they need. Your estate-planning attorney can assist you with this.

Your Personal Legacy

Beyond the financial legacy, you have a personal legacy—consisting of your sense of values and your accumulated wisdom and advice—that you will bequeath your children and grandchildren. That bequest will perhaps be even more important than any material things they inherit from you.

Hugh Downs, the well-known television star, gave a wonderful legacy in his wise book, *Letter to a Great Grandson.*[180] This book is worth reading for its ideas about how to pass along wisdom as well as because it is a most enjoyable book.

A personal legacy for our children and grandchildren comes primarily from what they have seen us do throughout our own lives. Did we contribute to certain charities and organizations? Were we involved in politics and social action? Were we assertive in standing up for our beliefs? Were we tolerant of the behaviors of others? Were we supportive of family? Were we good role models? How did we live our life?

Often we convey our values simply in what we say or how we say it. Our generation, and the ones that preceded it, often communicated values through proverbs, quotes, or other sayings which were typically passed down to us by our parents. Grandparents are often virtual storehouses of such accumulated pithy wisdom, particularly if they lived in the South or in rural settings, where such sayings are still common. "A stitch in time saves nine," or "People who live in glass houses should not throw stones," or "Every cloud has a silver lining," or "Everything in moderation," or "The school of experience is a harsh one, but fools will learn in no other." These maxims communicate wisdom, morals, ethics, and ideals in ways that are likely to be remembered by our grandchildren to guide them during their lives.

Grandchildren usually ask their grandparents lots of questions, and grandparents' values are communicated in both the manner in which we answer and the content of our answers. The experiences that we share with our grandchildren give us opportunities to demonstrate what is important to us and provide time for important conversations. Some of these conversations will likely be about our perspectives and the choices that we have made, as well as about the choices that we are still making. Because of the broader experiences that come with age, these conversations may concern matters that parents are not yet thinking about, such as the importance of community, historical perspectives, long-standing family or cultural traditions, or even about topics like death or spirituality. Though parents may shy away from such topics, or they may simply be too pressed with immediate demands to discuss them fully, grandparents can answer these deep questions thoughtfully, giving full attention to the child. Questions like, "Grandma, what religion are you?" will inevitably lead to other questions and perhaps an ongoing discussion.

Grandparents are often able to talk more freely, offering more than one perspective. For example, there is much in our modern society that denies our grandchildren the opportunity to learn the natural cycle of life. When we grandparents were young, we saw life and death. Our experiences of life's transitions were close-up and personal. Babies were born at home. Sick people died at home. The wake was held in the living room, and everyone gathered in the kitchen after the funeral. Now our grandchildren may see birth or death in the media through movies and television, but it is unlikely that they have attended either a birth or a funeral. They see the new baby in the hospital or when it comes home from the hospital. They don't see severely ill relatives, since hospitals exclude children under 12.

Willard Scott, beloved weatherman on national TV and author of *If I Knew It Was Going to Be This Much Fun, I Would Have Become a Grandparent First*,[181] described how he once took his grandchildren with him when he visited a cemetery. He took them in order to teach them about their ancestors, to "know where they came from," and to understand the Importance of valuing of one's family and community. Family visits to the cemetery used to be a common custom, but today, they are rare. Yet seeing gravestones of family relatives reminds children that life is fleeting and that it is important to value things that are lasting rather than transitory.

Children today see less of real life than we did at their age. Their experiences of homelessness, poverty, extreme worry over an illness, or the exhilaration of a child's birth are likely to be second hand unless their parents or grandparents have involved them in charity or social service work. Our modern way of life protects our youngsters, but it may not help them understand the importance of their family and community. In previous generations, the shared experiences of joy and sorrow galvanized families into a sense of caring, closeness, and belonging. Today, we can cultivate that sense of continuity of family traditions and values, but it may take conscious effort to do so, using some of the ideas in this book, since with families spread out across several states, getting together is not easy.

Sometimes you might feel that you cannot talk about heavy topics such as illness, death, spirituality, what type of funeral or burial you want for yourself when you die, or other last wishes, etc.[182] Perhaps you have experienced a recent loss or some other upsetting event. Or perhaps your views are so different from those of your children that you are concerned about creating strife if you do express your views. Don't feel that you must force such a conversation; wait until you are ready and the situation is appropriate. Of course, you will need to be sensitive to the parents' values, particularly if they differ from your own. Life has a way of providing many opportunities to think about and confront such topics. Perhaps the topic will come up in a news or radio program, or maybe it will come from a family member reading a book like Shel Silverstein's *The Giving Tree*,[183] Judith Viorst's *Necessary Losses*[184] or *Suddenly Sixty and Other Shocks of Later Life*,[185] or Mary Pipher's *Another Country*.[186] However you approach these topics, it is important for us as the elders to help our younger generation understand the cycle of life and to contemplate their own existence. This is particularly valuable for bright, creative, gifted children; they often confront these issues within themselves but feel that they are alone and unique in such thoughts.

One interesting and positive way for you to bring some of the issues of life and death into the open is by writing your own Ethical Will.

Ethical Wills

In Medieval times, and even before, wills were written to impart instructions of an ethical and religious nature to the children and their descendants, as well as directives about disposing of one's tangible, worldly goods. These ethical testaments are called "Ethical Wills" and are still written by some families today. We think an ethical will can be a valuable and important contribution to a family. Such a will can even be written jointly by one or more generations of the family.

In families, the grandparents are most often the primary keepers of the family traditions, including values. It is important for families to talk about what they value, or what is important to them and why. An Ethical Will lists values, dreams, and hopes for one's children, as well as descriptions of the particular meaning of whatever material goods you hope to pass on to them. An Ethical Will often also includes descriptions of personal and spiritual experiences, as well as statements about one's hopes, love, and forgiveness. If a family is interested in drawing up an ethical will, guidelines for doing so can be found on the Internet at www.ethicalwill.com.

We were not familiar with Ethical Wills before doing the research for this book. When we heard about it, we thought it was something that many grandparents would like to know about. You might think of an Ethical Will as a love letter to your family, but one that can (and should) be read before your death. In an Ethical Will, you may wish to write a few words or sentences about your most central beliefs and opinions, things you have learned about life, and people from your own experience. Perhaps you will want to include favorite quotes or clippings or cartoons. If you use a three ring binder, you can add things as you wish. When your grandchildren are a little older, you might even encourage them to write their own Ethical Will.

Following are some suggestions to help you create your Ethical Will. These ideas come from Barry Baines, author of *Ethical Wills: Putting Your Values on Paper.*[187]

➤ Every few days or weeks, write down ideas—even a few words or a sentence or two—about things like:

—Your beliefs and opinions.

—Things you did to act on your values.

—Something you learned from grandparents/parents/ siblings/spouse/children.

—Something you learned from experience.

—Something you are grateful for.

—Your hopes for the future for your family and yourself, including specifically your children, grandchildren, and great-grandchildren.

➤ Write about important events in your life, including comments about why they were important to you and your family.

➤ Imagine that you only had a limited time left to live. Is there anything you regret not having done?

➤ Save items that represent your feelings and values, e.g., quotes, cartoons, clippings, etc.

➤ Review what you've collected after a few weeks or months.

➤ Cluster related items together to see what patterns or categories emerge.

➤ Revise and expand these related categories into paragraphs.

➤ Arrange the paragraphs in an order that makes sense to you.

➤ Add an introduction written to those who are likely to read what you have written, and a conclusion.

➤ Put this aside for a few weeks, and then review and revise.

An ethical will seems to us a wonderful way to let future generations know what you believed in, and for those who come after you to reflect on the same values or traditions. It will remain as your legacy long after you are gone.

The Future Is in Their Hands (But Also in Yours)

As we become grandparents, we are, of course, increasingly aware of our own mortality. We know that we may be gone in another 20, 30, 40 years, depending on health and other factors. It is humbling to realize that the world now belongs to our children, but even more to our grandchildren. The future—for better or for worse—is in their hands. What kind of future will it be? We grandparents hope that the leaders of the future will come from today's bright and creative children who care about humanity and this planet earth. It has been said that our brightest minds are our nation's—and the world's—greatest resource. We hope that families will nurture them and that schools and communities will support their education and training as well. We want public and private education to strive for high standards for all children, including the bright and gifted children. We are concerned that some recent education initiatives have encouraged minimal standards and mediocrity over higher standards of excellence. The world will surely need bright and creative minds to solve its many problems.

As grandparents, we still have an opportunity to shape the world of the future. We have influenced the world—for better or for worse—by what we have done thus far during our lives. Now we have a new opportunity. We can influence those who will come after us—our grandchildren and our great-grandchildren.

We hope you enjoy your grandchildren and that they enjoy their time with you.

Glossary

(Additional glossary terms can be found at: http://members.aol.com/svennord/ed/giftedglossary.htm)

ability grouping—the flexible regrouping of students based on individual instructional needs.

acceleration—moving at a faster pace through academic content.

achievement test—tests used to measure how much a student has learned in various specific school subjects.

affective needs—the social and emotional considerations of an individual.

articulation—the transitional process of students between grades and learning levels.

cluster grouping—the intentional placement of a group of similar-ability students in an otherwise heterogeneous (mixed-ability) classroom for a particular learning activity.

cognitive needs—the intellectual needs of an individual.

cooperative learning—an instructional strategy in which small, usually heterogeneous, groups of students work collaboratively to learn.

cross-grade/multi-age grouping—grouping strategy that mixes children of different ages for instruction. Other variations include family or teacher grouping.

curriculum compacting—an instructional strategy in which a student's grasp of a subject area is assessed prior to teaching, and if the student demonstrates mastery of the subject, the student is allowed to progress to higher level work or is given more in-depth work in the same subject area.

differentiation—the modification of programming and instruction based on a student's academic need and intellectual ability.

due process—a process that requires at least an opportunity for both parties in a disputed issue to present their views or objections to the other.

enrichment—the enhancement of the curricular program with additional opportunities and avenues of learning.

heterogeneous/homogeneous grouping—heterogeneous groups are groups of mixed ability students; homogenous groups are groups of students of similar ability.

individual educational plan—an individualized educational plan written with the teacher and parent that may include such options as acceleration, differentiated instruction, enrichment activities, and affective counseling and guidance. Not all states and school districts require an IEP for the gifted.

intelligence test—a measure of intellectual ability which produces an IQ score.

mediation—a process whereby a mediator who is a neutral party works with two conflicting parties and attempts to arrive at a satisfactory solution or compromise.

mentorship—a cooperative arrangement between a student and a professional adult for the purpose of sharing common interests in a particular skill, topic, or career orientation.

middle-school philosophy—an educational philosophy based on the growth and developmental characteristics of the adolescent learner. The curricular program emphasizes transition from elementary to high school, exploratory experiences, and development of positive self-esteem through a team-teaching approach.

out-of-level testing, also called **above-level testing**—Testing used to assess abilities of younger students at a higher level than their developmental peers to determine their actual level of knowledge or capability. A second-grade gifted student could be given the fifth-grade math achievement test to see if he or she is already operating at that level in that subject.

pull-out/resource programs—classes and activities held during the school day but outside of the regular classroom. Children move from one classroom to another for the activities.

school reform—may include many different approaches and ideologies and may serve as an avenue for open dialogue and opportunities for change.

site-based management—management that is locally controlled at the school level (instead of central office) and involves shared decision-making by representative members of the school community such as parents, teachers, and community members.

standards-based education—a mechanism for which students demonstrate what they know and are able to do with regard to particular content areas such as reading, writing, mathematics, science, history, geography, and foreign language. For gifted students, this system of establishing identifiable and assessable skills and knowledge offers a framework for flexibility and instruction based on need.

tracking—a rigid, inflexible system in which students are selected for semi-permanent grouping based on ability. In the past, students with high ability in one subject might have been selected for the high track in all subjects.

twice exceptional—children who are both gifted and handicapped or disabled in some way.

underachievement—a discrepancy between a child's school performance and his or her ability as shown by standardized test scores.

Appendix A
Websites for Grandparents

www.aarp.org/confacts/programs/grandraising.html

www.crm.mb.ca/granny/granny.com

www.cyberparent.com/gran

www.earlychildhoodlinks.com/parents/grandparent hood.htm

www.igrandparents.com

www.grandboomers.com

www.grandkidsandme.com

www.grandloving.com

www.grandmommy.com

www.grandparentagain.com

www.grandparenting.about.com

www.grandparenting.org

www.grandparentsandmore.com

www.grandparentsedge.com

www.grandparentsintl.com

www.grandparentsuniversal.com

www.grandparentworld.com

www.grandsplace.com

www.grandtimes.com

www.grc4usa.org

www.gu.org

www.mygrandchild.com

www.seehowtheygrow.com

www.sonic.net/thom/oor.com

www.tcpnow.com/grandparenting

www.uwex.edu/ces/flp/granparent.com

www.wz.com/people/BeingaGrandParent.html

Appendix B
Grandparent Support Groups and National Organizations

AARP Grandparent Information Center (GIC)
601 E Street NW
Washington, DC 20049
202.434.2296
www.aarp.org

American Grandparents Resource Center
National Charitable Organization
P.O. Box 27064
Denver, CO 80227
303.980.5707
www.grc4usa.org

Foster Grandparents
Corp. for National Community Service
1202 New York Avenue NW
Washington, DC 20525
202.606.5000
www.seniorcorps.org

Generations United

National Organization
122 C Street NW, Suite 820
Washington, DC 20001
202.638.1263
www.gu.org

The Grandparenting Foundation

108 Fainham Road
Ojai, CA 93023
www.grandparenting.org

National Grandparents Day

First Sunday after Labor Day
www.igrandparents.com

Appendix C
Recommended Readings for Grandparents and Parents

Grandparent Book List

Berman, E. (1997). *Grandparenting today: Making the most of your grandparenting skills with grandchildren of all ages.* Collingdale, PA: Diane Publishing.

Berman, E. (1998). *Grandparenting ABCs: A beginner's handbook.* New York: Berkley Publishing Group.

Brovero, M., & Dorman, W. (1998). *Grandma and Grandpa, may I come over?* Bloomington, IN: Grayson Bernard Publisher.

Callander, J. (1999). *Second time around: Help for grandparents who raise their children's kids.* Wilsonville, OR: BookPartners.

Canfield, J., Hansen, M. V., McCarty, M., & McCarty, H. (2002). *Chicken soup for the grandparents' soul: Stories to open the hearts and rekindle the spirit of grandparents.* Deerfield Beach, FL: Health Communications.

Carlson, R. (2001). *The don't sweat guide for grandparents: Making the most of your time with grandchildren.* New York: Hyperion.

Carson, L. (1996). *The essential grandparent: A guide to making a difference.* Deerfield Beach, FL: Health Communications.

Carson, L. (1999). *The essential grandparent's guide to divorce: Making a difference in the family.* Deerfield Beach, FL: Health Communications.

Cox, C. (2000a). *Empowering grandparents raising children: A training manual for group leaders.* New York: Springer Publishing.

Cox, C. (2000b). *To grandmother's house we go and stay.* New York: Springer Publishing.

Dalton, R. & Dalton, P. (1990). *Encyclopedia of grandparenting: Hundreds of ideas.* Hayward, CA: Bristol Publishing Enterprises.

Doucette-Dudman, D. (1996). *Raising our children's children.* Minneapolis, MN: Fairview Press.

Downs, H. (2004). *Letter to a Great Grandson.* Scribner.

Elgin, S. (2000). *The grandmother principles.* New York: Abbeville Press.

Elkind, D. (1989). *Grandparenting: Understanding today's children.* Washington, DC: American Association of Retired Persons.

Epstein, P. (2003). *Great ideas for grandkids! 150 ways to entertain, educate, and enjoy your grandchildren—without setting foot in a toy store!* New York: McGraw-Hill/Contemporary Books.

Faulk, U. A. & Faulk, G. (2002). *Grandparents: A new look at the supporting generation.* Amherst, NY: Prometheus Books.

Faust, R. & Faust, T. (2001). *Grand parenting: Finding roots and wings for an open choice generation.* Shawnee Mission, KS: Leathers Publishing.

Fay, J. (1997). *Grandparenting with love & logic: Practical solutions to today's grandparenting challenges.* Golden, CO: Love & Logic Press.

Fridstein, M. (1997). *Grandparenting: A survival guide: How better to understand yourself, your children, and your children's children.* Glenwood Springs, CO: Tageh Press.

Fry, P. (1997). *Creative grandparenting across the miles: Ideas for sharing love, faith and family traditions.* Liguori, MO: Liguori Publications.

Hanks, R. (1997). *Connecting the generations: Grandparenting for the new millennium.* Gainesville, GA: Warren Featherstone.

Harris, G. (2002). *Grandparenting: How to meet its responsibilities.* Franklin, TN: Americas Group.

Harrison, T. (1997). *Grandparents' memory book: Did you really walk five miles to school?* Grantsburg, WI: STA-Kris.

Hartt, W., Hartt, M., & Cross, W. (1997). *Complete idiot's guide to grandparenting.* New York: Macmillan Publishing.

Jarvis, T. (2003). *The gift of grandparenting.* Notre Dame, IN: Sorin Books.

Johnson, S. (2003). *Grandloving: Making memories with y our grandchildren (3rd ed.).* Fairport, NY: Heartstrings Press.

Kettman, S. M. (1999). *The twelve rules of grandparenting: A new look at traditional roles and how to break them.* New York: Checkmark Books.

Kornhaber, A. (2002). *The grandparent guide: The definitive guide to coping with challenges of modern grandparenting.* McGraw-Hill/Contemporary Books.

LeShan, E. (1997). *Grandparenting in a changing world.* New York: Newmarket Press.

Linsley, L. & Aron, J. (1997). *Totally cool grandparenting: A practical handbook of time-tested tips, activities, and memorable moments to share for the modern grandparent.* New York: Saint Martin's Press.

Malone, G. (2003). *Off my rocker: Grandparenting ain't what it used to be.* Colorado Springs, CO: Navpress.

Nelson, J., Allen-Goad, P., & Kornhaber, A. (1999). *New-fashioned grandparenting: Changing America one grandchild at a time.* Grand Blanc, MI: Allyn Group Publications.

Newman, S. (1996). *Little things mean a lot: Creating happy memories with your grandchildren.* New York: Crown Publishing Group.

O'Connor, K. (1996). *Innovative grandparenting: How today's grandparents build personal relationships with their grandkids (Great! Grandparent).* St. Louis, MO: Concordia Publishing House.

Osborne, H. (2003). *Ticklebelly hill: Grandparents raising grandchildren.* Bloomington, IN: 1stBooks Library.

Rayner, C. (1997). *Successful grandparenting: The essential guide to one of life's most rewarding relationships.* London: David & Charles.

Sasser, S. (1999). *Grand activities: More than 150 fabulous fun activities for kids to do with their grandparents.* Franklin Lakes, NJ: Career Press.

Schmitz, D. (2003). *The new face of grandparenting. Why parents need their own parents.* St Paul, MN: Grandkidsandme.

Slorah, P. O. (2003). *Grandparents' rights: What every grandparent needs to know.* Bloomington, IN: 1stBooks Library.

Smith, G. (1999). *Learnings from little ones: Tales from a grandfather's heart.* Frisco, CO: Papaco Press.

Spence, L. (1997). *Legacy: A step-by-step guide to writing personal history.* Chicago: Swallow Press.

Spurlock, V. S. & Spurlock, V. (2001). *AAA traveling with your grandchild.* Heathrow, FL: American Automobile Association.

Steen, V. (1996). *How to be a way cool grandfather.* Memphis, TN: Mustang Publishing.

Westheimer, R. & Kaplan, S. (1998). *Grandparenthood.* New York: Routledge.

Wiggin, E. E. & Chapman, G. D. (2001). *The gift of grandparenting: Building meaningful relationships with your grandchildren.* Wheaton, IL: Tyndale House.

Zullo, K. & Zullo, A. (1994). *The nanas and the papas: A boomer's guide to grandparenting.* Kansas City, MO: Andrews McMeel Publishing.

Parent Booklist

Abelman, B. (1995). *Reclaiming the wasteland: TV and gifted children.* Cresskill, NJ: Hampton Press.

Adderholt-Elliott, M. (1987). *Perfectionism: What's bad about being too good?* Minneapolis, MN: Free Spirit Publishing.

Berger, S. L. (1994). *College planning for gifted students (2nd ed.).* Reston, VA: Council for Exceptional Children.

Bluestein, J. (1997). *The parent's little book of lists: Do's and don'ts of effective parenting.* Minneapolis, MN: Free Spirit Publishing.

Csikszentminalyi, M. (1996). *Talented teenagers.* New York: Cambridge University.

Delisle, D. & Delisle, J. (1996). *Growing good kids.* Minneapolis, MN: Free Spirit Publishing.

Dreikurs, R. & Soltz, V. (1991). *Children: The challenge.* New York: Plume.

Dunn, R., Dunn, K., & Treffinger, D. (1992). *Bringing out the giftedness in your child.* New York: John Wiley & Sons.

Elyé, B. (2000). *Teen success! Ideas to jumpstart your mind.* Scottsdale, AZ: Great Potential Press.

Feldman, D. H. (1991). *Nature's gambit: Child prodigies and the development of human potential.* New York: Teachers College Press.

Galbraith, J. (1984). *The gifted kids survival guide (for ages ten and under).* Minneapolis, MN: Free Spirit Publishing.

Galbraith, J. & Delisle, J. (1996). *The gifted kids' survival guide: A teen handbook (for ages 11-18).* Minneapolis, MN: Free Spirit Publishing.

Goertzel, V., Goertzel, M., Goertzel, T., & Hansen, A. M. W. (2004). *Cradles of eminence: Childhoods of more than 700 famous men and women (2nd ed.).* Scottsdale, AZ: Great Potential Press.

Halsted, J. W. (2002). *Some of my best friends are books: Guiding gifted readers from preschool to high school (2nd ed.)*. Scottsdale, AZ: Great Potential Press.

Isaacson, K. (2002). *Raisin' brains: Surviving my smart family*. Scottsdale, AZ: Great Potential Press.

Karnes, F. A. & Bean, S. M. (1993) *Girls and young women leading the way*. Minneapolis, MN: Free Spirit Publishing.

Karnes, F. A. & Bean, S. M. (1995). *Girls & young women inventing*. Minneapolis, MN: Free Spirit Publishing.

Karnes, F. A. & Bean, S. M. (1995). *Leadership for students: A practical guide*. Waco, TX: Prufrock Press.

Karnes, F. A. & Bean, S. M. (1997). *Girls and young women entrepreneurs*. Minneapolis, MN: Free Spirit Publishing.

Karnes, F. A. & Riley, T. L. (1996). *Competitions: Maximizing your abilities through academic and other competitions*. Waco, TX: Prufrock Press.

Kaufman, G. & Raphael, L. (1992). *Stick up for yourself!* Minneapolis, MN: Free Spirit Publishing.

Kelly, L. (1996). *Challenging minds: A year's worth of thinking skills and enrichment activities*. Waco, TX: Prufrock Press.

Kerr, B. A. (1997). *Smart Girls: A new psychology of girls, women and giftedness*. Scottsdale, AZ: Great Potential Press.

Kerr, B. A. & Cohn, S. J. (2001). *Smart boys: Talent, manhood, and the search for meaning.* Scottsdale, AZ: Great Potential Press.

Kurcinka, M. S. (1992). *Raising your spirited child: A guide for parents whose child is more intense, sensitive, perceptive, persistent, energetic.* New York: Harper Collins.

Lewis, B. (1991). *The kid's guide to social action: How to solve the social problems you choose—and turn creative thinking into positive action.* Minneapolis, MN: Free Spirit Publishing.

McCutcheon, R. (1990). *Get off my brain: A survival guide for lazy students.* Minneapolis, MN: Free Spirit Publishing.

O'Dean, K. (1997). *Great books for girls.* New York: Ballantine Books.

O'Dean, K. (1998). *Great books for boys.* New York: Ballantine Books.

Olenchak, F. R. (1996). *They say my kid's gifted: Now what?* Washington, DC: National Association for Gifted Children.

Perry, S. K. (1991). *Playing smart: A parents' guide to enriching, offbeat learning activities.* Minneapolis, MN: Free Spirit Publishing.

Peterson, J. S. (1993). *Talk with teens about self and stress.* Minneapolis, MN: Free Spirit Publishing.

Piirto, J. (2004). *Understanding creativity.* Scottsdale, AZ: Great Potential Press.

Radencich, M. & Schumm, J. (1988). *How to help your child with homework: Every caring parent's guide to encouraging good study habits and ending the homework wars.* Minneapolis, MN: Free Spirit Publishing.

Ricci, I. (1997). *Mom's house, dad's house.* New York: Simon & Shuster.

Rimm, S. B. (1990). *Exploring feelings: Discussion book for gifted kids have feelings, too.* Watertown, WI: Apple Publishing.

Rimm, S. B. (1990). *Gifted children have feelings, too: And other not-so-fictitious stories for and about teenagers.* Watertown, WI: Apple Publishing.

Rimm, S. B. (1990). *How to parent so children will learn.* Watertown, WI: Apple Publishing.

Rimm, S. B. (1994). *Keys to parenting the gifted child.* Hauppauge, NY: Barrons.

Rimm, S. B. (1996). *Why bright kids get poor grades.* New York: Crown Publishers.

Rimm, S. B. (1997). *Raising preschoolers: Parenting for today.* New York: Random House

Rivero, L. (2002). *Creative home schooling: A resource guide for smart families.* Scottsdale, AZ: Great Potential Press.

Rogers, K. B. (2002). *Re-forming gifted education: How parents and teachers can match the program to the child.* Scottsdale, AZ: Great Potential Press.

Romain, T. (1997). *How to do homework without throwing up.* Minneapolis, MN: Free Spirit Publishing.

Rothman, R. W. & Lavin, C. (1990). *Fostering young learners: Activities for parents and teachers in partnership.* Unionville, NY: Royal Fireworks Publishing.

Saunders, J. & Espeland, P. (1991). *Bringing out the best: A resource guide for parents of young gifted children.* Minneapolis, MN: Free Spirit Publishing.

Schmitz, C. C. & Galbraith, J. (1985). *Managing the social and emotional needs of the gifted.* Minneapolis, MN: Free Spirit Publishing.

Schumm, J. & Radencich, M. (1992). *School power: Strategies for succeeding in school.* Minneapolis, MN: Free Spirit Publishing.

Smutny, J. F. (1991). *Your gifted child: How to recognize and develop the special talents in your child from birth to age seven.* Westminster, MD: Ballentine.

Smutny, J. F. (1993). *Your gifted student: A guide for parents.* New York: Facts on File.

Smutny, J. F. (1997). *Teaching young gifted children in the regular classroom.* Minneapolis, MN: Free Spirit Publishing.

Smutny, J. F. & Blocksom, R. (1990). *Education of the gifted: Programs and practices.* Bloomington, IN: Phi Delta Kappa.

Smutny, J. F., Veenker, K., & Veenker, S. (1989). *Your gifted child.* New York: Facts on File.

Strip, C. & Hirsch, G. (2000). *Helping gifted children soar: A practical guide for parents and teachers.* Scottsdale, AZ: Great Potential Press.

VanTassel-Baska, J. L. (1989). *Patterns of influence on gifted learners: The home, the self, and the school.* New York: Teachers College Press.

Walker, S. Y. (1991). *The survival guide for parents of gifted kids.* Minneapolis, MN: Free Spirit Publishing.

Warren, S. (1987). *Being gifted: "Because you're special from the rest."* Unionville, NY: Royal Fireworks Publishing.

Warren, S. (1990). *The parents' guide to teachers of the gifted. The teachers' guide to parents of the gifted.* Unionville, NY: Royal Fireworks Publishing.

Webb, J. T. (2000a). *Do gifted children need special help?* (Video). Scottsdale, AZ: Great Potential Press.

Webb, J. T. (2000b). *Is my child gifted? If so, what can I expect?* (Video). Scottsdale, AZ: Great Potential Press.

Webb, J. T. (2000d). *Parenting successful children.* (Video) Scottsdale, AZ: Great Potential Press.

Webb, J. T., Amend, E. R., Webb, N. E., Beljan, P., Goerss, J. & Olenchak, F. R. (2004). *Misdiagnosis and dual diagnoses of gifted children and adults: ADHD, Bipolar, OCD, Asperger's, Depression, and other disorders.* Scottsdale, AZ: Great Potential Press.

Webb, J. T., Meckstroth, E. A., & Tolan, S. S. (1982). *Guiding the gifted child: A practical source for parents and teachers.* Scottsdale, AZ: Great Potential Press.

Winebrenner, S. (2000). *Teaching gifted children in the regular classroom: Strategies and techniques that every teacher can use to meet the academic needs of the gifted and talented.* Minneapolis, MN: Free Spirit Publishing.

Endnotes

Introduction

1. This survey was conducted among 823 grandparents age 50+ and was reported in *The AARP grandparenting survey: The sharing and caring between mature grandparents and their grandchildren* (1999).

2. The life expectancy for Americans increased nearly 30 years during the 20th Century ("Planning for the extra long retirement," ProtectAssets.com). Of the 4.3 million baby boomers born in 1960, more than 300,000 can expect to live to at least 90. And according to the Census Bureau, the number of people 100 years old or older nearly doubled in the 1990s. Additionally, the number of Americans over age 100 is expected to rise from 65,000 in 2000 to 129,000 in 2010 and to 5.3 million in 2100 ("Changing tune for longer life: When I'm 104," *Investor's Business Daily*, December 1, 2003, pp. A1-A2).

3. Goertzel, Goertzel, Goertzel & Hansen (2004); Piirto (2004); Tannenbaum (1983).

4. Davidson, Davidson, & Vanderkam (2004).

Chapter 1. You and Your Grandchild

5. Westberg & Daoust (2003).
6. Rogers (2002).
7. Webb, Meckstroth, & Tolan (1982).
8. Rivero (2002).
9. Rogers (2002).
10. Pipher (2000).
11. U.S. Census (2001).
12. Covey (1990).
13. Pipher (1996).
14. AARP (1999).

Chapter 2. Is My Grandchild Gifted?

15. Gopnik, Meltzoff, & Kuhl (1999).
16. For example, Colombo (1993).
17. Hall & Skinner (1980).
18. Webb & Kleine (1992).
19. Webb (2000b).
20. Gardner (1983).
21. Webb (2000b).
22. Halsted (2002).
23. Strip & Hirsch (2000).
24. Strip & Hirsch (2000).
25. Goleman (1995).
26. Such as Webb (2000b).
27. Baum, Owen, & Dixon (1991).

Chapter 3. *Some Areas of Concern for Gifted Childrend*

28. Rogers (2002).
29. Adderholdt-Elliott (1999).
30. Silverman (1993).
31. Jones (1994; 1998); Panati (1987).
32. Goertzel et al. (2004).
33. Kerr (1997).
34. Halsted (2002).
35. Silverman (1993).
36. Kerr (1997); Kerr & Cohn (2001).
37. Kerr (1997).
38. Kerr & Cohn (2001).
39. Allen (2001).
40. Rimm (1994).
41. Whitmore (1980).
42. Webb et al. (1982).
43. Miller (1996).
44. Betts (1985).
45. Rimm (1996).
46. Kaufmann (1992).
47. Strip & Hirsch (2000).
48. Webb et al. (1982).
49. Kerr & Cohn (2001).
50. Scott (2004).
51. Karnes & Bean (2000).
52. Strip & Hirsch (2000).

Chapter 4. Expanding the World for Gifted Children

53. For example, Lind (2001).
54. Clark (2001).
55. For example, Silverman (1993).
56. Bloom (1985).
57. Smutny, Veenker, & Veenker (1989).
58. AARP (1999).
59. AARP (1999).
60. Such as Healy (1999a; 1999b).
61. Christakis, Zimmerman, DiGiuseppe, & McCarty (2004).
62. American Academy of Pediatrics (1999).
63. Pipher (1996).
64. Karnes & Riley (1996).
65. Rogers (2002).
66. Rivero (2002).
67. Kerr & Cohn (2001).

Chapter 5. Maximizing Grandparenting

68. In the AARP Grandparenting Survey (1999), grandparents were asked, in an open-ended, free-response question, what were the most important values or ethics that they would like to pass on to their grandchildren. In response, 42% said that they wanted to pass on morals and integrity, 21% wanted to pass on success/ambition, 20% chose

religion, 14% to be considerate of others, and 10% to be responsible or trustworthy.

69. Schmitz (2003).
70. Lucas, Morley, Cole, Lister, & Leeson-Payne, (1992); Tanner & Finn-Stevenson (2002).
71. Carson (1997).
72. Webb (2000d).
73. AARP (1999).
74. *New York Times,* Aug. 31, 1924.
75. AARP (1999).
76. AARP (1999).
77. Rogers (2002).
78. Klein (2002).

Chapter 6. When a Grandparent Becomes the Parent
79. Bath (1995); Brenner & Fox (1998); Deater-Deckard & Dodge (1997); DeVet,(1997).
80. Betts (1985).
81. Webb et al. (1982).
82. Dreikurs & Soltz (1991).
83. Happasalo & Tremblay (1994); McCord, McCord, & Zola (1959).
84. Dreikurs (1991).
85. Barkley (1998).
86. Ginott (1969; 1982).
87. MacKenzie (1998).
88. Schwarzchild (1995).
89. Dreikurs (1991).

90. Severe (2003).
91. MacKenzie (2001).
92. Cornell (1983).
93. Rimm (1996).
94. Webb et al. (1982).
95. Webb et al. (1982, pp. 127–128).
96. Ginott (1982).
97. Covey (2004).
98. Webb et al. (1982).
99. Kerr (1997).
100. Kerr & Cohn (2001).
101. Halsted (2002).
102. Webb (2000b).
103. Webb (2000a).
104. Webb (2000d).
105. "Mental health: Does therapy help?" in *Consumer Reports* (Nov. 1995, pp. 734–739).
106. Webb et al. (1982).
107. Webb (2000c).
108. Rogers (2002).
109. Rivero (2002).

Chapter 7. Educational Planning
110. For example, Karnes & Marquardt (1991a; 1991b; 1999); Rogers (2002); Rivero (2002); Webb et al. (1982).
111. Gagne (1991); Roedell, Jackson, & Robinson (1980).

112. Silverman (1993); Strip & Hirsch (2000); Rogers (2002); Rivero (2002).

113. National Association for Gifted Children (1998).

114. Cox, Daniel, & Boston (1985).

115. Johnsen (2004).

116. Renzulli, Smith, Callahan, White, & Hartman (2002).

117. Gagne (1991).

118. Webb et al. (1982).

119. Tomlinson (2001).

120. Rogers (2002).

121. Davis & Rimm (2003); Schiever & Maker (1997).

122. Cox et al. (1985).

123. Clark (2001).

124. Tomlinson, Kaplan, Renzulli, Purcell, Leppien, & Burns (2002).

125. Cox et al. (1985); Rogers (2002); Strip & Hirsch (2000).

126. Schiever & Maker (1997).

127. Rogers (2002).

128. Oakes (1985); Slavin (1987).

129. Kulik & Kulik (1991).

130. Kulik & Kulik (1991, p. 191).

131. Reilly (1992).

132. NAGC (1998).

133. NAGC (1998).

134. Schiever & Maker (1997).

135. Cox et al. (1985); Gallagher & Gallagher (1994); Pollins (1983).
136. Assouline, Colangelo, Lupkowski–Shoplik, Lipscomb, & Forstadt (2003).
137. Benbow (1991, p. 163).
138. Assouline et al. (2003).
139. Renzulli & Reis (1991).
140. Assouline et al. (2003).
141. *Time* Magazine (May, 2003).
142. Benbow (1991).
143. Benbow & Stanley (1983); Brody & Stanley (1991); Cohn (1991); Mezynski & Stanley (1980).
144. Rogers (2002).
145. Cox et al. (1985).
146. Stanley (1985).
147. Kerr (1997).
148. Cox et al. (1985).
149. Johnson (1989); Rivero (2002).
150. For example, Field (1998); Moore & Moore (1987); Rivero (2002).
151. Rivero (2002).
152. Johnson (1989).
153. Strip & Hirsch (2000).
154. Rogers (2002).

Chapter 8. Other Resources for Gifted Children
155. Halsted (2002).
156. Konigsburg (1967).

157. *Newsweek* (April 26, 2004).
158. Westphal (2001).

Chapter 9. Advocating for Your Gifted Grandchild

159. Strip & Hirsch (2000).
160. Rogers (2002).
161. Rivero (2002).
162. Strip & Hirsch (2000).
163. Rogers (2002).
164. Winebrenner (2000).
165. Cox et al. (1985); Strip & Hirsch (2000).
166. Clark (2001); Rogers (2002).
167. Rivero (2002).
168. Karnes & Marquardt (1991a; 1991b; 1999).
169. Rogers (2002).
170. For instance, Lewis & Karnes (2001); Karnes & Stephens (2003).
171. Karnes & Marquardt (1991a; 1991b; 1999).
172. Goertzel et al. (2004).
173. Lewis & Karnes (1995).
174. Meadows & Karnes (1992).
175. U.S. Department of Education (1993).
176. Council for Exceptional Children (1999).
177. Cox et al. (1985).
178. Davidson & Davidson (2004).

Chapter 10. Planning for the Future of Your Gifted Grandchild

179. Davidson & Davidson (2004).
180. Downs (2004).
181. Scott (2004).
182. According to the AARP Grandparenting Survey (1999), there are several topics that grandparents find difficult to discuss with grandchildren. These include death and dying (17%), drugs, alcohol, and sex (16%), saving money (11%), religion and spiritual matters (10%), and the child's personal problems (10%).
183. Silverstein (1964).
184. Viorst (1998).
185. Viorst (2000).
186. Pipher (2000).
187. Baines (2001).

References

AARP. (1999). *The AARP grandparenting survey: The sharing and caring between mature grandparents and their grandchildren.* Washington, DC: American Association of Retired Persons.

Adderholdt-Elliott, M. (1999). *What's bad about being too good?* Minneapolis, MN: Free Spirit Publishing.

Allen, S. (2001). *Vulgarians at the gate: Trash TV and raunch radio: Raising standards of popular culture.* New York: Prometheus.

American Academy of Pediatrics Committee on Public Education. (1999). Media education. *Pediatrics, 104,* 341–343.

Assouline, S., Colangelo, N., Lupkowski-Shoplik, A., Lipscomb, J., & Forstadt, L. (2003). *The Iowa Acceleration Scale: A guide for whole grade acceleration K-8 (2nd ed.).* Scottsdale, AZ: Great Potential Press.

Baines, B. K. (2001). *Ethical wills: Putting your values on paper.* New York: Perseus Publishing.

Barkley, R. A. (1998). *Your defiant child: 8 steps to better behavior.* New York: Guilford Press.

Bath, H. (1995). Everyday discipline or control with care. *Journal of Child and Youth Care, 10(2),* 23-32.

Baum, S. M., Owen, S. V., & Dixon, J. (1991). *To be gifted and learning disabled* Mansfield Center, CT: Creative Learning Press.

Benbow, C. P. (1991). Mathematically talented children: Can acceleration meet their educational needs? In N. Colangelo & G. A. Davis (Eds.), *Handbook of gifted education* (pp. 154-165). Boston: Allyn & Bacon.

C. P. Benbow & J. C. Stanley (Eds.), *Academic precocity: Aspects of its development* Baltimore: Johns Hopkins University Press.

Betts, G. T. (1985). *The autonomous learner model for the gifted and talented* Greeley, CO: Alps Publishing.

Bloom, B. (1985). *Developing talent in young people.* New York: Ballantine.

Brenner, V. & Fox, R. A. (1998). Parental discipline and behavior problems in young children *Journal of Genetic Psychology, 159(2),* 251-256.

Brody, L. E. & Stanley, J. C. (1991). Young college students: Assessing factors that contribute to success. In W. T. Southern & E. D. Jones (Eds.), *The academic acceleration of gifted children* (pp. 102-132). New York: Teachers College Press.

Carson, L. (1997). *The essential grandparent: A guide to making a difference* Deerfield Beach, FL: Health Communications.

Christakis, D.A., Zimmerman, F. J., DiGiuseppe, D. L., & McCarty, C. A. (2004). Early television exposure and subsequent attentional problems in children. *Pediatrics, 113(4),* 708-713.

Clark, B. A. (2001). *Growing up gifted: Developing the potential of children at home and at school (6th ed.).* New York: Prentice Hall.

Cohn, S. J. (1991). Talent searches. In N. Colangelo & G. A. Davis (Eds.), *Handbook of gifted education* (pp. 166-177). Boston: Allyn & Bacon.

Colombo, J. (1993). *Infant cognition: Predicting later intellectual functioning.* Thousand Oaks, CA: Sage.

Consumer Reports. (1995, Nov.). Mental health: Does therapy help? pp. 734-739.

Cornell, D. (1983). Gifted children: The impact of positive labeling on the family system. *American Journal of Orthopsychiatry, 53,* 322-335.

Council for Exceptional Children. (1999). *Educating exceptional children: A statistical profile.* ED-99-CO-0026. U.S. Department of Education, OERI.

Covey, S. R. (2004). Three keys to partnering with your kids in raising your grandchildren. In W. Scott (Ed.), *If I knew it was going to the this much fun, I would have become a grandparent first.* New York: Hyperion.

Covey, S. R. (1990). *Seven habits of highly effective people.* New York: Simon & Schuster.

Cox, J., Daniel, N., & Boston, B. O. (1985). *Educating able learners: Programs and promising practices.* Austin, TX: University of Texas Press.

Davidson, J., Davidson, B., & Vanderkam, L. (2004). *Genius denied: How to stop wasting our brightest minds.* New York: Simon & Shuster.

Davis, G. A. & Rimm, S. B. (2003). *Education of the gifted and talented (5th ed.).* Pearson, Boston: Allyn & Bacon.

Deater-Deckard, K. & Dodge, K. A. (1997). Spare the rod, spoil the authors: Emerging themes in research on parenting and child development. *Psychological Inquiry, 8(3),* 230-235.

DeVet, K. A. (1997). Parent-adolescent relationships, physical disciplinary history, and adjustment of adolescents. *Family Process, 36(3),* 311-322.

Dreikurs, R. & Soltz, V. (1991). *Children: The challenge.* New York: Plume.

Field, C. M. (1998). *A field guide to home schooling.* Grand Rapids, MI: Fleming H. Revell.

Gagne, F. (1991). Toward a differentiated model of giftedness and talent. In N. Colangelo & G. A. Davis (Eds.), *Handbook of gifted education* (pp. 65-80). Boston: Allyn & Bacon.

Gallagher, J. J. & Gallagher, S. A. (1994). *Teaching the gifted child (4th ed.)*. Boston: Allyn & Bacon.

Gardner, H. (1983). *Frames of mind: The theory of multiple intelligences*. New York: Basic Books.

Ginott, H. (1969). *Between parent and teenager*. New York: Macmillan.

Ginott, H. (1982). *Between parent and child*. New York: Avon Publishing.

Goertzel, V., Goertzel, M. G., Goertzel, T. G., & Hansen, A. M. W. (2004). *Cradles of eminence: The childhoods of more than 700 eminent men and women* Scottsdale, AZ: Great Potential Press.

Goleman, D. (1995). *Emotional intelligence: Why it can matter more than IQ*. New York: Bantam.

Gopnik, A., Meltzoff, A. N., & Kuhl, P. K. (1999). *The scientist in the crib: Minds, brains and how children learn*. New York: William Morrow.

Hall, E. G. & Skinner, N. (1980). *Somewhere to turn: Strategies for parents of the gifted and talented*. New York: Teachers College Press.

Halsted, J. W. (2002). *Some of my best friends are books: Guiding gifted readers from preschool through high school (2nd ed.)*. Scottsdale, AZ: Great Potential Press.

Happasalo, J. & Tremblay, R. E. (1994). Physically aggressive boys from ages 6 to 12: Family background, parenting behavior, and prediction of delinquency. *Journal of Consulting and Clinical Psychology, 62(5)*, 1044–1052.

Healy, J. M. (1999a). *Endangered minds: Why our children don't think and what we can do about it.* New York: Simon & Schuster.

Healy, J. M. (1999b). *Failure to connect: How computers affect our children's minds.* New York: Simon & Schuster.

Johnsen, S. K. (2004). *Identifying gifted students: A practical guide.* Waco, TX: Prufrock Press.

Johnson, N. L. (1989). *The faces of gifted.* Dayton, OH: Creative Learning Consultants.

Jones, C. (1994). *Mistakes that worked.* New York: Doubleday.

Jones, C. (1998). *Accidents may happen: Fifty inventions discovered by mistake.* New York: Delacorte Press.

Karnes, F. A. & Bean, S. M. (2000). *Adventures and challenges: Real life stories by girls and young women.* Scottsdale, AZ: Great Potential Press.

Karnes, F. A. & Marquardt, R. G. (1991a). *Gifted children and the law: Mediation, due process and court cases.* Scottsdale, AZ: Great Potential Press.

Karnes, F. A. & Marquardt, R. G. (1991b). *Gifted children and legal issues in education: Parents' stories of hope.* Scottsdale, AZ: Great Potential Press.

Karnes, F. A. & Marquardt, R. G. (1999). *Gifted children and legal issues: An update.* Scottsdale, AZ: Great Potential Press.

Karnes, F. A. & Riley, T. L. (1996). *Competitions: Maximizing your abilities through academic and other competitions.* Waco, TX: Prufrock Press.

Karnes, F. A. & Stephens, K. R. (2003). *The ultimate guide to getting money for your classroom and school.* Waco, TX: Prufrock Press.

Kaufmann, F. (1992). What educators can learn from gifted adults. In F. Monks & W. Peters (Eds.), *Talent for the future.* The Netherlands: Van Gorcum.

Kerr, B. A. (1997). *Smart girls: A new psychology of girls, women and giftedness.* Scottsdale, AZ: Great Potential Press.

Kerr, B. A. & Cohn, S. J. (2001). *Smart boys: Talent, manhood, and the search for meaning.* Scottsdale, AZ: Great Potential Press.

Klein, A. (2002). *A forgotten voice: A biography of Leta Stetter Hollingworth.* Scottsdale, AZ: Great Potential Press.

Konigsburg, E. L. (1967). *From the mixed up files of Mrs. Basil E. Frankweiler.* New York: McMillan.

Kulik, J. A. & Kulik, C. C. (1991). Ability grouping and gifted students. In N. Colangelo & G. A. Davis (Eds.), *Handbook of gifted education* (pp. 178-196). Boston: Allyn & Bacon.

Lewis, J. & Karnes, F. A. (1995). Examining the media coverage of gifted education. *Gifted Child Today, 18(6),* 28-30, 40.

Lewis, J. D. & Karnes, F. A. (2001). Public relations and advocacy. In F. A. Karnes & S. M. Bean (Eds.), *Methods and materials for teaching the gifted.* Waco, TX: Prufrock Press.

Lind, S. (2001). Overexcitability and the gifted. *SENG Newsletter, 1(1),* 3-6.

Lucas, A., Morley, R., Cole, T. J., Lister, G., & Leeson-Payne, C. (1992). Breast milk and subsequent intelligence quotient in children born preterm. *The Lancet,* 339, 261-264.

MacKenzie, R. J. (1998). *Setting limits: How to raise responsible, independent children by providing clear boundaries* Rocklin, CA: Prima Publishing.

Mackenzie, R. J. (2001). *Setting limits with your strong-willed child: Eliminating conflict by establishing clear, firm, and respectful boundaries.* Rocklin, CA: Prima Publishing.

McCord, W., McCord, J., & Zola, I. K. (1959). *Origins of crime.* New York: Columbia University Press.

Meadows, S. & Karnes, F. A. (1992). Influencing public opinion of gifted education through the newspaper. *Gifted Child Today, 15(1)*, 44-45.

Mezynski, K. & Stanley, J. C. (1980). Advanced placement orientation calculus for high school students. *Journal for Research in Mathematics Education, 11*, 347-355.

Miller, A. (1996). *The drama of the gifted child: The search for the true self.* New York: Basic Books.

Moore, R. S. & Moore, D. N. (1987). *School can wait.* Provo, UT: Brigham Young University Press.

National Association for Gifted Children. (1998). *Position statements of the National Association for Gifted Children.* Washington, DC: National Association for Gifted Children.

Oakes, J. (1985). *Keeping track.* New Haven, CT: Yale University Press.

Panati, C. (1987). *Extraordinary origins of everyday things.* New York: Harper & Row.

Piirto, J. (2004). *Understanding creativity.* Scottsdale, AZ: Great Potential Press.

Pipher, M. B. (1996). *The shelter of each other: Rebuilding our families.* New York: Putnam.

Pipher, M. (2000). *Another country: Navigating the emotional terrain of our elders.* New York: Riverhead.

Pollins, L. M. (1983). The effects of acceleration on the social and emotional development of gifted students. In C. P. Benbow & J. C. Stanley (Eds.), *Academic precocity: Aspects of its development* (pp. 160-178). Baltimore: Johns Hopkins University Press.

Reilly, J. (1992). *Mentorship: The essential guide for schools and business.* Scottsdale, AZ: Great Potential Press.

Renzulli, J. S. & Reis, S. M. (1991). The schoolwide enrichment model: A comprehensive plan for the development of creative productivity. In N. Colangelo & G. A. Davis (Eds.), *Handbook of gifted education* (pp. 111-141). Boston: Allyn & Bacon.

Renzulli, J. S., Smith, L. H., Callahan, C., White, A., & Hartman, R. (2002). *Scales for rating the behavioral characteristics of superior students: Revised edition.* Mansfield Center, CT: Creative Learning.

Rimm, S. (1994). *Why bright kids get poor grades: And what you can do about it.* New York: Crown.

Rimm, S. (1996). *Dr. Sylvia Rimm's smart parenting. How to raise a happy, achieving child.* New York: Crown.

Rivero, L. (2002). *Creative home schooling: A resource guide for smart families* Scottsdale, AZ: Great Potential Press.

Roedell, W. C., Jackson, N. E., & Robinson, H. B. (1980). *Gifted young children* New York: Teachers College, Columbia University.

Rogers, K. B. (2002). *Re-forming gifted education: How parents and teachers can match the program to the child.* Scottsdale, AZ: Great Potential Press.

Schiever, S. W. & Maker, C. J. (1997). Enrichment and acceleration: An overview and new directions. In N. Colangelo & G. A. Davis (Eds.), *Handbook of gifted education* (2nd ed., pp. 113–125). Boston: Allyn & Bacon.

Schmitz, D. (2003). *The new face of grandparenting.* St. Paul, MN: Grandkidsandme.

Schwarzchild, M. (1995). *Helping your difficult child behave: A guide to improving children's self-control without losing your own.* Rocklin, CA: Prima Publishing.

Scott, W. J. (2004). *If I knew it was going to be this much fun, I would have become a grandparent first.* New York: Hyperion.

Severe, S. (2003). *How to behave so your children will, too!* New York: Penguin.

Silverman, L. K. (1993). *Counseling the gifted and talented.* Denver, CO: Love Publishing.

Silverstein, S. (1964). *The giving tree.* New York: Harpercollins.

Slavin, R. E. (1987). Ability grouping and student achievement in elementary schools: A best evidence synthesis. *Review of Educational Research, 57,* 293-336.

Stanley, J. (1985). Acceleration: The historical backbone to gifted child education. In P. J. Perry (Ed.), *Full flowering: A parent and teacher guide to programs for the gifted* (pp. 78-90). Minneapolis, MN: Wetherall Publishing.

Strip, C. A. & Hirsch, G. (2000). *Helping gifted children soar: A practical source for parents and teachers.* Scottsdale, AZ: Great Potential Press.

Smutny, J. F., Veenker, K., & Veenker, S. (1989). *Your gifted child: How to recognize and develop the special talents in your child from birth to age seven.* New York: Facts on File.

Tannenbaum, A. J. (1983). *Gifted children: Psychological and educational perspectives.* New York: Macmillan.

Tanner, E. M. & Finn-Stevenson, M. (2002). Nutrition and brain development: Social policy implications. *American Journal of Orthopsychiatry, 72(2),* 182-193.

Tomlinson, C. A. (2001). *How to differentiate instruction in mixed-ability classrooms (2nd ed.).* Alexandria, VA: Association for Supervision and Curriculum Development.

Tomlinson, C. A., Kaplan, S. N., Renzulli, J. S., Purcell, J., Leppien, J., & Burns, D. (2002). *The parallel curriculum: A design to develop high potential and challenge high-ability learners.* Thousand Oaks, CA: Corwin Press.

Treffinger, D. J. (2003). *25 tough questions more important than "Is my child in the gifted program."* (www.creativelearning.com).

U.S. Census. (2001). *Population profile of the United States.* Washington, DC: U.S. Census Bureau.

U.S. Department of Education. (1993). *National excellence: A case for developing America's talent.* Washington, D.C. USGPO, PIP 93–1201.

Viorst, J. (1998). *Necessary losses: The losses, illusions, dependencies, and impossible expectations that all of us have to give up in order to grow.* New York: Free Press.

Viorst, J. (2000). *Suddenly sixty and other shocks of later life.* New York: Simon & Schuster.

Webb, J. T. (2000a). *Do gifted children need special help?* (Video). Scottsdale, AZ: Great Potential Press.

Webb, J. T. (2000b). *Is my child gifted? If so, what can I expect?* (Video). Scottsdale, AZ: Great Potential Press.

Webb, J. T. (2000c). *Mis-diagnosis and dual diagnosis of gifted children: Gifted and LD, ADHD, OCD, Oppositional-Defiant Disorder.* ERIC Digest 448–382.

Webb, J. T. (2000d). *Parenting successful children.* (Video). Scottsdale, AZ: Great Potential Press.

Webb, J. T. & DeVries, A. R. (1998). *Gifted parent groups: The SENG model.* Scottsdale, AZ: Great Potential Press.

Webb, J. T. & Kleine, P. A. (1992). Assessing gifted and talented children. In D. J. Willis & J. L. Culbertson (Eds.), *Testing young children* (pp. 383-407). Austin, TX: PRO-ED.

Webb, J. T., Meckstroth, E. A., & Tolan, S. S. (1982). *Guiding the gifted child. A practical source for parents and teachers.* Scottsdale, AZ: Great Potential Press.

Westberg, K. L. & Daoust, M. E. (2003). *The results of the replication of the classroom practices survey: Replication in two states* Storrs, CT: National Research Center on Gifted and Talented. www.gifted.uconn.edu/nrcgt/newsletter/fall03/fall032.html.

Westphal, C. (2001). *A family year abroad: How to live outside the borders.* Scottsdale, AZ: Great Potential Press.

Whitmore, J. R. (1980). *Giftedness, conflict and underachievement.* Rockleigh, NJ: Allyn & Bacon.

Winebrenner, S. (2000). *Teaching gifted children in the regular classroom: Strategies and techniques that every teacher can use to meet the academic needs of the gifted and talented.* Minneapolis, MN: Free Spirit Publishing.

Index

D

E

About the Authors

James T. Webb, Ph.D., a grandparent who is also a nationally known psychologist, has served on the Board of Directors for the National Association for Gifted Children and was President of the American Association for Gifted Children. He also is the founder of the non-profit organization SENG (Supporting Emotional Needs of Gifted). Dr. Webb is President of Great Potential Press, Inc., and he is one of the authors of the award-winning *Guiding the Gifted Child: A Practical Source for Parents and Teachers*, which has been translated into several languages and which has sold over 100,000 copies. He has been recognized as one of the 25 most influential psychologists in the field of gifted education.

Born in Memphis, Tennessee, Dr. Webb graduated from Rhodes College and received his doctorate degree from the University of Alabama.

Janet L. Gore, M.A., M.Ed., is a grandparent who has more than 20 years experience with gifted and talented students as a teacher, school administrator, guidance counselor, policy maker, parent, and grandparent. For five years, she was a designated counselor for gifted high school students in Tucson, Arizona, and for three years, she served as State Director of Gifted Education in Arizona, where she was responsible for developing the quality of educational programs for gifted children throughout the state.

Mrs. Gore graduated from Carleton College in Northfield, Minnesota, and she received her M.A. in English from the University of Iowa and her M.Ed. in Guidance and Counseling from the University of Arizona.

Frances A. Karnes, Ph.D., a very active grandparent, is Professor of Curriculum, Instruction, and Special Education and Director of The Frances A. Karnes Center for Gifted Studies at The University of Southern Mississippi. Dr. Karnes' rich background of experience in leadership roles includes service as a member of the Board of Directors of the National Association for Gifted Children, the Operational Volunteer

Board of the Girl Scouts of the United Sates of America, and the Board of Trustees of Quincy University.

Dr. Karnes, who is the author of numerous books and articles on the education of gifted children, graduated from Quincy University in Quincy, Illinois, and received her M.Ed. and Ph.D. degrees from the University of Illinois in Urbana. She also was awarded an honorary doctorate degree from Quincy University.

A. Stephen McDaniel, J.D., A.E.P, E.P.L.S., is a grandparent who is the senior partner with the Memphis, Tennessee, law firm of Williams, McDaniel, Wolfe & Womack, P.C. He is the President of the National Association of Estate Planners and Councils, and Past President of the Estate Law Specialist Board, Inc. Mr. McDaniel is a Fellow in the American College of Trust and Estate Council, a Certified Estate Planning Specialist, and an Accredited Estate Planner. His practice is limited to estate planning and probate administration. Mr. McDaniel has written articles for several publications, including the *Journal of the American Society of CLU, Broker World*, and *Life Association News*, and has been quoted in

Kiplinger's Personal Finance magazine and *USA Today*.

Born in Memphis, Tennessee, Mr. McDaniel received his undergraduate and law degrees from the University of Memphis. He served for many years as an adjunct faculty member of the University of Memphis School of Law teaching estate planning and estate and gift taxation.

Other Books About Gifted Children
From Great Potential Press